Sylvia Plath

Poetry and Existence

by
David Holbrook

THE ATHLONE PRESS
London and Atlantic Highlands, NJ

This paperback edition first published 1988 by
THE ATHLONE PRESS
1 Park Drive, London NW11 7SG
and 165 First Avenue, Atlantic Highlands, NJ 07716

ISBN 0 485 12062 3

Originally published 1976 by The Athlone Press
Reprinted 1991
© *David Holbrook 1976*

British Library Cataloguing-in-Publication Data

Holbrook, David
Sylvia Plath : poetry and existence.
1. Plath, Sylvia—Criticism and
interpretation
I. Title
811′.54   PS3566.L27Z/

ISBN 0–485–12062–3

Library of Congress Cataloging-in-Publication Data

Holbrook, David
Sylvia Plath : poetry and existence.

Bibliography: p.
Includes index.
1. Plath, Sylvia—Criticism a
2. Psychoanalysis and literatu
[PS3566.L27Z7 1988]
ISBN 0–485–12062–3 (pbk

Reprinted and bound in
at the University Press

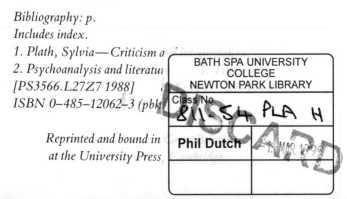

The strife of thought, accusing and excusing, began afresh, and gathered fierceness. The soul of Lilith lay naked to the torture of pure interpenetrating inward light. She began to moan, and sigh deep sighs, then murmur as if holding colloquy with a dividual self: her queendom was no longer whole; it was divided against itself. One moment she would exult as over her worst enemy, and weep; the next she would writhe as if in the embrace of a fiend whom her soul hated and laugh like a demon. At length she began what seemed a tale about herself, in a language so strange, and in forms so shadowy, that I could but here and there understand a little . . .

Gradually my soul grew aware of an invisible darkness, a something more terrible than aught that had yet made itself felt. A horrible Nothingness, a Negation positive infolded her; the border of its being that was yet no being, touched me, and for one ghastly instant I seemed alone with Death Absolute! It was not the absence of everything I felt, but the presence of Nothing. The princess dashed herself from the settle to the floor with an exceeding great and bitter cry. It was the recoil of Being from Annihilation.

George Macdonald, Lilith

Acknowledgements

I should like to thank the many students in Cambridge, Australia and Devon, from whom I have learnt much in discussing the poems of Sylvia Plath. I should like to acknowledge the generous support of Masud Khan, the distinguished psychoanalyst and Editor of the International Library of Psychoanalysis. I have learnt something from a study by Connie Richmond, *The Worlds of Sylvia Plath*, an essay for the Certificate of Education, University of Kent. I am also under a considerable debt to my wife, from whom I have tried to learn about woman over twenty-five years, and from whose responses to this book I have gained fresh insights into feminine modes and meanings.

I am also indebted for help from Dr Peter Lomas, the psychotherapist, who read the manuscript for me, and to Miss Olwyn Hughes for information about certain aspects of the poet's life.

D.H.

NOTE

Contents

I

Who is Sylvia?

This book attempts to use interpretations from psychoanalysis and kindred disciplines to improve our understanding of the poetry of Sylvia Plath. It is an extended essay in literary criticism undertaken because I value Sylvia Plath's work as an artist, and believe that she has important things to tell us about her particular kind of experience. I also believe that she suffered a characteristic sense of existential insecurity in our world, the most significant aspect of which was her feeling that she might lose her sense of meaning in life and her capacity to throw her imagination over the world—the capacity to perceive in an intentional way. Not unrelated to this, as I believe, she had, in her private phenomenology, a fatally false sequence in her logic: she believed that death could be a pathway to rebirth, so that her suicide was a schizoid suicide. Again, this cannot be discussed without reference to the atmosphere of the contemporary arts, which displays at this moment a dangerous rejection of life, moving towards nihilism and an abandonment to hate.

My first paragraph, however, reveals a dilemma. Who or what do we mean, when we speak of 'Sylvia Plath'? My material is the poetry and the novel: I am not a biographer. But it will be clear that if I deduce from certain kinds of symbolism in the poetry that Sylvia Plath had schizoid characteristics and the special kind of problems which belong to this condition, I am extrapolating from the poems to the person, and here there may be, or may not be, confirmation or illumination from biographical facts. Yet the poems are often fictions, while others are clearly autobiographical. The lovely poem *The Night Dances* is evidently about her own actual baby: and this is confirmed by a note by her husband.

Leaving Early, by contrast, would seem to be a poem about an imaginary person who visited the woman upstairs.

But, evidently, if I am to examine the meanings of the poems in the light both of the psychology of their author and of her groping towards a philosophy of existence, I must also talk about the woman as revealed in the poems and novel. This is the more important now that 'Sylvia Plath' is the object of a fashionable cult, not least because of her suicide and her schizoid tendencies, and is also a heroine of women's liberation movements. Her rejection of certain kinds of femininity (and, as I would put it, her hatred of certain aspects of woman), for example, have been presented at certain poetry festivals as important human truths. My view, which I shall try to justify by extended analysis of her poetry, is that very often what she says about male and female and other subjects is grossly distorted and false. My interpretation of these falsities is part of a whole series of works, in which I am trying to distinguish between true and false solutions to the problem of existence, between philosophies based on love and those based on hate.

Another reason for discussing the 'actual woman', despite the dangers and difficulties, is that Sylvia Plath's work presents us with a disturbing problem, not least in education. If we believe that the reading of literature refines the emotions and helps to civilise us, what then do we expect to gain when we offer adolescent students works for study which seriously falsify experience? In schools today, students are often obliged to apply themselves for examination purposes to essentially nihilistic works from modern writing, in an atmosphere in which they are not urged to examine these works from their own lights, because that might annoy the examiner, but must simply absorb them and submit to the implication that these works are offering profound human truths. Yet, in the light of philosophical anthropology, such as I try to invoke here, these works may be offering falsifications or forms of moral inversion which are absurd, or even deranged, and may even do harm to the sensitive and responsive young person. For all her immense creative effort, Sylvia Plath could not save herself. What, then, do we say about the effects of her art on us? And especially on the young? Can we detach ourselves from the seductive idolization of suicide and infanticide in *Edge (Ariel,*

p. 85), written only two weeks before she committed the former act herself? How do we regard the zany idolizations of suicidal techniques in *The Bell Jar*? Some might say that this doesn't matter—art is only art and does not affect us so directly. Yet, if we give assent to the libidinal attachment to death in *Edge*, what values can we invoke to condemn those who blow up children with terrorist bombs or harm their consciousness with cruel exploitation? And what do we say about her own act, which deprived the world of a fine creative spirit, orphaned her own children, and jeopardised the life of a neighbour? We can surely only disconnect our response to a poem like *Edge* from events in life which follow from it as a direct consequence, either by a cultivated aestheticism which cold-bloodedly refuses to recognise links between culture and living, or by a lapse into moral inversion which is prepared to sacrifice life to the indulgence of the senses or the solipsistic mind. Both these tendencies are, of course, found in contemporary culture. But the terrible cruelty in the former is made clear enough in the character of Gilbert Osmond in Henry James's *Portrait of a Lady*, leading to a serious forfeiture of capacities for living (as in Isabel Archer), and also in the character of Prince Daniyal in L. H. Myers's *The Near and The Far*, in whom the aesthete's indulgence goes with cruelty. The latter, analysed recently in Phillip Rieff's *Fellow Teachers*, with its Roman antecedents, is a form of egoistical nihilism that could mean the end of civilization itself. To abjure discrimination is no service to the artist herself, in this case, who saw love, in her best work, as 'the one/Solid the spaces lean on . . .'

The essential value to invoke is concern and, as we shall see, the poem *Edge* is false because it conceals in its seductive beauty a false logical step—luring us into accepting that the beauty-enjoying 'I' has the right to destroy the life in others. As the expression of inner truths, art cannot be exempted any more than any other human activity from the need to pursue truth: art may illuminate falsities, but if it seeks to glamorise or enshrine falsity, then it must be questioned—not least at a time when survival itself is in question. Care and concern, in the light of philosophical biology, are primary realities of the evolutionary process: if care and concern are jeopardised, as they are by the substitution of hate for love in the ideology of much contemporary art, we need to examine the likely consequences. As John Vyvyan says, discussing the emergence of birds and mammals in his *Sketch for A World-Picture* (1972), one of the requirements for a more complicated adult form in animals was 'a longer span of childhood, demanding a steady increase in parental care, and from this sprang a unique set of relationships. It is evident that these relationships, when they were further developed in the group, have led to vices as well as virtues; but it is fair to emphasise the virtues. In a mammalian family, the parents must love and teach; the young must respect and learn; and dispositions appropriate to these needs are woven into the fabric of a mammalian community. There is nothing mysterious, therefore, in the evolution of what we call the virtues. The higher forms of life could not have come into existence without them; and it would require only one generation of purely selfish parents for all the mammals—and most of the birds—to become extinct' (p. 143).

This view of the evolutionary basis for love would seem to be reconcilable with the work of philosophical biologists like F. J. J. Buytendijk, the psychoanalysts and existentialist analysts, and with phenomenology. Yet, in a great deal of contemporary art it is the vices which are stressed. And at the centre of this movement in the arts there is to be found a hatred especially of the child: for example, Ted Hughes's play *Orghast*, as described in *Orghast in Persepolis*, focusses on a hatred of the infant and displays immense guilt about this. In his wife Sylvia Plath we find a hatred and fear of an infant within her, unborn and menacing with its hunger, combined with an out-going love of her own children, finding them at times fulcrums for her whole existence (*Nick and the Candlestick*). In *Edge* these two ambivalent streams converge, and the love of her children becomes an intense, but insane, desire to merge them into her own perfect birth-death. Fortunately, she was spared the enaction of this terrible confusion and left her children alive.

From this brief digression into the realms where poetry and philosophy—and *psychology*—merge and meet, it will be evident that for my purposes I cannot restrict myself to a mere literary analysis. We cannot solve the problems which arise from even a single phrase ('masturbating a glitter', for example) without moving beyond the words into the realms of investigative psychology, and this will mean, in some spheres, conjecturing, about the life, as I did in my study of Dylan Thomas. And in analysing the psychology of Sylvia Plath I shall take certain works, like the poem *Tulips*, or the novel *The Bell Jar*, as largely autobiographical, while reminding myself that there is also a sense in which they are fictions, too.

But there are places where Sylvia Plath makes it plain—sometimes by slips—that these works are autobiographical.* For example, in *The Bell Jar*, the 'I'-voice talks of the presents she received as a girl working in journalism:

> For a long time afterwards I hid them away, but later, when I was all right again, I brought them out, and I still have them around the house. I use the lipsticks now and then, and last week I cut the plastic starfish off the sunglasses case for the baby to play with. (pp. 3–4)

But whose baby? At the end of the novel there is no question of 'Esther' being married, or having a baby. The slip betrays quite clearly that Esther 'is' Sylvia Plath, and that when she speaks of 'being all right again' she is speaking of her own breakdown and recovery: the baby was Mrs Ted Hughes's.

My justifications for employing insights from various forms of psychotherapy are several. First, I believe that we cannot understand her poetry well, and at times not at all, unless we recognise that she has a topography of her own, which is that of the world as the schizoid individual sees it. Secondly, as I have suggested already, we must defend ourselves against her falsifications, especially when they are the object of cults, in an atmosphere in which we are being urged to cultivate our psychoses and endorse decadence and moral inversion. Here, as with *Edge*, it is often a question of re-examining our 'cool'—that is, our tendency to accept a certain low-key tone of voice. One of the aims of the schizoid individual is to persuade us to accept his sometimes fanatical inversions of reality and truth, as common-sense. Thus, in discussing suicide, Sylvia Plath writes: 'The trouble about jumping was that if you didn't pick the right number of storeys, you might still be

---

* She described *The Bell Jar* as 'an autobiographical apprentice work which I had to write in order to free myself from the past' (quoted in Nancy Hunter Steiner (1973), p. 85).

alive when you hit bottom. I thought seven storeys must be a safe distance' (*The Bell Jar*, p. 144).

There are some paragraphs of Jonathan Swift, another schizoid writer, in which one is invited to follow along with the same coolness, as throughout *A Modest Proposal*. But here we need to pay especial attention to the words 'right' and 'safe'. Here, the 'right' number of storeys is that number which make up a height that will certainly kill you: 'safe' means that there will be no chance of survival, and thus the word takes on a grotesque ambiguity. But, once we unravel the schizoid false logic, it is possible to see where these ambiguities come from: for her, it was 'safe' to be dead, as we shall see. But from our point of view, we must insist, to be smashed to death is not 'safe', and since we do not share her myths about suicide, we would expect to be alive when we hit bottom.

The delusions which make such a series of sentences insane, however, are beneath the surface, belonging to the inner psychic reality. And they belong to another schizoid characteristic of Sylvia Plath—her dissociation from her own body, and the inner reality of 'somewhere else'. Esther speaks as if she wants to kill something 'in' her own body: 'It was as if what I wanted to kill wasn't in that skin or the thin blue pulse that jumped under my thumb, but somewhere else, deeper, more secret, and a whole lot harder to get at' (*The Bell Jar*, p. 156). 'A whole lot harder to get at' is a light-hearted way of saying something that is terribly true —that we can exert no power over the 'psychic tissue' and all its inherent faults: but her use of the phrase is ominous, implying a murderous impulse. Because any approach to psychic reality is so disturbing to us, even to begin to explore such problems of existence as those of Sylvia Plath often arouses fierce resistance and opposition. (It is quite common for people to have to leave seminars on her poems, because they cannot bear the inevitable confrontation with psychic reality.)

Fortunately, we are able to examine the truths of psychic reality more coolly today, as a result of the work of a number of investigators since Freud. And we are particularly fortunate in having a number of recent studies which have penetrated the schizoid problem: R. D. Laing's *The Divided Self*; Harry Guntrip's *Schizoid Phenomena, Object-relations and the Self*; W. R. D. Fairbairn's *Psychoanalytical Studies of the Personality*, and various papers by D. W. Winnicott, Robert Daly, Aaron Esterson, Marion Milner, Melanie Klein, and Rollo May. All this work will be here referred to as the 'schizoid diagnosis': I believe that a phenomenological analysis of the poetry and symbolism of Sylvia Plath also extends the schizoid diagnosis, and already (according to Masud Khan) the present work has been applied, on being circulated in manuscript, in clinical work. Sylvia Plath's message about schizoid experience, if we can hear it, may unlock many private languages, and help schizoid individuals to find what they most desperately need—the opportunity to communicate.

It is immediately clear that Sylvia Plath had a 'dividual self'. Throughout her work there are images of selves which are petrified, cracked, automaton, patched up, and divided against themselves. Perhaps one of the most characteristic is the double self in *In Plaster* in which the real body-self inside the plaster cast is the 'tenant', and without whom the outer self would 'perish with emptiness'. At the heart of the self in *Poem for a Birthday* there are all kinds of objects, including a (male) puppy, while elsewhere inanimate objects, like darning dollies, take on a terrifying life of their own—while the self in despair becomes a bundle of weapons ('I fly about like clubs', *Elm*). The tenant in her dividual self at times seems only to bloom 'out of her as a rose/Blooms out of a vase of not very valuable porcelain . . .'—and this theme of inner worthlessness is often struck, as she searches within herself for substantiality, sometimes finding only the vacuum at the heart of a tornado.

It should be clear by this point that I am not simply saying that Sylvia Plath was 'ill', or dismissing her work as 'sick'. There is a schizoid condition in her: but this cannot be discussed without reference to the problem which the schizoid individual is singularly equipped to recognise—the problem today of living in a schizoid society, in a world which seems to have lost its meaning. As Harry Guntrip shows, from the case-histories he discusses (1961), there are some individuals who are extremely successful in their professional work yet who go to the psychotherapist and declare 'I am nobody'. This type, he says, is found in high proportion in intellectual life, which attracts those who, because they are schizoid, create an abstract world in which to live, because they cannot find themselves real, in a real body, in a real world, in ordinary existence. But as Viktor Frankl (1969) declares, a person may at times be ill, or may in some aspects of his existence be disturbed—yet his actual existential anguish cannot be dismissed as 'sick'. To be tormented by the problem of the meaning of life, or by existential dread, is to be human, or even especially human. So, we need to examine both the disturbed falsities and their philosophical extrapolations, and to search for what Fairbairn detects in any schizoid person: 'deep down, the schizoid needs to love and be loved'. To this we may add the need for meaning, as emphasised by existentialist therapy and *Dasein*-analysis.* Masud Khan has said (in a private communication) that Sylvia Plath 'pushed to its extreme a process of nihilistic purity of self which started with Rousseau . . . the Utopian notion of an idolized inner self invariably entails an unacknowledged and permissive random hate of the actual given human reality and all that it offers'. This may be applied not only to Sylvia Plath but to our culture in general, as it is affected by fashionable nihilism and the cult of 'schizophrenia'. Discussing the problems of the psychotherapist in working with schizophrenics in an essay 'The Mad Psychiatrist', Leslie Farber (1966) relates how the therapist may come to fall in love with the high drama of his patients, so that ordinary life comes to seem 'pallid and artificial'. This is the danger of a schizoid culture: it comes to put that care and love on which human existence depends into contempt, by contrast with the great dramas of hate. The greatest danger in this is that even our best human potentialities, satisfactions, and meanings may become inaccessible to us.

This is not the place for a detailed examination of theories of the origins of the condition known as schizophrenia, or of the schizoid state. I have examined various theories elsewhere. The most fashionable attitude today (developed from some of the 'politics of experience' of R. D. Laing and especially from the work on the 'death of the family' of David Cooper) is that 'society' creates situations in which some families tend to mystify certain weaker members, and make them into scapegoats. Peter Lomas, in *True and False Experience* (1973), takes a more moderate

* *Dasein*-analysis takes it cue from Heidegger's concept of 'being-unto-death'. Its central concern is with the individual's need to assert a meaningful sense of 'being *there*' against nothingness, of significant existence. See p. 295 below.

view that 'a family which has such a powerful capacity to undermine the adolescent has probably failed to provide the child, at an
early age, with a strong sense of identity: in other words, the process is a cumulative one' (p. 123). The weakness of identity comes
before the social processes of mystification and scape-goating: we
need to look at deeper existence problems.

Various incidents and elements in a child's life may impair his or
her capacities to acquire this strength of identity: the too-early
birth of a sibling, a parent's illness or death, or even the child's
own hypersensitive expectations may well contribute to feelings
of emptiness and weakness. With Sylvia Plath, this is a delicate
problem to discuss. Even if one only interprets the writings, as I
intend to do, it is impossible to avoid noticing that her protagonists
tend to blame others, especially the mother, and later (as in *Daddy*)
the father. Yet it is also clear from (*The Bell Jar* for example) that
the actual mother did everything she could to help her daughter—
and, indeed, reports say that the poet had a happy relationship
with her mother, who now has to bear not only the anguish of her
suicide but also the unhappiness of seeing the evident hatred in the
poetry made plain. In truth, it would seem that the angry blame
directed at mother and father in some of Sylvia Plath's writings
has no grounds, but arises out of the same delusions which made
her regard suicide with such rapture or fantasy her father as a
Nazi. For some reason, because of some failure of the normal processes of growth of identity, she felt 'let down' by 'life'—and this
blame turned against those from whom she had expected something she felt she did not get. In no normal dimensions of experience is there any evidence that anyone did less than a human being
could do: the origins of her schizoid state, I suggest, lay in processes which no-one can consciously alter, between infant and
mother. Peter Lomas (1967) quotes from Thomas Blackburn's
poem *For a Child*:

> And have I put upon your shoulders then,
> What in myself I have refused to bear,
> My own and the confusion of dead men,
> You of all these, my daughter, made my heir,
> The furies and the griefs of which I stayed
> Quite unaware?

It is important to stress here, at the beginning, in order to try to alleviate some of the inevitable distress caused not by interpretation, but by the mere existence of the work, that the processes and experiences of existence which Sylvia Plath expresses and with which we must deal in analysis belong to a sphere quite beyond the categories of blame or attribution of faults and neglect. *She* expresses such blame: a great deal of what we have to say exonerates those who brought her up and lived with her. *She* expresses hate: we declare this without justification. Those who did bring her up may console themselves by the emphasis placed in our criticism on the immense creativity of her questing spirit—that in itself is tribute to their care and love.

The confusion in her soul over life and death was a basic fault which arose out of processes so subtle that they are quite beyond human volition, as are catastrophes such as *spina bifida* or mongolism. While her own capacity for love and joy was given her by her family and those with whom she lived, the conditions in her inner reality were evidently so deep that no-one could have done anything to alleviate or cure them, unless it were a psychotherapist of profound insight and infinite patience, like the late D. W. Winnicott. We only have to read such cases as the very complex ones of 'Lola Voss' or 'Susanne Urban' in the work of Ludwig Binswanger, to realise how much effort would have been required, far beyond the resources of any untrained person.

So, while we need to recognise that to be spiritually distressed is only to be human, it is also clear that Sylvia Plath was mentally ill, as she herself tells us, at times. She had periods of not being able to cope, and she attempted, and eventually managed, suicide, and these were clear signs, whatever Alvarez may say, of psychopathological states.

Yet because of her schizoid condition, she was also able to have insights which make her seem at times more sane than we ordinary people are. We need only consider the way in which she penetrates to the cold-bloodedness of the world of fashion journalism, in *The Bell Jar*. 'Fashion blurbs, silver and full of nothing, sent up their fishy bubbles in my brain. They surfaced with a hollow pop' (p. 104). The emptiness of this world, she shows, is an emptiness of consciousness—and has at its heart a fundamental and poisonous spiritual vacancy, symbolised by the meal of ptomaine-contaminated crab-meat which the girls consume as part of a promotion racket. (When they nearly prove 'expendable' to the advertising world, they are sent 'presents' to help them get well—all of which empty hedonism the novelist delineates with a dry, caustic irony.) It is in such a world that much more dehumanized atrocities can be carried out, like the execution of the Rosenbergs, while those who are corrupted by its ethos are indifferent, and live comfortably by the morality of hate: ' "I'm so glad they're going to die." Hilda arched her cat-limbs in a yawn' (p. 104).

As we shall see, because of her schizoid condition, this writer is able to plumb the deeper problems of being-in-the-world. Yet the poems and *The Bell Jar* present us with a number of perplexing difficulties, too—of how to respond. While we can easily share the author's horror at the dehumanization of the American scene, our problem is that we cannot share her solutions. Her protagonist's enthusiasm for suicide, and the way in which this enthusiasm is glamourised, are a desperate and inverted 'remedy'. Nor can we share what goes with these—the protective *sang-froid* of her prose whose flippancy belongs itself to the dehumanization (and is akin to the terrible 'objective' language of 'body-count' and 'overkill'): 'The idea of being electrocuted makes me sick ... I thought it must be the worst thing in the world' (*The Bell Jar*, p. 1). Perhaps we put this failure of tone down to the callowness of a young girl, trying to be sophisticated. Is Sylvia Plath guying the kind of individual who adopts the 'cool' of fashionable journalism? We may be less sure when we come to this: 'for a while it seemed to me that the only way to stop it would be to take the column of skin and sinew from which it rose and twist it to silence between my hands' (p. 130). This is how Esther thinks about her mother, when she cannot sleep, and the older woman's snoring annoys her. But why does Esther hate her mother so much? ('I could see the pin curls on her head glittering like a row of little bayonets', p. 129).*

* In view of my remarks above (see page 10) about the autobiographical nature of much of Sylvia Plath's work it is perhaps desirable that I should note explicitly that in her own writings the frequent references to mothers and mother-figures have a complex motivation and must not be construed as references to Sylvia Plath's real mother. Nor must any comments I base on them be taken in this sense. As I try to show, profound questions of the artistic identity and of the development of the human psyche are involved here. The forces at work are largely

Of course, the American suburbs are oppressive with their silence, and Esther finds a menace to her freedom in the creaking of Dodo Conway's domestic pram wheels—one can see why Sylvia Plath appeals to the Germaine Greers of our world. But why is she made to say: 'I made a point of never living in the same house with my mother for more than a week' (p. 125)?

The answers to our perplexities in responding to such work, I believe, may be found eventually, if we pay sufficient attention to her signs and symbols. A persona is trying to say something to us (of which the author could have been unconscious). The word 'glittering', for example, is a key word.

One theme we shall have to pursue is that of the child, the infant, within us and, to use Fairbairn's most important insight, the 'regressed libidinal ego'. This is a dynamic of the personality which embodies the hungriest part of us, which is still in a sense a baby whose hunger has never been satisfied. The hunger is essential existence-hunger, a hunger for substantiality of identity and for meaning: but because the infant existence-experience is so embodied, it feels like a hungry mouth. Yet because of its fear of encountering the world, in all its insubstantiality, it retreats into the womb, whence it becomes a menace to on-going existence. This unborn baby thus becomes the focus of dread in the schizoid person. And this baby, as shall see, is the focus of a great amount of hate in much modern culture, representing, indeed, that sensitivity and even creativity—not least of 'female element being'—which we cannot bear, because the world is so unwilling to accept it. Yet again, as is clear from Sylvia Plath's work, those who are preoccupied with meaning, like her, yearn for that very creativity, and yearn for that infant to be brought to birth. Indeed, all her effort, both positive, in her poetry, and negative, in her suicide, was directed to loving this regressed libidinal ego, and bringing him into existence: the significance of that 'him' will appear later.

But, of course, such dynamics mingled as they are with hate, are extremely dangerous. This explains a great deal. When Esther

---

unconscious: we see their outcome but are only just beginning to understand their causes and the processes by which they operate. Where we can only with difficulty understand, we should be careful not to offer judgements based on the rough-and-ready criteria of normal daily existence.

is staying in her mother's house, fearing to become like her by identification, a mere domestic woman, condemned to a baby-raising life like Dodo Conway, she regresses. The fear of identifying with her mother and becoming a woman (which we shall examine later) is associated with a fear of becoming a child again, because the immature child is in a fierce desperate need, and menaces by its hunger. This explains the regression in Esther's hand-writing:

> But when I took up my pen, my hand made big, jerky letters like those of a child, and the lines sloped down the page from left to right almost diagonally, as if they were loops of string lying on the paper, and someone had come along and blown them askew. (p. 137)

This, as we shall see, is a characteristic image of Sylvia Plath: a sense that writing on the page has somehow come unstuck, so that it lies there, and one could even crawl into it—or it might even crawl off the page.* But the regression symbolised in the hand-writing is the message: 'there is a child in me'. Later Esther puts this child-writing on Doctor Gordon's desk, but he is too insulated in his vanity to understand the signal:

> I thought Dr Gordon must immediately see how bad the handwriting was, but he only said, 'I think I would like to speak to your mother. Do you mind?'
> 'No.' But I didn't like the idea of Doctor Gordon talking to my mother one bit. I thought he might tell her I should be locked up. I picked up every scrap of my letter to Doreen, so Doctor Gordon couldn't piece them together and see I was planning to run away, and walked out of his office without another word. (pp. 142–3)

'Without another word' is a significant phrase. Communication has broken down, because the phemenological meaning has not been taken. Now the processes so well examined by Esterson and Laing (1964) are about to begin—in the next paragraph Esther's mother is crying, because her daughter, she has been told, must have electro-convulsive therapy. Yet the mother eagerly assents

---

* Cf. 'The little paragraphs between the pictures ended before the letters had a chance to get cocky and wiggle about.' *The Bell Jar*, p. 145.

to the institutionalization which she also feels is a disgrace. That is, in response to her message (that Esther has within her an ungrown infant) the 'patient' is met with a process of labelling, treatment and coercion—directed at her because she is 'wrong', so that she now becomes a kind of scapegoat. In the light of the work of Winnicott and Fairbairn, however, I believe that the patient is not only being 'punished' for failure to conform to social and family norms (as Laing and Esterson might urge)—but for revealing the horrors of the inner void, and the urgent needs of that hungry unborn child-self within, and even for expressing a tragic aware-ness of the human predicament which this brings. This infant hungers to be *seen*: the solution to the existence problem depends upon it, and yet the psychiatrist does not *understand*.

In *Poem for a Birthday*, as we shall see, a desperate feeling haunts Sylvia Plath—if only her clear messages could be *heard*. If people could only see how terrible were the things she was speaking of, they could see what was wrong: her tragedy was that they were unable to. Her poems thus bear a significant relationship to Esther's handwriting at this moment of regression. This is not to say that the poems are regressed: but their symbolism has its own message, that things are 'bad', and when she despaired of this message being received, she sank into nihilistic despair and distor-tion. The world, instead, acclaimed her blackest falsification, while failing to hear the voice of catastrophic regression, and loss of hope and meaning.

The blankness faces Esther. The Doctor cannot understand. The mother (despite her care and concern) is the butt of resentment, because communication seems to have failed. Now, the mother is in collaboration with the psychiatric powers that offer Esther ECT. The mother knows very well that there is a serious danger (as the Doctor has said) that Esther may have to go to hospital: but she hasn't fully taken her daughter into her confidence—so there is a kind of 'double bind': ' "Don't I *always* tell you the truth?" my mother said and burst into tears' (p. 143).

The 'collusion' between the mother and the psychiatric authori-ties is the kind of process criticised by psychologists like Esterson (1964).

But what is crucial, as *The Divided Self* itself showed, is that in the mystifying processes the patient's true meanings are lost. We do not hear what is really wrong: and it is this that is disastrous. The present work is offered as an attempt to understand the meanings of such a self, in some ways unborn. It is clear from *The Bell Jar* that everything goes wrong with Esther from this moment, when she expected to be understood—and was not. Fundamentally, I shall argue, this failure to be understood meant that Sylvia Plath had to work out, unaided, her sense of how to bring the unborn self to birth. A false conclusion to the problem of self-definition developed, because, as I hope to show, death became confused with birth, and regression took the path to the tomb. To find meaning in life, she had to die.

We can see this confusion quite clearly, after the horrible moment at which Esther wants to strangle her mother:

> I feigned sleep until my mother left for school, but even my eyelids didn't shut out the light. They hung the raw, red screen of their tiny vessels in front of me like a wound. I crawled between the mattress and the padded bedstead and let the mattress fall across me like a tombstone. It felt dark and safe under there, but the mattress was not heavy enough.
> It needed about a ton more weight to make me sleep ...
> (p. 130)

Somehow, for Esther to overcome her breakdown (which is a total failure of perception), she needs to get into some kind of a cave—here, the womb-like cavity under the mattress (matrix). But at the same time this is described in tomb-like terms, and to be really effective, the mattress would have to become a tomb lid.

A few days later, she reads about a suicide in the newspaper:
> I brought the newspaper close up to my eyes to get a better view of George Pollucci's face, spotlighted like a three-quarter moon against a vague background of brick and black sky. I felt he had something important to tell me, and that whatever it was might just be written on his face. (p. 144).

As we shall see, the moon-image is important here, as is the curious exploration of the man suicide's face. The message about the need for re-birth is not being understood: perhaps the message she seeks, in answer to her existential problems, is to be found in that face of the man who has killed himself, who is 'in death'.

Esther's father, like Sylvia Plath's, is in his grave, and she has
not been really happy since the age of nine, when he died. 'Daddy'
is in the world of death—and the suicide has just gone there. Since
the mother has shown no understanding in her face, and Doctor
Gordon does not understand the message of the handwriting—
perhaps the answer is there, in George Pollucci's look as he *faces
death*? Perhaps the answer to the problem of existence lies 'through'
that face, in the death world?

In *The Bell Jar* there are many indications that Esther's problem
is that of an insubstantial identity, which is craving to become
substantial enough to live: 'I felt myself melting into the shadows
like the negative of a person I'd never seen before in my life' (p. 10).
On pp. 21–2 she takes a hot bath which is described as if it were a
re-birth, and hears voices whispering two different names at her
door, 'as if I had a split personality or something'. Another
character is described as staring 'at her reflection in the glossed
shop windows as if to make sure, moment by moment, that she
continued to exist' (p. 105). These are recurrent themes in Sylvia
Plath's work.

Reading the novel we are continually aware, that Sylvia Plath's
world was full of the possibility of non-existence. But this is also
associated, in Esther, with a hopeless loss of faith in the future, just
as death-as-rebirth is resorted to from fear of a loss of intentional
vision. The figs on her imaginary tree of fulfilment turn black and
drop (p. 80); and like the protagonist of the poem *The Disquieting
Muses*, Esther tries to become a woman—but cannot (pp. 78–9).
Increasingly, there is a loss of the capacity for creative becoming,
of *future*. Trying, in her insomniac fantasies, to imagine a future
stretching away like telegraph poles, Esther says,

> I saw the years of my life spaced along a road in the form of
> telephone poles, threaded together by wires. I counted one,
> two, three ... nineteen telephone poles, and then the wires
> dangled into space, and try as I would, I couldn't see a single
> pole beyond the nineteenth. (p. 129)

There is something very strange and sinister in Sylvia Plath's
ritualistic thinking about periodicity and her lack of confidence in
a future after a certain 'number' of years. Her father died when
she was nearly nine: Esther cannot see beyond nineteen: Lady

Lazarus 'dies' every ten years: somewhere, again, in this numerical magic is the clue to *beginning*. At about her third decade Sylvia really dies. All these belong to attempts to sustain creativity: in the end hope of this is lost, too. I have discussed the way in which Esther 'is' Sylvia Plath, and there is magic in this, too. When Esther is speaking of writing a novel she says: 'My heroine would be myself, only in disguise. She would be called Elaine. Elaine. I counted the letters on my fingers. There were six letters in Esther, too. It seemed a lucky thing' (pp. 126–7). There are six letters in 'Sylvia', and it shares some of its letters with 'Elaine'.

Here Sylvia Plath reveals that she used a kind of childish magic, in incantations and rituals employed to deal with life's problems. This element of magic and the deficiency of a sense of identity we may link with the central theme of this study, the failure of confidence in the imagination, and in the future. From moment to moment, Sylvia Plath's protagonists cannot deal from a secure self with a world recognised as real. Sometimes they try to throw fantasy over the world: sometimes the world seems to contain terrible, irrepressible ghosts, which she cannot allay or assuage. Psychoanalytical theory asserts that the capacity to see the world in a meaningful way is linked with the capacity to love and the experience of being loved. Without this kind of rich security of love-experience, and the capacity for meaningful seeing that can follow from it, her poetry represents an immense attempt to overcome what she calls 'neutrality', and to exert creative intentionality in perception:

> . . . I only know that a rook
> Ordering its black feathers can so shine
> As to seize my senses, haul
> My eyelids up, and grant
>
> A brief respite from fear
> Of total neutrality.
> (*Black Rook in Rainy Weather, The Colossus*, p. 42)

She does not ask for a miracle, 'To set the sight on fire/In my eye', but she knows that the Blakean vision is possible, to transcend normal reality:

A certain minor light may still
Leap incandescent

Out of kitchen table or chair
As if a celestial burning took
Possession of the most obtuse objects now and then—
Thus hallowing an interval
Otherwise inconsequent

By bestowing largesse, honour,
One might say love.

She hoped that angels might flare at her elbow: and she sought to find everyday objects manifestations of heavenly truth. She knows that life is worth living because of its 'peak moments': but these perhaps she finds rare? Yet she wanted ordinary life to be meaningful:

> For me, the real issues of our time are the issues of every time —the hurt and wonder of loving; making in all its forms, children, loaves of bread, paintings, building; and the conservation of life of all people in all places.
>
> (*London Magazine*, 'Context', February, 1962)

Yet in the end what she calls 'neutrality' overtook her, perhaps because, as she says in the same poem, she could only 'patch, together a content of sorts'. She dreads the loss of meaning. Her problem becomes one which has been expressed by many poets. In a story by Walter de la Mare a character says, 'I have come to the end of things. For me the spirit, the meaning, whatever you like to call it—has vanished, gone clean out of the world, out of what we call reality'. This is the central problem for the modern artist, that when a confidence in love fails, there can also be a loss of confidence in a benign universe, and so meaning seems to dissolve, while the hold on reality breaks down, and hope dissolves into futility. This schizoid feeling about the experience of reality yields those terrifying moments in the work of Sylvia Plath when the sense of the self-in-the-world falls apart:

> For a minute the sky pours into the hole like plasma.
> There is no hope, it is given up.
>
> (*Berck-Plage, Ariel*, p. 30)

In a poem like *Getting There*, it seems that she felt her whole
working life was, or should be, a spiritual journey, like that of
William Blake. But she ends up, we may say, overwhelmed by
the literal, the 'objective', the material dominance of 'matter in
motion', and in dismay, like the heroine of *The Wishing Box*, she
seeks renewal in death. By my phenomenological analysis of her
poetry, I hope to try to show why this happened.

She had the conscious desire expressed above, to 'conserve the
life of all people'. But it is obvious from her poetry that, beneath
her sociable exterior, and her capacity for joy and creativity, there
were intensely negative dynamics. The question arises of the
degree to which these were exacerbated by outside influences.

I do not discuss many biographical facts about this poet. It is
clear from the poems that Sylvia Plath was deeply affected by the
breakdown of her marriage: but there are as obviously destructive
dynamics in herself that may well have contributed to that
breakdown. Here what interests me most is the question of the
destructive dynamics in our culture, in which there are many
powerful advocates of actually 'cultivating' derangement. It is
often denied that cultural influences can harm anyone: but to
believe this would seem impossible to anyone who believes that
culture is primary in human existence. Moreover, it is quite clear
from certain studies of the operations of the human consciousness,
that it is possible for certain individuals, who have adopted a life-
style and philosophy based on moral inversion, to influence
others. One of the slogans of the German Baader-Meinhof
terrorist gang was '24 hours of HATE each day': and we have this
kind of moral inversion in culture as well as politics.

Perhaps the strangest aspect of our world today is that, even as
violence and hate increase, people deny that there can be any
influences on consciousness which could bring these events about,
or make the situation worse. Yet in the arts there are those like
Peter Brook who actually teach the actor to 'discover something
of his own potential madness', while A. Alvarez encourages the
artist to 'cultivate his psychosis'.

If the logic of schizoid inversion of values is taught, then it will
be learned. This is clear from Fairbairn's analysis (1952) of
schizoid states and their intellectual implications. The origin of
schizoid conditions lies in the failure of the infant to find himself

accepted and loved, 'in his own right'. When his love, and his need to love, seemed to be rejected, he concluded by infantile logic, that love is harmful. From then on, he must needs base his moral system on hate. Hate is not the opposite of love, but its inversion— and basically it manifests an aggressive and hostile attempt to coerce 'the other' into supplying what, it is felt, should be supplied—care and concern.* But one of the motives behind this reliance on hate is highly moral: the schizoid person feels that since love is so 'bad' that it may damage the 'other', it is better, ethically, to hate, since this is less dangerous.

But, when the individual becomes desperate, he may adopt an immoral position: 'The immoral motive is determined by the consideration that, since the joy of loving seems hopelessly barred to him, he may as well deliver himself over to the joys of hating and obtain what satisfaction he can out of that' (op. cit., p. 27).

As I have tried to show elsewhere, the present evident tendency towards extremism, violence, gross indecency and moral inversion in the arts has developed out of a loss of faith, not only religious faith, but faith of any kind in human qualities and imagination. The brutality in our culture is a manifestation of having nothing to say, and of a loss of confidence in trying to say anything. As a substitute for the satisfactions of creativity based on love, on human 'meeting', and essential collaboration in symbolism, many have taken to forms of intoxication. Nietzsche said that when man loses a sense of whither he is going, he may try to overcome his feeling of emptiness by 'intoxication by music, intoxication by cruelty'. The cruelty in much present-day fashionable art is examined by Phillip Rieff in *Fellow Teachers*: speaking of those who follow 'radical chic', he writes, 'I fear their minds, which are prepared to be violated by any idea'—while they grow 'violent in their expression'. A similar fear is expressed by Theodore Roszak in *Where the Wasteland Ends*, who says of many young directors in the theatre, 'A madhouse imagery of mass murder, canni-balism, necrophilia, Grand Guignol fills their work . . . they forget that art has any other function than to mirror the horrors . . .'

Yet, of course, resort to violence and nihilism need not be the

---

* See the psychoanalytical theories of Michael Balint in *Primary Love and Psychoanalytic Technique* (1952). The schizoid in fact cannot avoid the conclusions of his 'infantile logic' because he knows of no other alternative premises.

consequence of loss of faith. As I have tried to show, elsewhere, the composer Gustav Mahler was only too aware of the menace of nihilistic promptings that there might be no meanin in existence: but he placed this threat of chaos, by Olympian effort, and strove, albeit without God, to find a sense of meaning in existence, having its roots in love.

Many artists today, not least Sylvia Plath's husband, Ted Hughes, stand at a cross-roads in this dilemma, between their own true-self creativity and the false-self solutions offered by what Phillip Rieff calls 'wasp culture'—a significant phrase in the present context, as we shall see. In Ted Hughes's work, there is a tendency to lapse into a glorification of the solutions symbolised by the 'iron horseman', or by Crow, or Krogon, who armour themselves, and deny their vulnerability; while being appalled by their affinity with aggressive animals:

> To Krogon it is his prisoners, the earth, his own body, his bond with animal life on the one hand, with spirit on the other: a compound crime he refuses to recognise, which is slowly dementing him. (*Orghast at Persepolis*, p. 97)

The curative theme shows through:

> Agoluz's role is to convert the Krogonishness inherent in himself (his real father being Krogon) to a sane, rational, albeit limited and partial order, which is workable. (ibid., p. 96)

But here, as in *Crow*, the universe is alien, and if one examines one's links with other men, or with the animal world, all one finds is increasing guilt, and increasing meaninglessness. The relationship between man and the universe can be seen—as it is, say in Marjorie Grene's *Approaches to a Philosophical Biology*, or in John Vyvyan's *Sketch for a World-Picture*, as a marvellous mani-festation of evolving life-forms, in which 'virtue' emerges almost as a creative principle of the universe. Love, for example, seems a product of the growth processes of the higher mammals, and especially man. But this is not the world-view that lies behind the work of Sylvia Plath and her widower.* Yet they, too, in despair

* See, for instance, Ted Hughes's playlet *Eat Crow* (Rainbow Press, 1971) and *A Crow Hymn* (Sceptre Press, 1970), both expressing a view that everything, by cosmic entropy, leads to death.

and doubt, have sought to find meaning and order, by creative effort, however distorted.

To help the artist today to be genuinely creative, rather than fall into dismay, we need to attend carefully to his meanings, and try to understand them. If we make a phenomenological analysis of the meanings of consciousness, as manifest in their symbolism, we may be able to hear the true voice of creativity and compare it with the false meanings of hate and nihilism. This is what I try to do in this analysis of the meanings of the poetry of Sylvia Plath. I try to show that at times she went beyond sanity, towards a higher vision: and yet also, at other times, that she completely falsified the problem of existence—albeit with the aim of trying to begin to live, when she felt she was alive but not yet living. Her predicament was terrible: but even more terrible was the way in which our society applauded her most for the falsifications, while remaining deaf to her truth.

2

Poem for a False Birth

No sooner do I turn to the poems than I am beset with almost insoluble difficulties. I have to try to relate two languages: that of literary criticism and that of those disciplines which investigate the meanings of consciousness. Moreover, I have to set out to bridge two methods, trying to foster the reader's possession of poetic meaning, while endeavouring to discuss universal truths about the dynamics of human personality as seen by 'philosophical anthropology'.

The only way I can convince my reader is by making him feel that the poetry is illuminated by what I am saying, and that the human condition of which poetry speaks is susceptible to understanding. So, my best way to begin is to find a poem central to the *oeuvre* and pursue a discussion of it, even if for the moment I find myself writing an interpretation which will seem strange, if not mad, to the reader.

I propose to begin by making an analysis of the poem at the end of Sylvia Plath's collection *The Colossus, Poem for a Birthday* (pp. 80–8). By a phenomenological approach, exploring the ambiguities and meanings of every word here, I shall try to demonstrate that this poem delineates Sylvia Plath's predicament in all its complexity and takes us into the heart of the dilemma posed by her work. At the same time it will become evident that we need more than literary critical disciplines to fully understand her.

I ask the reader to bear with my analysis of this poem, ignoring for the moment certain problems of the concepts and theory I shall be using. I shall return to these later. For the time being I want to show that Sylvia Plath was indeed, as she believed, speaking of unknown areas of human experience. But yet so acute is the difficulty of such speaking that only by supplying sense from newly available knowledge of schizoid states can we hear what she is saying. Once we can hear we can discuss what is being said. Once we are familiar with unusual areas of awareness the poem can stand on its own as a penetrating record—often of manifestations of existence into which we enter only with reluctance and pain. Yet unless we explore these areas we cannot solve the problems of existence she raises. We cannot go back to the situation before her questions were asked and pretend they have never been uttered.

We may begin with the title: whose birthday is it? The significant phrases in the poem are 'Tell me my name', and 'I shall be as good as new'. The protagonist is in a mental hospital and hopes there to be reborn: or, rather, to be *born*. (I have little doubt the poem is about the poet's own experience of mental breakdown and treatment, of which a fictionalised account is also given in the novel, *The Bell Jar*.) Fairbairn (1952) speaks of how the schizoid individual, because he has not developed a certain capacity to defend himself against painful insights, can see with remarkable clarity into his own condition. In this poem such a person writes of the dreadful experience of being subjected to being 'made anew' by processes which yet never touch on her essential problem of having, at the core, no adequate sense of *being*.

The first section is titled: *Who*. There is no question mark, as if there is no hope that the question may be answered. Just as, later, her child is defined in a poem title, *You're . . .*, here she defines herself as *Who . . .*, (King Lear can ask, 'Who is it that can tell me who I am?': but this contains the verb I AM, and the question demands 'reflection'—a response from 'encounter'.) In the background perhaps is 'Who is Sylvia?'. But the question-mark-less *Who* suggests she has no hope of reflection, and there is no sense of I AM.

At this point an introductory note is necessary on the phrases in this poem: 'the mother of mouths', 'the mother of otherness', 'the mother of pestles'. At a time of rebirth she turns to the potential source of being:

> Mother, you are the one mouth
> I would be a tongue to.

What does she mean in *Who*, by the above lines, and those that follow?

> Mother of otherness
> Eat me . . .

To understand these lines we have to enter into very early feelings of a bodily kind about being born—as we do in Dylan Thomas's *If My Head Hurt a Hair's Foot*. Fairbairn says, 'The child's ego is a mouth-ego'. In all of us there is the remnant of an unsatisfied infant hunger and this 'unborn' dynamic in oneself (the 'regressed libidinal ego') feels like a hungry, all-devouring mouth. As Guntrip (1966) notes, schizoid patients who are seriously unfulfilled and, so, psychically hungry, may dream of this unborn self as a baby, perhaps locked away in a steel drawer. This 'baby' in them has a tremendous hunger to exist—so, once it is recognised, the patient may feel like 'one great mouth, wanting to eat up everything and everybody'.

Individuals who feel inside themselves such a voracious hunger to exist, with its roots in primitive urges to suck, have intense feelings about the gates of the body and also the hungry 'mouth-ego' echoed everywhere in their world. Since the schizoid individual feels such intense hunger directed at his 'objects' (those he would relate to—the 'significant other' and the 'world-as-object'), he comes to feel that the 'object' (the 'other') must have similar voracious feelings directed at him. Love seems a mutual eating—and, so, terribly dangerous. Ted Hughes explores such intense feelings of mutual incorporation in his *Lovesong* (*Crow*, p. 74):

> His kisses sucked out her whole past or future . . .
>
> . . .
> She bit him she gnawed him she sucked
> She wanted him complete inside her
>
> . . .
> In the morning they were each other's face . . .

In *The Divided Self* R. D. Laing discusses how, to the schizoid individual, love or indeed any human contact can seem full of the dangers of mutual incorporation. Every normal person feels this to a degree: lovers feel they want to 'eat one another up'. But insofar as the feeling is full of fear, this arises from infant anxieties of an unconscious kind about the parents' sexual relationship. At a time when sex can only be conceived as a kind of eating, children fear that the parents may eat one another—and, if they become excited and involved, they feel the combined parents may turn round to eat them, because of their involvement. Sylvia Plath's recurrent imagery of mouths is imbued with this kind of intense, primitive, bodily feeling belonging to infancy—although, of course, what she is symbolising are psychic states of being unborn. These bodily feelings are powerfully sexual.

We have known since Freud that children have strong sexual feelings of maleness and femaleness and that these take Oedipal and Electral forms.* These are of great importance in Sylvia Plath, because of her problems of identity, as we shall see. She had intense Electral feelings for her father, full of sexual (or sensual) under-currents, oral and genital feelings. These are evident in *The Beekeeper's Daughter* (*The Colossus*, p. 75)

> A garden of mouthings. Purple, scarlet-speckled, black
> The great corollas dilate, peeling back their silks.
> . . .
> You move among the many breasted hives . . .

These 'mouths', like the tulips in *Tulips*, are female sexual organs, which dilate like eyes and 'peel back their silks', yearning for the father.

> Trumpet-throats open to the beaks of birds.

The birds sucking the honey from the flowers are using a male proboscis to eat the pollen out of the female flowers.

> The anthers nod their heads, potent as kings
> To father dynasties.

The male, phallic, parts of the flowers are potent, and fertile: 'The air is rich' with pollen (semen). 'Here is a queenship no mother can contest...' But since this queenship of the flowers, with which she identifies, has the male-anther potency within itself, it is a *male* femaleness. And since all its yearning is directed at the

---

* Fairbairn's point should be borne in mind, that 'sensual' might be a better term than 'sexual' when discussing such infantile body feelings.

father, it is Electral, incestuous, and therefore matricidal: 'A fruit that's death to taste . . .' The mother is ousted.

But there is a penalty, of paying the price for the taboo on incest, and for the matricide. The fruit that is tasted is not only death to the mother if she tries to taste it: but it is death to the daughter.

The Golden Rain Tree drips its powders down.*

This is an image of the phallus, casting seed: but it is also an image of urinary rain, of a retributive kind.† The great corollas, with which she identifies, which 'peel back their silks' are, strangely, also male penises, peeling back their foreskins. Her identification is so intense that not only does she yearn for Daddy like the female flowers. She becomes a strange male-anther flower, involved in terrible dangers—which are the dangers of exposing oneself to being dealt with in a way of whose nature and purpose one is uncertain: it could be hate: it could be jealous revenge: it could be castration. The significance of these feelings will appear later.‡

Here there are intense complexities. Love—as to all schizoid individuals—is dangerous, a mouth-consuming thing. So, to enter into sexual relationship with the father is dangerous anyway. Secondly, he might well become angry and guilty at being seduced by his daughter, while she becomes guilty too. Further dangers lurk in her identification with the yearning flowers and the male creatures in intercourse with them. Thirdly, there is competition with the ousted mother, who might then appear in a castrating guise—perhaps even from the heart of a flower, since the flowers, and the daughter who identifies with them, represent the female object to which the father is drawn. Fourthly, Sylvia Plath (as I shall argue) seems to have experienced the mother's handling in infancy, for whatever reason, as something meaning-

* In Jung's *Man and His Symbols* (p. 280) there is an illustration of Jan Gossaert's painting (now in the Alte Pinakothek, Munich) showing Danae being impregnated by Zeus in the form of a shower of gold. This symbolises the marriage of heaven and earth.

† The proper word here would be 'talion', the Freudian term from *lex talionis*, 'An eye for an eye and a tooth for a tooth'. The child is believed to fear talion retribution from those on whom he directs his sadistic urges to empty, to eat—or to enjoy sexually, since this is a form of eating.

‡ Astonishingly, this poem, with its richness of Electral passion, is called by Ted Hughes 'one of her chilliest' (*The Art of Sylvia Plath*, p. 190).

less and bewildering, largely composed of 'impingement', a kind of (male) 'doing', substituted for (female) being. Instead of a female 'being for', what she experienced was 'doing' scraps of maleness. Thus, what fascinates her about the flowers is the maleness to be found in them. Fifthly, her own identity, having been composed of male fragments, tends to give the flowers a male quality when she identifies with them. And since such 'impingement is experienced as hate' (as Winnicott tells us), this makes the flowers full of hate-dynamics and 'a fruit that's death to taste'. Moreover, since Daddy is dead, to identify with him, and to have such yearnings for intercourse with him even in memory, threatens petrifaction and death. The poem thus takes us into the other world of death which will be found important in her work.

Tasting is something one does by the mouth: so, tasting the flowers as the birds do with their male beaks, and as she wants to do, is full of dangers—of being subjected to a retributory attack from the same source as the seed: of being annihilated, even in enjoying the flowers which her father moved among and which his bees enjoyed. She is a woman inclined to do male things—but fearing terrible consequences, as we shall often see. (If she sucks at the father's penis in using him as a substitute for the mother with her breast, may not his 'milk' be a taste of death?)

The focus of these complex primitive feelings is the need to be, reflected by one's parents, in *becoming a female being*. It is this confusion which lies behind the dreadful section of *Poem for a Birthday*, *Who*, and its sterility and hopelessness, and, indeed, behind many of Sylvia Plath's poems. The mother is the 'Mother of otherness': that is, mother of the-other-being-that-I-would-like-to-be—not this 'dead head' in the toolshed. But what she wants of the mother is that she should 'Eat me . . .' How does the desire to be born have to do with eating? Sex, as we have said, is a kind of eating, to a child and, so, relating to the flowers (which are a rich source of life), is eating, and full of potential destructiveness. Yet (she feels) there must be a clue here somewhere to the deeply desired birth. It is somewhere in entering or being in, or emerging from, between 'two lips' like the mouths of flowers (tulips)—somewhere in the 'mouth' experience (which is also the genital experience). Eating is how one grows: so, it becomes a symbol of the way to psychic growth. This is all focussed in that one phrase 'mother of mouths'.

Of course, Sylvia Plath knew consciously about copulation, conception and birth. But the adult can still have an unsatisfied curiosity at the deeper levels of the psyche. He can go on in adult life, in symbol and fantasy, trying to answer problems he engaged with as an infant, even though intellectually he knows the answers. The primitive curiosity is not satisfied.* So, the little unborn self reminds itself:

> I said: I must remember this, being small.
> There were such enormous flowers,
> Purple and red mouths, utterly lovely.
>
> The hoops of blackberry stems made me cry.
> (*Who*)

Once upon a time she loved, as a child, the great flowers and their mouths, in which there seemed to be the secret of *coming into life*. Now she is reduced to being small again, to being a little girl punished by conventional psychiatric treatment, so she tries to remember this early promise, and its secret. She remembers, too, dimly, the blackberry stems which, bent like hoops (and seen thus by a child), made her cry—by scratching her. That is, she has here a dim remembrance of the threat of impinging hate which we have noticed in *The Beekeeper's Daughter*. But the berries are also dimly associated with black eyes that *see* (see p. 48) and with blackberrying with Daddy (see p. 242).

The blackberry hoops merge with an image of the wires of the electro-convulsive therapy apparatus and the 'berries of the dark' which her (?insulin) treatment brings her. These too are 'fruits that are death to taste'. That is, they are punishments, inflicted upon her by those she trusts (who are thus parents), in the same way that (she fears) the parents will punish her for her involvement in their sex.

> Now they light me up like an electric bulb.
> For weeks I can remember nothing at all.

---

* See Chapter 10, 'Primitive Fantasy', in *The Masks of Hate*; also p. 91, where I discuss Melanie Klein's theory, and suggest Ian Fleming's paranoid-schizoid fantasies are based on 'unsatisfied infantile curiosity' about parental sex.

Electro-convulsive therapy brings the same impingement of hate which she feared as a death from the flowers. And it destroys the delightful visions she had as a child round these Electral images. Now she is 'Without dreams of any sort'. Yet she knows her predicament, and here we can return to the image with which we began our reading.

> Mother, you are the one mouth
> I would be a tongue to.

Noticeably, the phrase is 'a tongue'. In *The Beekeeper's Daughter* she identifies with various kinds of flower or parts of flowers, anthers, petals. But here she wants to be 'a tongue' in the mother's mouth. This means that she wants to be spoken, out of her mother's mouth, as a creature that can herself say I AM. But the image of the tongue merges into that of a penis. Here physical feelings are involved, in complex with forms of activity to do with the gates of the body—eating, kissing, sucking, speaking, having sexual intercourse, being born, thrusting one's beak into a flower, displaying one's potent anthers, having dripped upon one a golden rain from heaven. Although being a tongue in the mother's mouth is in some respects a passive image—it is also a male image, of thrusting one's tongue into the mother's mouth like a lover, or thrusting one's penis into the mother's sexual organ, or thrusting one's body, by 'reptation' through it, for the yearning is to be born out of the mother's birth passage, as well as for being confirmed by the mother's speaking of one, in creative reflection. Mouth and vagina are paths to an inner world, the container, inside, cavern, vacuum, or tomb: but also through into another world, hopefully a new world.

In *The Beekeeper's Daughter*, as we have seen, the father is dead. To enter too closely into union with him might bring one into the world of the dead. The 'otherness' which is sought, then, might lead not to life-in-life, but to death-in-life.* Later we shall see the terrible consequences of such lack of confidence in both parents and their internal imagos. As paths to life (as they are to the child) they could also be paths to death.

* See the phenomenology of 'Rudolph' below, p. 169ff. The marriage of heaven and earth could give one greater life on earth, but could also take one, like Eurydice, into the other world beyond death.

In *Tulips* the flowers sent to the protagonist in hospital as a 'get-well' gift are resented and seem hateful and threatening. In *The Bell Jar* when Esther's mother brings her a bunch of roses as a get-well gift, she rejects them and thrusts them into the waste-paper basket. Relationship is at times intolerable:

> 'You're not to have any more visitors for a while.'
> I stared at Doctor Nolan in surprise. 'Why that's wonderful.'
> 'I thought you'd be pleased.' She smiled.
> Then I looked, and Doctor Nolan looked, at the waste-basket beside my bureau. Out of the waste-basket poked the blood-red buds of a dozen long-stemmed roses.
> That afternoon my mother had come to visit me.
>
> (*The Bell Jar*, p. 214)

Here, the roses are not female genitals or mouths, as are the flowers in *Tulips*, but male phalluses ('poked . . . buds . . . long-stemmed'). The hatred directed at them springs perhaps from 'Electral' envy at the mother's possession of the father, as if she has his penis inside her. But, as will appear more fully as we proceed, I believe there is a deeper resentment, which is rooted in a belief that in infancy the mother proved unable to give her anything but 'pseudo-male impingement'.

As we shall see, the most disturbing aspect of *The Bell Jar* is Esther's hatred of her mother. And this hatred of the mother-imago pervades Sylvia Plath's poetry, mingled with dread, resentment, and rage. In *The Bell Jar* the roses are symbols of that death which belongs to hate, directed in revenge against the mother who (she believes) has not been able to love.

> That afternoon my mother had brought me the roses.
> 'Save them for my funeral,' I'd said.
> My mother's face puckered, and she looked ready to cry.
> 'But, Esther, don't you remember what day it is today?'
> 'No.'
> I thought it might be Saint Valentine's day.
> 'It's your *birth*day.'
> And that was when I had dumped the roses in the waste-basket.
> 'That was a silly thing for her to do,' I said to Doctor Nolan.

Doctor Nolan nodded. She seemed to know what I meant. 'I hate her,' I said, and waited for the blow to fall.

But Doctor Nolan only smiled at me as if something had pleased her very, very much, and said, 'I suppose you do.'

(p. 215)

Here we have an account of the moment also referred to in *Poem for a Birthday*, by the phrase 'wastebasket gaper'.

It is at this kind of point that the literary critic, faced with a work in which the negative and distorted dynamics are so intense, begins to wish he had the benefits of the therapist who knows his patient and has years of training and experience behind him. We need to strive to see the individual using symbols in the here and now as an adult, to try to find solutions to life-problems of an intense kind. Phenomenologically, it will not do to explain these symbols in terms of their 'cause' in infantile experience. It would not do to conclude that Sylvia Plath's problems are explained by some postulated failure of her mother's care. The blow to her infant happiness from her father's death has coloured her own interpretation of her early relationship with her mother, and also distorts her account of her own attitudes to her mother, insofar as she 'is' Esther. She loved her father passionately, and there were intense Electral feelings in that (of a little girl wanting her father as a lover and supplanting the mother). But now, after his death, she wants to follow him into the world of death, to get from him the 'reflection' she still needs and could not get from the mother.

While she expected normal retaliatory vengeance from her shadow (or 'castrating') mother imago, for the Electral feelings, what happens to these feelings now that Daddy is dead? Adult sexuality was associated for the infant with eating up and annihilating: her fantasy involvement in it had brought fears of retribution from the combined parents. But now the mother has become a 'Shadow of doorways' because she has eaten the dead Daddy and has him inside her. In her impassioned desire to go down into his tomb, she also wants to get into her mother's womb where Daddy, or Daddy's penis, is hidden. And she herself, we remember, wants to get back into the womb to be reborn.

This is the answer to our problems over the hate expressed in the poetry and fiction for the mother: and it is also the answer to the whole problem of Sylvia Plath's hopeless logic—for in the very place she seeks is death, and the black dead Daddy whom in the end she rejects. He blocks the place from which, she hoped, she might emerge again. But she is also afraid of the mother who, having eaten Daddy, might eat her ('Mother of otherness/Eat me'), thus absorbing her into the shadows. The flowers are the mothers' genital ('two lips') which might, like her own heart, eat her, out of sheer love (these phrases come from the poem *Tulips*), and take her down to that world where dead Daddy is. So, the mother must be forestalled, nor least in her love, because of this menace.

The hatred directed at the mother belongs to the same paranoid-schizoid delusion which makes her think suicide a way to re-birth. The mother is a threatening shadow: the flowers are tigers: 'keep them for my funeral'. The same kind of frightened, and vengeful, rejection of the mother is to be found in *Edge* (*Ariel*, p. 85), where we find clues that her suicide may also in part be a form of vengeance directed at the mother, 'who is used to this sort of thing'—because she has eaten the father. All this, of course, belongs to the logic of a deeply distressed infant who cannot explain things otherwise. All we can say is that here we are dealing with primitive experiences which we are only just beginning to understand: something like the experience which according to D. W. Winnicott, his patient, 'George', had as a baby: 'From my point of view it was just there that George was experiencing and re-experiencing being nothing, which is what it feels like for a child when there is a dead imago in the mother's inner psychic reality' (1971, p. 391).

This sentence illuminates much in the consciousness of certain artists. Such dead imagos haunt the work of Gustav Mahler (as in the *Kindertotenlieder*), the poems of Dylan Thomas, the stories of George Macdonald and the plays of Barrie. The shadows in Sylvia Plath's work symbolise voids in the mother's 'inside' which she believed she experienced. They represent fragments of the experience of emptiness where there should have been 'honey', or 'reflection'. Where she should have experienced 'being for', to enable her to feel 'I am', she experienced 'impingement', as a kind of hate, and a false maleness. Her 'realisation' should have brought all the experiences of being handled together in the same body, in the same world.* But it did not. In the absence of a substantial sense of being loved and 'seen' in her own right she feels she had had to steal whatever forms of 'male doing' she could grasp. Mother's femininity for some reason is not accessible: she had had to 'steal' maleness from mother (a breast that is a penis) and whatever she can in this way from Daddy (beans, rose-buds, clubs, old tools, handles, tusks, pestles—a 'cupboard of rubbish'). There are fragments from the mother's comings and goings and fading, half-remembered fragments of memory of Daddy which never cohere into anything but a cracked colossus or automaton.

So, there is an urgent need for tenderness, a need to begin physical love play all over again to become whole by loving handling: mouth-play at the nipple, kissing, speaking and being spoken of. To be the tongue in the mother's mouth is to identify so closely with the mother that one *is* she: and yet, as she utters, and gives tongue, she 'speaks' one—she makes her child. To want to be a tongue to the mother's mouth is to want to be *made*, between two lips.

So, we come to the central theme of the need to be given an identity by *liebende Wirheit*, loving communion. 'You are the one mouth I would be a tongue to' means 'I would like to be spoken of by you, being part of you, so closely identified with you that it would be as if I were speaking, or being spoken, from within you.' And, 'I would like to be confirmed (born) out of the lips of your mouth (womb)'. Since the poem is about psychic parturition, this takes us into the area of primary psychogenesis—what Guntrip calls 'the very start of the human identity'.

As I was writing this chapter a newspaper reported how a woman's baby was restored to her four days after being stolen from his pram. In an interview she said: 'At first I *could not speak* and *dare not look at him. Then I fed him* . . . When he was away I felt I must have *imagined having him* . . .' (my italics). Such comments reveal that the child's discovery of his identity is based on a creative psychic process: if a baby is taken away from her a mother suffers a 'schizoid illness'—and begins to lose the meaningful baby

* See Winnicott, 'Primitive Emotional Development' in 1968a pp. 145 ff., and 'Creativity and its Origins', in 1971a, p. 65. If a girl-baby looked into her mother's mind and found an unconscious desire to have a boy it could lead to such problems as are discussed in the latter, and in this chapter.

she has created in imagination (or 'spoken'). When this woman's baby was returned to her, she couldn't at first 'find' him, as the meaningful baby she had created. When she feeds him she 'makes' him by feeding him and re-establishes his real existence for her. She 'speaks' him. Or rather, perhaps, she has to re-enter into that strange relationship in which she allows him to believe that *he is she*, or *has made her*, which we shall discuss further below.

With Sylvia Plath, I believe, something undermined catastrophically, for whatever reason, her experience of this primary parturition at the start, perhaps 'from the moment of birth', leaving what Laing has called 'a vortex of non-being', which was deepened and intensified by her father's death, and left her with a baffled feeling—desperately needing reflection from the mother but fearing this intense hunger might rebound on her, not least because the father is buried inside the mother. So, despite her evident concern, the mother was kept at arm's length.

I. WHO

In *The Bell Jar* Esther rejects her birthday because it can only be a 'non-birthday'. Here, the harvest is a non-harvest. It is October:

> The month of flowering's finished. The fruit's in,
> Eaten or rotten. I am all mouth.
> October's the month for storage.

Perhaps in the background is Keat's *Ode to Autumn*: 'and fill all fruit with ripeness to the core'. But she is not full. She is 'all mouth': her whole being yearns to come into existence. And where is she?

> This shed's fusty as a mummy's stomach:
>
> . . .
>
> These halls are full of women who think
>   they are birds.

At first the poem seems to be about being in a garden shed in autumn. But gradually we come to see it is about a mental hospital ward. What is stored there is no harvest, nor are the creatures hibernating, so as to come alive in the spring. There is a fusty hopelessness about the poem—about ever satisfying the regressed libidinal ego who hungers for fulfilment.

A mummy is a dried corpse, with a fusty stomach. But the word obviously takes on the meaning of 'Mummy!' in the light of 'I am all mouth' and what follows. The 'shed' is like a dry-as-dust womb, and the mental ward is like the inside of a mummified mother. The short time (month) of being out in the world as a living creature is ended: the individual with a dead identity is gathered in with the others, as part of a grotesque harvest of 'dead heads'.

I am at home here among the dead heads.

She is with the fruit, which is either eaten or rotten: one is either loved or else one decays. But to be loved is to risk being eaten, and yet she wants the mother to eat her. Yet in the shed (or ward) she is merely put away inside a fusty and sterile space, which is no good to her (as useless as she felt Mummy was). As Laing notes, of the Jonah theme in the symbolism of schizophrenia, 'to be eaten does not necessarily mean to lose one's identity'. Here Sylvia Plath examines the nature of being eaten (in all the complex sense I have discussed above) in terms of being born (or 'spoken'). The odds and ends of dead heads in the mental ward (or in the cupboard of herself) seem to amount to nothing. They do not seem edible.

Fairbairn says that the schizoid individual, out of desperation, and because he is not loved, steals the paternal penis and the mother's breasts, in order to assemble something, as the basis of identity. He takes by force that which was due to him by right but not freely given. But trying to steal love, he steals part-objects. Masud Khan attributes a girl's promiscuity in one case to her need to steal men's penises, in order to fill a void in herself (Khan, 1971). Other case-histories discuss a disturbed sense of 'inner space' in the schizoid individual. Here, the 'shed' is not only the mental ward, but also the identity, in which are stored odd stolen tools, handles, and teeth which have gone rusty from neglect ('rusty tusks'). Later there is a reference to herself as 'hairtusk's bride'. Who is 'Hairtusk'? Is he the father's stolen penis? Or is he Fido Littlesoul, the puppyish infant self that gnaws away at the root of the self? As we shall see, the disturbing fact is that he is a *he*.

It is evident as we take the poem symbol by symbol that all the fragments belong to an assemblage that is self-enclosed. We should not take 'hairtusk's bride' as an invitation to start looking round for a real husband. Nothing enters from outside, or hardly anything—her world is a largely encapsulated one, inside her garden shed. Laing relates this self-enclosure to the schizoid's urge to be omnipotent.

> He tried to be omnipotent by enclosing within his own being, without recourse to a creative relationship with others, modes of relationship that require the effective presence to him of other people and of the outer world. He would appear to be, in an unreal, impossible way, all persons and things to himself.
>
> (Laing, 1960, p. 78)

To Sylvia Plath, being incarcerated (harvested) in the mental ward echoes this incarceration of the world within herself. Give-and-take is too full of dangers: so, an inner world must be maintained, cut off in its closed circuit from the outer world. The self itself has shrunk to something tiny and insignificant, like an elf.

> Let me sit in a flowerpot,
> The spiders won't notice.

The spiders will neither pounce on her and eat her, nor stop spinning their webs. Here there are no big flowers, 'utterly lovely': there is only lifeless aridity:

> My heart is a stopped geranium.

—as if it has been nipped out.

She is at the end of a period of 'treatment': yet instead of opening her heart as a 'bowl of blooms' (which 'opens and closes for sheer love of me'—see *Tulips*) the geranium is 'stopped' and the flowerpot is empty. Yet she feels impingement, as Dylan Thomas felt it, as having to do with *breathing* difficulties.* There is an inversion of normal responses—the petals bloom upside down: the

---

*Winnicott believed he had discovered links between birth traumata and breathing difficulties. See 'Birth Memories, Birth Traumata and Anxiety', *Collected Papers*, p. 174. See also the discussion of this in my *Dylan Thomas: the Code of Night*, pp. 168 ff.

feelings are those of resistance to what others would feel to be care:

> If only the wind would leave my lungs alone.
> Dogbody noses the petals. They bloom upside down.
> They rattle like hydrangea bushes.

We may compare this with lines in *Tulips* (*Ariel*, p. 20):

> I didn't want any flowers, I only wanted
> To lie with my hands turned up and be utterly empty . . .

> The vivid tulips eat my oxygen.

> Before they came the air was calm enough,
> Coming and going, breath by breath, without any fuss.

Breathing is unwanted. It even seems an impingement to breathe. 'Dogbody' smelling the petals is resented—as in *Tulips*, the love-gift impinges, and the flowers threaten to eat the life-giving air, while the space around the patient is disturbed by resented eddies of life. In *Who* the flower-bushes are rattling like dead plants.

Who is Dogbody? A busybody who seeks to do good to you in God's name? A dogsbody in hospital—an orderly? In Ted Hughes's *Gog* there is a reference to the 'dog's God'. In T. S. Eliot's *The Waste Land* we read, 'O keep the Dog far hence . . .', which some critics interpret because of its capital initial letter as a reversal of 'God'. Anybody who comes along (doctor, mother, orderly, nurse, the Fido Littlesoul inside you) impinges on you.

What consolation is there? The poem is hopeless: the only consolation is the deadness itself:

> Mouldering heads console me,
> Nailed to the rafters yesterday:

The women in the mental ward are vegetables: yet they have a strange beauty:

> Cabbageheads: wormy purple, silver-glaze,
> A dressing of mule ears, mothy pelts, but green-hearted,
> Their veins white as pork fat.

> O the beauty of usage!

The simple fact of vegetable existence, with a green heart, still seems to indicate hope somewhere, usage, usefulness. There is no usage here, certainly, except ill-usage perhaps. She remembers cabbages in toolsheds, somewhere, being beautiful: somewhere is earthy life. One feels at home in relation to the earth-object. But there seems little chance of reflection—of eyes seeing one:

> The orange pumpkins have no eyes.

And within herself she has been taught to be petrified:

> This is a dull school.
> I am a root, a stone, an owl pellet,
> Without dreams of any sort.

What Sylvia Plath is telling us is that the inhabitants of the ward have the beauty of living creatures. They are deluded (they think they are birds). But conventional psychiatry has destroyed their visions—so she becomes a dull root, a dead stone or a pellet of skin and bone, rather than wisdom—vomited, eaten and dead, out of an owl's inside ('I am round as an owl').

The only hope was in the mother. So, she tries to go back to being little. Now, she can remember nothing at all—and yet feels she is being *taught* something ('I must remember this . . .', 'made me cry . . .'). Yet what in fact is happening is that her little real self shrinks into a flowerpot, under a stone, or under a potlid, to avoid persecution. Being punished when in a hopeless situation makes the adult patient feel like a naughty little girl—so Sylvia Plath feels she is a tot. This minuscule self seems to emerge elsewhere from bewilderment about the identity—as in *Alice in Wonderland* or when, in George Macdonald's *Phantastes*, the lost anima is discovered as a little naked figure in the cavity of a locked ancient desk. There is a sense in which Sylvia Plath spent all her life seeking her femininity (as queen bee, for instance) and never finding it. Yet it seemed not far away—'utterly lovely', in the flowers in the garden in her childhood, as her father moved among the 'many-breasted hives'. What she sought was a shower of gold from heaven that would marry heaven to earth in the sense of making heaven and earth meaningful. Instead, heaven, moon and earth remained sterile, fatherless, unreflecting, deathly, voracious —while there is no answer to 'who'.

2. DARK HOUSE

In the next section she speaks of how, consequently, she has had to establish an identity out of whatever comes to hand. Not having a substance from 'female element being' (which later we shall connect with *beeing*—and *honey*) she is a wasp making a self by (male) bustling and doing:

> This is a dark house, very big.
> I made it myself...

The inner edifice has to be made out of intellectual effort, by a 'thinking' version of that impingement 'which is experienced as hate'—which is why it is dark. It is a shadow self (see *Tulips*: 'I see myself... a cut-paper shadow')* and made of grey paper,

> Cell by cell from a quiet corner,
> Chewing at the grey paper,
> Oozing the glue drops,
> Whistling, wiggling my ears,
> Thinking of something else
> . . .
> I see by my own light.†

As we shall see, it is significant that the poet's father was an entomologist and professor of biology at Boston who wrote a book on bumblebees.‡ A bee is 'good'—it makes honey, and stings only when it is necessary to die for the purpose. A wasp only 'does', is a little tiger, yielding nothing useful like honey or wax but only its dry papery nest, and it stings much more aggressively. It is more 'male' than the bee. ('The bees are all women', *Wintering, Ariel*, p. 69.)

Elsewhere she says, 'This is the light of the mind, cold and planetary'. Since her self is a hollow, intellectual construct, made of paper (regurgitated 'inner contents', mental doing, containing empty breath) it could just as well become anything else, or,

---

* There are schizoid elements of a similar kind in the symbolism of shadows detached from the self in Barrie's *Peter Pan* and George Macdonald's *Phantastes*. See also Richard Strauss's opera, *Die Frau Ohne Schatten*. Not having a shadow is not being personalised and embodied—i.e. not psychically born.
† Two grey, papery bags—
    This is what I am made of... (*Apprehensions, Crossing the Water*, p. 57).
‡ *Bumblebees and Their Ways*, Macmillan, New York, 1934.

magically, could give birth to anything. (She is a writer who makes a world of paper and words which are breath.) By the same process of paper-making she could also make maps to show herself directions, or generate an identity:

> Any day I may litter puppies
> Or mother a horse. My belly moves.
> I must make more maps.

The haphazard imagery expresses her desperation at not knowing what she is, and her uncertainty about taking on any form, finding any direction, or creating anything from her body that was substantial and trustworthy.

Within her she has emptiness:

> . . . so many cellars,
> Such eelish delvings!

Through which she makes her way, groping and blind:

> Moley-handed, I eat my way.

The mind, however dissociated, is aware that there is a body within which there are tunnels and shafts: somewhere there must be a structure, yet as she explores it, she can find nothing secure or reliable (and she explores it by male symbols, eels and moles). Yet she can observe her predicament with a strange (and, to use her own word elsewhere, 'daft') wittiness: 'wiggling my ears'—the image of a wasp's antennae twitching as it works is hilarious, transferred to an introspective self-seeking to create a self by insect-like activity.

Somewhere 'down there' is the regressed libidinal ego, with its hunger for nourishment—licking what he can from the substance of the self: 'I am all mouth' and

> All-mouth licks up the bushes
> And the pots of meat.
> He lives in an old well,
> A stony hole. He's to blame.
> He's a fat sort.

This 'All-mouth' is the regressed libidinal ego, the 'dark thing', that 'sleeps', in her, 'looking out with its hooks for something to

love' (*Elm*). But there are here some strange things about 'him'—
not least the fact that he is a *he* (in poem 4, 'Fido Littlesoul' is also
a he). Why is Sylvia Plath's regressed libidinal ego a male? (Or it
could be a puppy or horse?) I have argued in relation to Dylan
Thomas that his problems of identity perhaps originated when his
mother handled him as if he were another sibling that had died.
Winnicott reports a man with a split-off female element, who was
handled as if he were a girl. A girl patient of Masud Khan had a
split-off male element, because she was handled as a boy.* I believe
we can argue, on the basis of my analyses above, that Sylvia Plath
has within her identity a split-off male element built on hate—and
this is *all* she has. She doesn't have any female core. A fragment of
maleness is the basis of her identity and this consists of an internalisation of the mother's 'pseudo-male doing'. But since she
identified so closely with her father later she also confuses this
with his identity, and with her internalisation of his male element.
So, she has a confused and fragmentary male identity, which is in
part bits of Daddy, the Colossus: in part formed of the father's
stolen penis; in part a little puppy—a 'fat sort', or little animal—
mumble-paws, Littlesoul, not knowing what it is. She knows
(however) that she is a girl, because of her body. So, she is only a
kind of mate to the stolen maleness: Hairtusk's' bride. (In *Birthday
Present* the 'tusk' is rejection, with death lurking in the background.)

All-mouth is a 'fat sort' who is hungry and lives in a hole, licks
up the bushes and the pots of meat. 'He's to blame' in some way:
what for? For her existence, I believe: and so he is the father's
penis, stolen and kept inside her, in a vacancy in the sterile and
petrified core of the self ('a stony hole') where the hunger *to be*
has never been satisfied, and femaleness has never been found.
The stolen father's penis with its hungry mouth is thus identified
with the regressed libidinal ego, which is also 'to blame' for the
present predicament: so, he is the butt of the anti-libidinal ego,
that is (according to Fairbairn), the dynamic in the self that hates
the weakness of the baby-self. He (Hairtusk—All-mouth—Fido
Littlesoul) is hated and feared because he is a hungry mouth, a

---

* See Winnicott, 1971a, p. 65; and Khan, 'En la regardant et en écoutant, je
pensais à une image en surimpression à la télévision: il y avait les deux personnes
distinctes superposées . . .' (1971), p. 53. (Now in English in Khan (1974), p 234.)

glutton for one's marrow. Yet he bears, as a 'fat sort', a resemblance to the tongue in the mother's mouth: a baby in a petrified matrix that cannot speak it forth.*

This complex primitive imagery surely symbolises Fairbairn's remarks, 'Deep down, the schizoid individual yearns to love and be loved'? The poem goes on

> Pebble smells, turnipy chambers.
> Small nostrils are breathing.
> Little humble loves!
> Footlings, boneless as noses . . .

In the last stanza we have a flood of tenderness—as if for her own unborn children. But the tenderness is rather for the unborn aspects of the self in regression. As noted below, Guntrip reports that schizoid patients dream of babies in steel drawers or waiting in some way to be born. It is such a baby she cherishes at the root of her being.

> It is warm and tolerable
> In the bowel of the root.
> Here's a cuddly mother.

By such strange visions of her interior world, Sylvia Plath penetrates to her own deepest problems, the need to be mothered—as psychiatry could not mother her. She tries to mother herself. She wants to bring her baby-self to birth, from her own bowels. At the time when being alive, and especially being 'treated', is intolerable, the regressed libidinal ego, symbolised as 'little humble loves', is warm and tolerable, 'drawn back inside' the cuddly bowels of the mother-self.

It is indeed strange that these regressed libidinal egos are plural She is a 'many-sounding-minded'-creature of several 'systems'.†
The 'boneless . . . noses' or 'footlings' are little baby penises or toes round which a true self could be built. She knows 'I have a

---

* In *All the Dear Dears*, a skeleton who stands for Death threatens to eat the marrow out of the poet's bones: later the skeleton's skull through the glass comes to look like the mother's face in a mirror. It is as if the *hunger to be reflected* itself is like a voracious Death while the mother's face is unreflectingly stony and bonelike.

† 'Many sounding minded' is a phrase from Dylan Thomas. The concept of several systems is from R. D. Laing (1960).

self to recover' (*Stings*) and cries 'There ought . . . to be a ritual for being born twice' (*The Bell Jar*)—hoping for 'a second chance to live' (Guntrip).

3. MAENAD

The name *Maenad* for a Bacchante is from μαίνομαι, 'to be mad': it contains the English word M(aen)ad. Section 3 simply means 'I went mad':

> Once I was ordinary . . .

—there was a time when I was not mad. How did I get like this? I sat as a child identifying with my father, taking in wisdom from him:

> Sat by my father's bean tree
> Eating the fingers of wisdom.

The 'bean tree' seems to have a special relevance for Sylvia Plath: it occurs again in *The Bee Meeting* (*Ariel*, p. 60) where memories of the father bee-keeper evoke vivid feelings about the beanfield in which there are:

> Feather dusters fanning their hands in a sea of bean flowers,
> Creamy bean flowers with black eyes and leaves like bored
> hearts.
> Is it blood clots the tendrils are dragging up that string?

In the same field are:

> Strips of tinfoil winking like people . . .

In this scene we have the juxtaposition of several images which are of intense significance to Sylvia Plath: shiny tinfoil like winking eyes; leaves like hearts with holes in; bloodclots (actually flowers that will one day be *edible*—as beans). The flowers and tinfoil strips are bright eyes (the significance of which will be evident later), associated with blood and the outflowings of the heart. Taking into account the underlying physical imagery, of primitive sexuality, what we have here are images of love-hunger. (To Jung the father was the source of spiritual wisdom, which becomes part of the woman's *animus*, her internalization of maleness taken from the father.) So, to sit by her father's bean tree, 'eating the fingers of wisdom', is not only to take in his instruction but to eat his penis—to take into herself the male elements of his identity, feeling that she was stealing these, because love had not been freely given.

Here, looking back on her childhood,

> The birds made milk.

'When I was a child', she is saying, 'I thought that the birds' white liquid droppings were milk.' This might be a natural thing for a little girl to think. But earlier we found the women in the mental hospital wards thinking they were birds. So, the birds that make milk seem like breasts. The women think they are birds; the child thought that the birds were a kind of part of woman. Because of the confusion of part-objects, I believe, the birds are not only breasts, but also represent the penis which is like a little bird and can in a sense make milk (and if one has stolen it instead of the breast, the confusion is understandable).

> When it thundered I hid under a flat stone.

A child is afraid because of guilt: when love has had to be stolen, the guilt arises from the fear of talion revenge which is expected from God (who is a kind of Daddy). A flat stone resembles a tombstone, so this is to play dead: but also in being flat it has no proud assertiveness—and such assertiveness might reveal the erect, colossus-like, phallic nature of her male identity. That is, if she stood up erect, it would be obvious that she had stolen the father's penis, a lingam, a pestle. Here we approach a strange underlying fear in Sylvia Plath: to be alive is to be 'wrong' because life is sustained by a stolen instrument of love that does not really belong to you. To hide under a flat stone is to assume a female prostrate posture, and so to escape. As we shall see, in *The Bell Jar* Sylvia Plath's protagonist's suicidal impulse comes immediately after her visit to her father's grave, as if to find the secret of her identity, which was perhaps in the 'female element' of the father, lying there under that stone, with flowers 'where the person's navel would be' (down inside mother earth).

Why did she go mad?

> The mother of mouths didn't love me.
> The old man shrank to a doll.

This is as clear a statement as any schizoid individual could make of the origins of her predicament. It says that 'when I was an infant, my intense oral needs, my hunger for survival, were not met by the mother who should have provided creative reflection for my mouth-ego. I had to build my identity on maleness, so I stole my father's "old man". But my father died and my memories of his image faded—so I found myself with no inward possession of him, based on secure identification, but with a stolen penis that became a little doll in my hands'. From this insight we can see that the colossus, the statue-man she puts together from scraps in her work, is a kind of 'transitional object'—a teddy-bear or doll.

Boys (Winnicott tells us) prefer hard transitional objects: girls prefer soft ones: the symbolism is that of differences of body and being. In Sylvia Plath's case, because a soft breast-object could not be taken into the self (or mouth-object from 'the mother of mouths'), she has to substitute a penis-object, a male dolly.* Masud Khan links sexual perversion to transitional object phenomena and so the plaything here may be seen to have sexual undertones. The 'old man' that 'shrinks to a doll' is the stolen penis which is used in a futile way to 'masturbate a glitter' (cf. *Death and Co.*); but (as we shall see) his eyes are bald and unreflecting. In discussing these fetichistic (and penis-envy) elements in Sylvia Plath, as they may be linked from this very revealing poem, I am trying to prepare the reader for the amazing meanings of her adoption of male modes, and the ferocious resentment which developed later out of desperation, when these failed her.

At last, in *Daddy* (*Ariel*, p. 54), in exasperation and frustration she decides that this way of 'communicating' through the 'black telephone' to her father in the other world must be given up, and she must castrate (or annihilate) herself of the male phallus-imago. Her repeated attempts to establish an identity by the use of the penis of the 'colossus' take her a long way beyond the pitiful hopelessness of *Poem for a Birthday*, towards murderous revenge:

---

* Cf. the 'darning-egg' witchwomen in *The Disquieting Muses*, *The Colossus*, p. 58. At the end of the short story *The Wishing Box* the protagonist, who has committed suicide, is dancing with 'her red-capped prince'—the father's penis.

Daddy, I have had to kill you.
You died before I had time—
Marble-heavy, a bag full of God,
Ghastly statue with one grey toe
Big as a Frisco seal

And a head in the freakish Atlantic
Where it pours bean green over blue . . .

Here Daddy is a petrified penis as big as a seal (in the *bean* green
Atlantic), corresponding to the big toe of a Colossus whom, she
feels, she could have made satisfactory *if she had had time*. (Her
father died of a disease which began in his toe.) She has a photo of
him with a cleft in his chin. She makes a joke of this cleft being
there instead of in his foot. But the cleft is the cleft in the stolen
penis, and the black telephone that is 'cut off at the root' is the
penis she castrates (and steals). But, in truth, this big, hate-
constructed, black, dead penis is her *own* split-off male element
(animus), against which all her spleen is directed, in ultimate hopelessness. Instead of femaleness, all she has is a cleft in the 'chin' of a
stolen phallus. This maleness as the basis of her woman's identity
is the secret behind her obsession with darning dollies and other
fetishistic symbols.

The hopelessness is there in *Maenad*:

O I am too big to go backward . . .

As Guntrip says, the schizoid individual, though he yearns for
rebirth, is yet terrified of being 'drawn back inside'—into a loss of
all objects, by ultimate regression. She realises there is no going
back: she is too big.

As a child she believed that bird's droppings were milk. But
now she is disillusioned, and the things dropping from the birds
are merely feathers. In many of her images she is seeking milk:
but what she gets is something you can neither eat, nor see your-
self in. From the birds she thought were breasts, she gets only
something of which she can make no use—like the feather dusters
in the beanfield in *The Bee Meeting* or the snow flakes that merely
settle on her own face in *The Night Dances*, rather than a richness
to be absorbed: also,

The bean leaves are dumb as hands.

the leaves of her father's bean tree cannot speak to her (as the mother's mouth could).

Now, in the mental hospital, instead of returning to begin again from the 'bowel of the root' and experiencing rebirth, she experiences an autumnal month that is 'fit for little'. (The word 'fit' evokes echoes of 'Why then I'll fit you with the remedy', from Kyd, borrowed in *The Waste Land*: 'Hieronomo's mad againe.')

The dead ripen in the grapeleaves.

Those who should seem like bunches of grapes ripening under the viticulturist's care, are dead.

A red tongue is among us.

This tongue is not the tongue of the mother of mouths, but a *tongue of flame*—and a male tongue, or impinging penis. It is the tongue of flame she associates with electro-convulsive therapy and being done to. It is the tongue of *false male doing*, and it is making her into an identity different from her own.

Mother, keep out of my barnyard,
I am becoming another.

She is not to take the path of being enabled by the 'mother of otherness', to find that other world of being, by being tongue to her mouth. She is becoming 'another' altogether—and the rejection of the mother and 'female element being' is necessary for this. 'Another' here means 'other than female'.

Instead of giving herself up to the 'mother of mouths' she is submitting herself to another devourer—'Dog-head'. Dog-head is a God-head, and he is a 'big love eater', but by *doing* He is her doctor:

Feed me the berries of dark.

In *Blackberrying* (*Crossing the Water*, p. 24) the berries are as big as the ball of her thumb, dumb eyes, and something like blood clots, 'squandering' their juices in love:

Big as the ball of my thumb, and dumb as eyes
Ebon in the hedges, fat

With blue-red juices. These they squander on my fingers.
I had not asked for such a blood sisterhood; they must love me.

The giving of 'inner contents' by the berries is love: they almost
offer her 'encounter'. Yet, to her, 'eyes' are dumb, even as blackberrying enhances her perception.

In *Tulips* the protagonist's head is an eye that cannot shut: 'it
has to take everything in'. Here, in the mental hospital her eyes
have to take in the berries of dark:

> Feed me the berries of dark.
> The lids won't shut.

The eyes that look for 'reflection' have darkness forced on them.
Instead of the eyes of berries she gets a crown of thorns: the 'hoops
of blackberry stems' are the cables of the ECT machine. When she
is given shocks, she can't remember anything for weeks: so, the
berries these 'hoops' force on her are berries of oblivion, forced on
her like light on an eye that won't shut. She has to see reality even
as it is meaningless to her.

> Time
> Unwinds from the great umbilicus of the sun
> Its endless glitter.

Death, in one of its aspects, is masturbating this glitter. In the
death circuit of *being done to*, in a pseudo-male way, Time becomes
a great, endless unwinding, beginning from the sun. 'Glitter' and
the umbilicus relate the image to the mother's eyes and body: but
the image is of a cosmic (male) impingement, which she must
accept. It is a cosmic male orgasm.

> I must swallow it all.

—she must *endure* 'life without feeling alive' and she must put up
with her treatment, swallowing the berries of the dark. The huge
pressure of a meaningless (and fatherless) universe must be allowed
to press in on her.

The others round her, also being treated by ECT and other forms
of shock treatment, lie in odd postures—'their limbs at odds'.
They seem to have no identities either. They are all in the 'moon's
vat'. For Sylvia Plath the moon is a stony, blank, hard-hearted,

indifferent face—her 'vat' thus a kind of witch's cauldron. (In *Edge*, the moon's 'blacks crackle and drag'; in *The Couriers*, there is a 'cauldron' 'crackling/All to itself' on the top of the Alps.)

In this light the blood is black . . .

The petrifying influence of the stony moonwitch is being exerted all around her: vast impingement. In being changed into 'another', along with all the others, she is being attacked by the castrating mother herself. The coercive influence of punitive psychiatry seems to her to belong to the same balefulness and is but another manifestation of the failure to love.

Tell me my name.

She has worked out by now that what she is being taught is that the 'correct' thing for her is to accept a conformist (or false male self) identity, by a ritual of degradation.* Here arise startling implications, to do with our concepts of 'cure' and what society regards as a normal identity, as we shall see.

4. THE BEAST

We have seen many images of the vacancy in the identity where the female element should be. *The Beast* is about the deficiencies of the male element. Here is the truth about the Colossus, who is not a Colossus at all, but 'Fido Littlesoul', a little animal, just a 'cupboard of rubbish'—a collection of stolen partial objects.

Sylvia Plath often discusses the way in which she seems 'married' to various things or people, from her plaster cast to the black telephone. For 'marry' here, I believe, we may read 'identify'. Her concept of marrying belongs to the infant's primitive belief that Mummy and Daddy virtually eat one another in marriage. Her capacity for relationship seems to have remained on the basis of primitive identification.† In *The Beekeeper's Daughter* (*The Colossus*, p. 75) she is married to her father:

* See Esterson (1970), p. 98.
† As Andrew Brink (1968) remarks of *Daddy*, 'With Love inoperative hatred comes into play and is directed against the doubly resented object, the father-husband'.

Father, bridegroom . . .

—and as queen bee she marries his old age:

The queen bee marries the winter of your year.

Failing in 'female element being', she is a summer-queen-bee married to a winter-father, who is in the 'dead season', for he is dead. As we see from her other poems she has virtually *made* her colossus. Here, in *The Beast*, she recognises that he doesn't really exist. He may have been the father who once paid her loving attention as a little girl:

He kept blowing me kisses.
I hardly knew him.

But now she is really

Duchess of Nothing,
Hairtusk's bride.

Hairtusk is maleness, again, the father's penis: but, like the bone and hair in the glass case at Cambridge (in *All The Dead Dears*) all that remains of her father's body. It is like a rhinoceros horn, a male proboscis thing, a hairy (? 'wisdom') tusk, one of the 'fingers of wisdom', becomes a dried fetish, useful for doing, but useless in the quest for being. She married only a cupboard full of fragments of impingement—memories of her father and fragments of the mother's 'male element'. These are all she has on which to build a self and at the bottom of it is still the hungry mouth ego. He's a destructive little puppy who gnaws at the darkness: and, as we have seen, he is male when he ought to be female.

Yet, since he is the only structure on which she can build her identity,

He won't be got rid of:
Mumblepaws, teary and sorry,
Fido Littlesoul, the bowel's familiar.
A dustbin's enough for him.
The dark's his bone
Call him any name, he'll come to it.

Here the 'beast' seems the animus, Jung's 'shadow of the male in the female'. It was formed from Daddy, and from the 'male element' of the mother as sources of identity. These scraps of 'doing', assembled together in her infancy, become her puppy-self (felt to be 'him').* This puppy-dog self is one element of her complex, pitiful, regressed libidinal ego, the true self that longs to be born. This beast, once 'bullman' and 'King of the dish' (that is, a penis who has feasted on femaleness), is not the idealised false self of hate which is the subject of *The Colossus* and *Daddy*. Here the protagonist is disillusioned enough to see that her belief in what at first was a god-like creature, magical and larger than life, cannot be sustained. (Interestingly enough he is inflated here, ironically, in a language borrowed from Dylan Thomas, who also used spells to try to create a world that was 'all him'.) Jung tells us that, through suffering, a woman can embrace her animus, as part of herself rather than a force that possesses her—and then 'he' can become an 'invaluable inner companion who endows her with the masculine qualities of initiative, courage, objectivity and spiritual wisdom' (1964, p. 194).

In this section of *Poem for a Birthday* Sylvia Plath has such a positive view of her animus. She was once hopeful.

> Breathing was easy in his airy holding.
> The sun sat in his armpit.
> Nothing went mouldy. The little invisibles
> Waited on him hand and foot.

But she cannot keep her confidence in the magic:

> Down here the sky is always falling.
> Hogwallow's at the window.
> The star bugs won't save me this month.

A grossness of bodily need has brought her down to the 'mud-sump' of hopelessness. Her animus being thus reduced, he is no invaluable companion. Hairtusk has nothing to offer, to help sustain Fido, the regressed libidinal ego, who has learnt to chew his meagre bone of hope in the darkness, and is even inclined to accept a conformist self in ultimate humiliation. 'Tell me my

---

* Guntrip reports a patient's dream of a little dog in a box which has been there since he possessed such a dog as a boy. 'The dog represented a specifically distinct ... a "true self" put in cold storage and awaiting a chance of rebirth' (1968), p. 209.

name', in *Maenad*, becomes here, 'Call him by any name, he'll come to it'.

Fido Littlesoul is familiar enough with the bowels and a dustbin is enough for him. The creativity of vision (the star bugs) have saved her in the past. But now, after ECT, she is beyond saving: she is merely a drab in the sty, in Time's gut-end. She has been taught debasement and brought down to the bottom—a fish puddle, a mud-sump, a sty, among emmets and molluscs, lesser creatures ('I know the bottom—I know it with my great tap-root': *Elm*). In this humiliated state her regressed libidinal ego, composed of little scraps of rubbishy maleness, will answer to any name, he is so hungry and needy: and abjectly conformist.

5. FLUTE NOTES FROM A REEDY POND

This hopelessness becomes in the next section something like aboulia,* a psychological paralysis. The mouth-hungry patients, dehumanised, become primitive creatures of the swamp:

> . . . frog-mouth and fish-mouth drink
> The liquor of indolence, and all things sink
>
> Into a soft caul of forgetfulness.

The patients are under sedation, shocked or drugged. There is no real recreation: they are only manipulated mechanically like automatons, masked by horn. Whether there is any reference here to a device worn by patients I do not know. What one sees inwardly is the beaked mask of characters in the Italian Comedy, or perhaps Bosch figures in paintings. The horn is a hard shield; it is aggressive and has sexual connotations: in a sense it is the front-line defensive face of false male doing.

> Puppets, loosed from the strings of the puppet-master,
> Wear masks of horn to bed.

It is a kind of living death. The essential reality of death (which thrusts the problem of meaning at us) is side-stepped, by spiritual death:

---

* 'Inability, usually pathological, to make or to act on decisions' (*Penguin Dictionary of Psychology*). Hamlet suffers from aboulia.

> This is not death, it is something safer.
> The wingy myths won't tug at us any more . . .

The poem is a record of the effects of conventional psychiatry in demythologising the psyche: no more Icarus impulses, no more soaring flights of imagination:

> Now coldness comes sifting down, layer after layer . . .

It is like snow, covering earth in forgetfulness, an image which occurs in *The Bell Jar*. The topography becomes unfamiliar: but yet the fall-out is menacing, bringing a cruel blankness. The flowers are gone, leaving only the skeletons of *umbelliferae*—and there is no shelter:

> Overhead the old umbrellas of summer
> Wither like pithless hands. There is little shelter.
> Hourly the eye of the sky enlarges its blank
> Dominion.

As the myths are destroyed, so are the delusions. The sky becomes a blank vacancy of unreflecting meaninglessness and the dead weeds, withered, offer no defence against its impingement. 'The stars are no nearer'—the modern scientific universe is simply matter in motion, a blank dominion, which simply *is*, and we can come no nearer understanding the stars nor do they lend themselves to our imaginings.*

What the protagonist has lost is the hope that was in death-as-resurrection:

> The moults are tongueless that sang from above the water
> Of golgotha at the tip of the reed,
> And how a god flimsy as a baby's finger
> Shall unhusk himself and steer into the air.

In this poem the nymphs (the women in the ward) are 'nodding to sleep like statues'. They are 'lamp-headed' because ECT has lit them up: but they have gone empty-headed and petrified. Each has a lamp at the head of her bed but their lights are out. What is lost is

---

* So, the sky is 'starless and fatherless' (*Sheep in Fog*, *Ariel*, p. 13) while each gesture 'flees down an alley of diminishing perspectives', and its significance 'Drains like water out of a hole at the far end'. (*Insomniac*, *Crossing the Water*, p. 21.)

the capacity to sing: the birds have lost their feathers (they are moults: these feathers were once believed to be milk) and they cannot sing any more of magical things. If we examine the 'wingy myths' that are lost 'in a soft caul of forgetfulness', they are myths of resurrection or rebirth-by-suicide. The dragonfly climbs to the tip of the reed, and flies away like a god: like Christ he unhusks himself of his old body to live a new life.

This section of the poem virtually says that, through psychiatric treatment, Sylvia Plath lost her belief that she could, like a dragonfly, one day 'unhusk' herself and, 'flimsy as a baby's finger',* be reborn. But this treatment did not rid her of her belief in the myth of schizoid suicide, though it might have sunk it for a time in a 'soft caul of forgetfulness'. Neither did it provide for the longed-for rebirth, while all it destroyed was lovely vision. There is now neither true creative intentionality, nor the fantasy of resurrection.

From everything her poetry tells of the experience of mental illness and conventional psychiatry, one gains a disturbing sense that 'treatment', based as it is felt to be on *doing* and *impingement* itself, is felt to be based on *hate*. Because it fails to find meaning, it seems to be blind to, and to menace, possibilities of finding a meaning in life. While it may suspend delusions, it may even so seem to confirm and reinforce the patient's own hate-solutions to the problems of existence by seeming to put beyond reach solutions based on creativity and love. It perhaps urged her closer to suicide as a choice to die, by dispelling the wingy (Icarus) myths of schizoid suicide, which have beneath them the will to live at least. The patient seems left yearning for the chimeras of which she has been 'cured'. However delusive, they at least contained meanings, in which hope was 'locked up'. Imprisoned in physicalism, conventional psychiatry seems to reduce the human being to a puppy, statue or humiliated moult or frog, and the world to a blank and meaningless mass of matter. 'Perception takes the place of apperception.' In the short story *The Wishing Box*, the protagonist commits suicide because she cannot throw meaningfulness over the world.

---

* The baby's finger, like the 'footlings, boneless as noses', is perhaps a source of re-creation she feels to be in the internalised father's penis. See *Loveletter* in *Crossing the Water*: 'I slept on like a bent finger', p. 44.

3

Anything to prove that her shaping imaginative powers were not irretrievably lost; that her eye was not merely an open camera lens which recorded surrounding phenomena and left it at that. 'A rose,' she found herself repeating hollowly, like a funeral dirge, 'is a rose is a rose—'
Agnes recalls 'her infinitely more creative childhood days'. She felt now 'a gaping void in her own head'. She could not bear the prospect of a long life of 'visionless days'. The story suggests that the loss of the capacity for meaningful seeing and for filling the seen world with imaginative significance is like 'some dark, malignant cancer'. Such a fear of failure of perception could perhaps have been made worse by the eradication of 'wingy myths', by ECT.

6. WITCH BURNING

This view is reinforced by the sixth section which suggests that Sylvia Plath was 'taught' by conventional psychiatry that the solution to the problem of ego-weakness is to submit masochistically to hate and that *hate can only be cast out by hate*. Of course, we must be careful here, because we are responding to schizoid utterance, and, as we shall see, there are occupational hazards in this, of 'falling in love' with the schizoid individual and of becoming involved in her paranoid feelings of being 'oppressed'.

But throughout all her work, even when she tells us it is 'mad', Sylvia Plath preserves her penetrating insights and her capacity for clear utterance, and utter sincerity. This is very terrible—like a martyr washing his hands in the flames and praying aloud even as his flesh burns. But our task is to listen, and to respond. Being 'normal', we are 'aware of the risks' as the schizoid person often is not. That is, we shall suffer pain and deep disturbance, because of our capacity for concern, which she sometimes lacks.

Witch Burning is about the hate-self being burned by the haters.

> In the marketplace they are piling the dry sticks.
> A thicket of shadows is a poor coat. I inhabit
> The wax image of myself, a doll's body.
> Sickness begins here: I am a dartboard for witches.
> Only the devil can eat the devil out.
> In the month of red leaves I climb to a bed of fire.

The poem is about the experience of being lit up 'like an electric bulb' by ECT. She hopes that she will be able to have her illness ('Sickness begins here'). But there is a poignant sense of not knowing where the 'I' is. Is she in the 'thicket of shadows' which is a 'poor coat'? Is she in the 'doll's body' (cf. *The Applicant, Ariel,* p. 36)? She feels that the body on the ECT couch or the bed on which she receives insulin therapy is a wax image of herself in which witches are sticking pins (hypodermic needles, shocks) as the mother gave the infant only impingement experienced as 'pestling'. It is October, when the leaves are red—the end of summer: she climbs on to a bed of flame, hoping for a change of season, towards maturity or spring perhaps—but she is uncertain whether this colour is on the way to winter and death, or whether it is a refining fire towards spring and birth. She hopes that this pain, this *being done to*, this hate, will purge her hate (the verb is *eat*—and one devil is eating another by oral hate which consumes rather than speaks). But that there was any true rebirth seems unlikely, for she herself at the end of the poem under discussion speaks with bitter irony when, after describing the mechanical processes of assembling parts into whole puppet-like creatures, she says,

I shall be good as new.

Following 'Tell me my name' this utters only a wry promise— 'I promise to be good': which is the answer such conventional psychiatry requires, by adopting the procedures of punishment and coercion.

If we study this feeling, in the light of Fairbairn's analysis of the strange logic of the schizoid individual, can we not perhaps see that the coercive 'doing' of shock treatment can teach a schizoid patient that 'It is better to give oneself over to the joys of hating' than to seek dangerous love? Only hate can cast out hate: a dangerous formula that could so easily lead to encapsulation within a death-circuit. In *The Bell Jar* the protagonist Esther says that under ECT she 'began to wonder what she had done', that she had to be punished so much. Here the protagonist concludes that she is being punished for having tried to commit suicide, or, to put it another way, for trying to get herself reborn. If you teach someone that they have been naughty trying to be born, are you not teaching them that next time *they had better make sure they die*?

> It is easy to blame the dark; the mouth of a door,
> The cellar's belly.

In *The Bell Jar* the protagonist crawls down into the cellar to take her poison and this cellar is evidently a womb; when she cannot sleep she makes her bed into a tomb; she cannot find her father anywhere, and when she gets to his grave she lays her cheek on the stone—and decides in the next paragraph to kill herself. Somewhere, she feels, there is a chance of rebirth, if only one could somehow re-enter the 'mouth' of the 'belly': so, here, she is speaking of the symbolism of schizoid suicide. Is it that she feels it is 'easy to blame' the suicidal impulse, if it is misinterpreted? What she was looking for in those shadows was a new light: but

> ... They've blown my sparkler out.

Or does she feel that 'they' have taken the universal presence of black threatening shadows in her world as an excuse to put out the 'sparkler' of her own flame—the very glitter that is the focus of hope? We noted earlier that 'all-mouth' was 'to blame': the menacing shadows which reflect his voracity in the outer world are to blame, too. The whole poem is full of schizoid guilt. As Laing says, this is likely to lead to self-enclosure. Might not shock therapy, by seeming to be punishment, be likely to make this worse?

Instead of being offered opportunities for rebirth, she is imprisoned: by a witch (the castrating mother figure), who is dead:

> A black-sharded lady keeps me in a parrot cage.
> What large eyes the dead have!
> I am intimate with a hairy spirit.
> Smoke wheels from the beak of this empty jar.

Being subjected to ECT is like being an imprisoned parrot ('Tell me my name'). It is a death, because she is meeting 'the dead' with large, unseeing eyes, in the dark. And it is like a rape: the hairy spirit, akin to Mahler's ape, is a paranoid projection of her own hate, and this is now 'intimate' with her. These images, like those of smoke wheeling from the *beak* of an *empty* jar,* arise from the

---

* There could be here an echo of the dreadful motto to *The Waste Land*, 'Nam Sibyllam, quidem Cumis ego, ipse oculis meis vidi, in ampulla pendere . . .', '. . . respondebat illa: ἀποθανεῖν θέλω.'

confused impressions of a patient strapped to the treatment couch: they are, significantly, of emptiness, death, rape, and meaningless 'doing'.

In response to this punishment, the true self tried to shrink and preserve itself by being too tiny to be hurt:

> If I am a little one, I can do no harm.

Here speaks the confused and terrified infant, who cannot understand why, when she wanted love, she was given violence:

> If I don't move about, I'll knock nothing over.

One may glimpse here, I believe, the severely deprived child, rocking on its bed in an institution, expressionless, listless out of fear of the consequences of 'moving about'

> So I said,
> Sitting under a potlid, tiny and inert as a rice grain.

Coercive therapy establishes inertness: yet, to the victim who hopes for a cure, this impingement, which fosters a conformist self, seems like the truth:

> They are turning the burners up, ring after ring.
> We are full of starch, my small white fellows. We grow.
> It hurts at first. The red tongues will teach the truth.

Being 'burnt' is like being heated as a grain of starch, which after a while bursts and expands. Instead of the growth of the true self she experiences a sense of being suddenly filled in inner space, from the 'inert . . . grain', with something like popcorn: by such imagery 'we grow' can surely only be taken as the bitterest irony?* Again, she speaks as though confessing after punishment. She is ready to interpret and confess her faults of feeling petrified, of having intercourse with death in the shadow of petrification—if only she can give *some* shape. (She has, in this poem, been a red tongue, a footling, a coat of shadows, a wax image, a doll's body, a dartboard, a parrot, a little one, a rice grain, a singeless moth.) But the end of the poem merely dissolves into the fire, in which the 'I' is lost.

* Cf. *The Bell Jar*. After ECT 'nothing had changed', p. 216.

7. THE STONES

The final poem about this episode of breakdown and psychiatric 'cure' is called *The Stones*. It contrasts the sterility of being 'done to' with the yearning of the regressed libidinal ego *to be*. 'Mending' is seen as 'patching': nothing fundamental is supplied for the existential needs.

> This is the city where men are mended.
> I lie on a great anvil.

When she broke down

> The flat blue sky-circle

> Flew off like the hat of a doll
> When I fell out of the light.

As the cosmos flew apart, she sought to retreat to the womb (the cellar and attempted suicide): to find a womb that could 'speak' her. But it was unable to.

>   I entered
> The stomach of indifference, the wordless cupboard.

In *The Bell Jar* Esther's suicide attempt follows an episode at home where she is overwhelmed by the sense of hate and indifference between herself and her mother. The novel conveys a dread of the mother's impingement. Here it is remembered as being crushed by the stone penis of a colossus, of immense male-element doing:

> The mother of pestles diminished me.
> I became a still pebble.
> The stones of the belly were peaceable,

> The head-stone quiet, jostled by nothing.

Here the image of petrified self inside the stony male-mother merges into an image of the father's tomb. There is a libidinal attachment, as in *Tulips*, to a withdrawal to a state of being utterly non-human and turned to stone, in ultimate inanition: 'jostled by nothing'.

Only, as she says here quite clearly, the hungry unborn infant within, the mouth-ego, cried out—even in the suicide attempt.

Only the mouth-hole piped out,
Importunate cricket

In a quarry of silences.
The people of the city heard it.
They hunted the stones, taciturn and separate,

The mouth-hole crying their locations.

Here she speaks of her 'mouth-hole' with affection, 'importunate
cricket', as if it did not belong to her, or was a little creature inside
her. Winnicott speaks of a false self which can be so heroic that it
will organise a suicide to 'save the true self from insult'. Surely
Sylvia Plath speaks at times from this false self, which has a deep
love of the true self, but yet cannot find it as part of the whole, or
bring it to birth?

The people who hear the true self crying are feared by her because they do not understand and are remote: they are 'taciturn
and separate'. In the cellar where she is seeking rebirth through
schizoid suicide her regressed libidinal ego lies in wait like a foetus
in a bottle (in alcohol?).

Drunk as a foetus
I suck at the paps of darkness.*

They take her to hospital and revive her. She portrays this as an
act of coercion exerted on an unwilling subject who wanted to be
a stone. Yet it is also a form of love—albeit misunderstanding
love: again, she is subjected to (male) 'doing':

The food tubes embrace me. Sponges kiss my lichens away.
The jewelmaster drives his chisel to pry
Open one stone eye.†

Being brought to life without real rebirth is a sterile and futile
procedure. The 'doing' is an impingement which she resents.
Again we have the dreadful image of the head being a ('stupid

*Cf.   Grown so wise grown so terrible
             Sucking death's mouldy tits.
          Sit on my finger, sing in my ear, O littleblood.
             (Ted Hughes, *Littleblood*, *Crow*, p. 94).
   † A chisel cracked down on my eye, and a slit of light opened like a mouth or
wound . . . Then the chisel struck again' (*The Bell Jar*, p. 181).

pupil') eye which cannot shut, cannot *stop seeing*. To her, to see light can be hell:

> This is the after-hell: I see the light.
> A wind unstoppers the chamber
> Of the ear, old worrier.
>
> Water mollifies the flint lip,
> And daylight lays its sameness on the wall.*

She sees therapy as a kind of insane, sadistic optimism—a mere 'grafting' and stitching of spare parts together:

> The grafters are cheerful,
>
> Heating the pincers, hoisting the delicate hammers.
> A current agitates the wires
> Volt upon volt. Catgut stitches my fissures.

There was never a more vivid picture of the state Laing speaks of as 'life without feeling alive', and of the schizoid feeling of self as partially divorced from body:

> A workman walks by carrying a pink torso.
> The storerooms are full of hearts.
> This is the city of spare parts.
>
> My swaddled legs and arms smell sweet as rubber.
> Here they can doctor heads, or any limb . . .

To one who does not feel 'ontological security' there is a bitter irony about a place where 'they can doctor heads'. (The women in the wards were 'dead heads' as a result.) The bitterness becomes sardonic:

> On Fridays the little children come
>
> To trade their hooks for hands.
> Dead men leave eyes for others.

---

* Hardy writes of the sense of schizoid futility which can be felt about daylight in deep grief, in *The Going*:
> And daylight hardens upon the wall . . .

To see unwillingly, because what is seen is meaningless, again, would seem to be connected with the substitution of *perception* for *apperception* which Winnicott sees as following the failure of creation reflection. See below, p. 142.

Her inner child has been given nothing: implicitly she jeers at the medical profession as a racket which only pretends to resurrect. 'Suffer little children to come unto me'—they get hands for hooks, do they? In *Tulips* the faces of her husband and children seem like 'little smiling hooks': here children whose arms end in cruel hooks can be given hands (hooks also fasten into eyes). The children are humanised (we remember how afraid she is of the 'dark thing', which is 'looking out with its hooks': also she inside herself is 'moley-handed') and their disabilities are removed. But the line is ironic—it is obvious she doesn't believe the miracle is possible. If a hand has not grown, the individual is touchless, ineffectual. (In his surrealist legend *Lilith* George Macdonald's protagonist grows a new hand when the old one, which could not open generously, is chopped off.) It is true that some can see because they have been given spare parts from the dead: but these mechanical marvels still leave the deepest existential needs untouched.

These need love: but here

> Love is the uniform of my bald nurse.

Here, love is the outward professional garb of an impinger who is an unattractive male: it does not come from feminine 'being for', and so cannot reach to the depths of need. ('Bald' is also almost synonymous with 'blind' in her work.) Yet, love is my problem: my need for it is the curse of my existence:

> Love is the bone and sinew of my curse.

'Fixed stars/Govern a life' (*Words*): deep in the psychic tissue there is a deficiency of love, and a fear of love. Psychiatry has merely 'mended' a 'case': there seems to be a flowering in it, but it is elusive ('flowering's finished'). Love and the true blossom have not been created there: there is only a mended pot with a rose stuck in it, whose essence still eludes:

> The vase, reconstructed, houses
> The elusive rose.

> Ten fingers shape a bowl for shadows.

In the centre of the shape formed by doing there are only shadows still:

My mendings itch. There is nothing to do.

There is nothing to be achieved by 'doing': there is nothing really to be done about my state. The last line is a bitter moan of despair:

I shall be good as new.

—and at the same time a promise to the psychiatric examination board.

3
The Baby in the Bell Jar:
the Symbolism of the Novel

As we have seen, one central theme in this writer's work is that of
'impingement': she who has had to make her identity out of
scraps of 'being done to' is continually preoccupied with the relationship between being forced to conform and the true self that
seeks to fulfil itself. So, she is fascinated by surgical operations,
birth, executions, the psychiatric interview, ECT, sadistic acts, and
suicide (the final doing-to-oneself). Although, since she is a
schizoid individual, she tends to give us a paranoid view of the
relation between 'society' and the individual, she also exposes some
of the weaknesses in our society—areas in which we fail to cherish
being, to give individuals a chance to find the path to being able to
say I AM, by loving encounter. These are the themes of her novel,
The Bell Jar.

One of the most important symbols here is that of birth, and we
may relate her preoccupation with it to some of D. W. Winnicott's insights. For example, he made the startling suggestion that
the experience of being satisfactorily born is itself a creative experience. One must not of course sentimentalise this insight: it is
obviously possible to survive a difficult or delayed birth without
damage, for instance. If Winnicott is right, however, what happens when childbirth is mechanised by surgery? Perhaps some
fundamental consequent problem of the American identity is
indicated by Sylvia Plath's description in her novel of a birth
which her protagonist, Esther Greenwood, observes in a teaching
hospital:

some men in lime-green coats and skullcaps and a few nurses came moving towards us in a ragged procession wheeling a trolley with a big white lump on it.

. . .

I was so struck by the sight of the table where they were lifting the woman I didn't say a word. It looked like some awful torture table, with these metal stirrups sticking up in mid-air at one end and all sorts of instruments and wires and tubes I couldn't make out properly at the other.

. . .

The woman's stomach stuck up so high I couldn't see her face or the upper part of her body at all. She seemed to have nothing but an enormous spider-fat stomach and two little ugly spindly legs propped in the high stirrups, and all the time the baby was being born she never stopped making this inhuman whooing noise.

Later Buddy told me the woman was on a drug that would make her forget she'd had any pain and that when she swore and groaned she didn't really know what she was doing because she was in a kind of twilight sleep. (pp. 67–8)

Her account shows an obsession with the parts and functions—the inert body and the clinical set-up. Her account is not coloured by disgust, nor does she seek to alienate us by dwelling on the sordid or horrifying. But her reality, while beautiful, is also terrible because it is depersonalised:

the baby's head stuck for some reason, and the doctor told Will he'd have to make a cut. I heard the scissors close on the woman's skin like cloth and the blood began to run down—a fierce, bright red. Then all at once the baby seemed to pop out into Will's hands, the colour of a blue plum and floured with white stuff and streaked with blood . . . (p. 68)

Her exactness is possible because of her uninhibited fascination with 'inner contents', not least blood and babies. Her cool detachment also displays a certain 'diminution of affect', a clinical term in psychotherapy for an abnormal lack of appropriate feeling-response. This typically American clinical birth takes its place in the symbolism of the novel alongside the execution of the Rosenbergs by electrocution and the 'treatment' of mental patients by insulin shock and electro-convulsive therapy. These too are forms of being done to, of impingement. Birth has been removed from the realm of 'being' and taken into that of 'male doing', and so it is for her representative of the attitude of American society to human beings, which has its own schizoid characteristics (as in its attitudes to sex).

Her symbolism throughout this novel thus yields understanding of her own predicament and is at the same time a criticism of her society. She also sees that what is lacking is creative reflection. 'meeting', confirmation:

> I didn't feel up to asking him if there were any other ways to have babies. For some reason the most important thing to me was actually seeing the baby come out of you yourself and making sure it was yours. I thought if you had to have all that pain anyway you might just as well stay awake.
>
> I had always imagined myself hitching up on to my elbows on the delivery table after it was all over—dead white, of course, with no make up and from the awful ordeal, but smiling and radiant, with my hair down to my waist, and reaching out for my first squirmy little child, and *saying its name*, whatever it was . . . (pp. 69–70, my italics)

Here we have the woman speaking, of the needs of being, and of the beginnings of identity in 'encounter'. In speaking of 'making sure it was yours' and 'saying its name' she intuitively realises that the mother has a mirror-role from birth ('Tell me my name').

She looks at the world as one driven by a need to answer the question, What is it to be human? And so she can reveal the lack of humanity in American society, its failures to put human considerations first.

She relates, for instance, Esther's difficulty in finding a doctor at a weekend, even for an emergency.

> Joan pulled up an Indian hassock and began to dial down the long list of Cambridge doctors. The first number didn't answer. Joan began to explain my case to the second number, which did answer, but then broke off and said 'I see' and hung up.
>
> 'What's the trouble?'

'He'll only come for regular customers or emergencies. It's Sunday.'

. . .

. . . Sunday—the doctor's paradise! Doctors at country clubs, doctors at the seaside, doctors with mistresses, doctors with wives, doctors in church, doctors in yachts, doctors everywhere resolutely being people, not doctors. (pp. 244–5)

As the delivery theatre is depersonalised, so is the doctor's role in the community. He is a doctor on Tuesday, Wednesday and Thursday: a playboy at weekends. This, of course, reflects a related split between social function and personal identity in many other fields.

Sylvia Plath's novel is haunted by the experience of the separation of intellect from body, by dissociation. The search is to find 'where her protagonist's problem *is*', as we have seen:

I wanted to tell her that if only something were wrong with my body it would be fine, I would rather have anything wrong with my body than something wrong with my head . . .

(p. 193)

Annoyed by the continual attention to her body in a mental hospital—the taking of temperature that always gives the answer 'normal' for instance—Esther upsets a tray of thermometers.

almost immediately two attendants came and wheeled me, bed and all, down to Mrs Mole's old room, but not before I had scooped up a ball of mercury . . .

I opened my fingers a crack, like a child with a secret, and smiled at the silver globe cupped in my palm. If I dropped it, *it would break into a million little replicas of itself, and if I pushed them near each other, they would fuse, without a crack, into one whole again* . . . (p. 194, my italics)

The globe of mercury is a symbol of the mother's eyes, reflecting the self. So, the self is 'in' it. Irritated by the term 'normal', she angrily demonstrates that her identity is exceptional in that it can break into a thousand fragments, or reform into a whole. Yet this self, being metallic, is pure and dehumanised and also dispersed like a swarm of bees. The breaking of the mercury is a strategy of survival: she evades the constraints of psychiatric coercion by being continually mercurial ('I am the magician's girl who does not flinch', *The Bee Meeting*). The image is of the 'intellectual collecting together of impingements', as Winnicott puts it, 'holding them in exact detail and sequence, in this way protecting the psyche until there is a return to the continuing-to-exist state'. The whole blob is this latter state: the mercury broken into a million globules is the psyche which seeks to survive by fragmentation.* The impulse to preserve the 'exact detail and sequence' of impingements is what generated the poems and the novel—it is in this way that Sylvia Plath uses her 'collecting intellect'. The mercury also symbolises that longed-for area of being, where 'creative reflection' is needed, to bring wholeness, and a secure feeling of being in one's own body: a metal 'filling', pure and valuable, like the core of the earth.

While still at college, Esther Greenwood is thrust, by the magic of pseudo-events (by winning a magazine competition), into the world of image-promotion. She wants to be a poet: ironically enough, and symptomatically enough, she finds herself in the world of American commercial journalism, and media promotion. Sylvia Plath's accounts of the depersonalised and schizoid 'fun' behaviour of this world of New York nite life is horrifying because of its stark realism. She has only a touch of the impulse of a Scott Fitzgerald to find a starry-eyed significance somewhere in this world of Big Spenders and manic 'liveliness'.

Her style develops with her insights. At the beginning it is somewhat slick and manifests the kind of dissociation evident in Madison Avenue. In fashionable journalism the writer, because he is dependent on advertising, must adopt the sophisticated air of 'loving' our 'sickness' that we find, for example, in *Esquire* and *The New Yorker*. The nervous, awkward qualities of the style make it difficult for us to respond to it at times: the underlying gravity is at odds with the emotional triviality of a callow, 'throw-away' language:

> It was a queer, sultry summer, the summer they electrocuted the Rosenbergs . . . I'm stupid about executions. The idea of being electrocuted makes me sick . . . I couldn't help wonder-

---

* 'The image/Flees and aborts like dropped mercury' (*Thalidomide*, *Winter Trees*, p. 32).

ing what it would be like, being burned alive all along your
nerves.

I thought it must be the worst thing in the world. (p. 1)

Later, however, the lighthearted throwaway style of this kind of
writing ('as if I had a split personality or something')—gives way
to a clarity whose simple directness convinces the reader that what
is said is really meant. She soon begins to abandon the 'flip' technique which is incapable of escaping from its gawkiness into anything deeper ('Girls like that make me sick'). She relinquishes this
mode for a direct and sparse gravity of her own, a simplicity with
a black depth, of which few American writers since Emily
Dickinson and Mark Twain have been capable—as in the prose
describing her first suicide attempt on skis (see below)

> I was descending, but the white sun rose no higher. It hung over
> the suspended waves of the hills, an insentient pivot without
> which the world would not exist. (p. 102)

From this gravity she is able to register, as against the cold perspective of an indifferent cosmos, the triviality, the hate, the violence and weakness in American 'fun' life. Esther's agony of
suicidal madness meets incomprehension in those around her. She
can record the manic desperation of flat-and-hotel life in New
York, and the violence beneath the world of *Ladies Day*, *Vogue*,
and the *Thirty Best Stories of the Year*. She is able to convey not
only the false bustle—but how, at the centre of it all, Esther
Greenwood feels a terrifying emptiness:

> I felt very still and very empty, the way the eye of a tornado
> must feel, moving dully along in the middle of the surrounding
> hullabaloo. (p. 3)

This is a more disturbing image than appears at first glance, because the eye of a tornado is a vacuum formed by the surrounding violence, and has a *sucking* power of gigantic destructiveness.
There is an emptiness at the heart: then what are 'inner contents'?
This preoccupation with what is 'good' or 'bad' within is a continual theme, so there is an uncanny consistency about all Sylvia
Plath's substance, emptiness, corruption or purity. When Esther
chooses a drink she chooses vodka, because it is glassy and
tasteless:

I'd seen a vodka ad once, just a glass full of vodka standing in the middle of a snowdrift in a blue light, and the vodka looked clear and pure as water, so I thought having vodka plain must be all right. (p. 11)

If she thinks of herself giving birth she is 'white'.

In *The Bell Jar*, Sylvia Plath is often preoccupied with air, water, snow, flowing blood, vomit, feelings of emptiness within, and menacing black shadows. Approaches to relationship brings a fear of 'loss of inner contents'. The schizoid individual fears that closeness to others may threaten him with 'emptying', because love is associated with intense hunger. When Esther's closest friend begins to jitterbug with a disk jockey, she dreads the incorporative oral element in the sexuality that emerges. She feels herself threatened: 'shrinking to a small black dot . . . I felt like a hole in the ground'. Doreen ends up on this night out in a manic whirl of sensual intensity with Lenny. Esther watches, fascinated by the oral savagery:

I noticed, in the routine way you notice the colour of somebody's eyes, that Doreen's breasts had popped out of her dress and were swinging out slightly like full brown melons as she circled belly-down on Lenny's shoulder . . . Lenny was trying to bite Doreen's hip through her skirt when I let myself out the door . . . (p. 18)

The account has undercurrents of fear and fascination which perhaps arise from infantile primal scene fantasies. Sexual activity to her seems both full of threatening dangers (of oral incorporation), and grotesque—because she cannot find the emotional meaning in it. When she 'summons' her 'little chorus of voices' they tell her that she will never be able to find meaning in physical sex. They also tell her that such sexuality is not *her* libidinal goal. The revulsion from sexuality found in such poems as *The Applicant* and *Berck-Plage* is apparent here in the novel. If this is the path to love, then there seems little hope that she will be able to satisfy her yearning. An inward voice mocks her first efforts at love:

You'll never get anywhere like that, you'll never get anywhere like that, you'll never get anywhere like that.
Once, on a hot summer night, I had spent an hour kissing a

hairy, ape-shaped law student from Yale because I felt sorry for
him, he was so ugly. When I had finished, he said, 'I have you
taped, baby. You'll be a prude at forty.' (p. 155)

But even because of her bewilderment Sylvia Plath reveals the
dilemma of individuals in a civilisation in which identity has become linked with sexual prowess and in which it can only be
expressed in terms of activity, or pseudo-male 'doing'. The deeper
self, the area of intimacy in the realm of 'being', is abused.

Virginity is a burden: one has to decide intellectually to lose it:
'I decided to seduce him.'

I felt the first man I slept with must be intelligent ... I wanted
somebody I didn't know and wouldn't go on knowing—a kind
of impersonal, priestlike official, as in the tales of tribal rites.

(p. 240)

When she is deflowered 'all I felt was a sharp, startingly bad pain'.
The experience is recorded with cold detachment—though Sylvia
Plath obviously does not feel that this is unusual, nor, I suppose,
(schizoid attitudes to sex being so predominant) do most of her
readers.

Esther suffers a severe haemorrhage, which is pronounced a
'chance in a million'. But the act was an insult to the body. Does
the author see that the haemorrhage may well have been a psycho-
somatic manifestation of the fear of contact and 'impingement'?
The deeply insightful persona of the artist does, I believe, see this:
but it cannot be clearly 'placed' consciously.* Indicatively, Esther's
most vivid relationships are with a man called Constantin, who
seems an 'unattainable pebble at the bottom of a deep well,' and
with a violent man called Marco who attacks her physically after
giving her a diamond in jest, bruising her arm in 'play'—but really
(evidently) in hate and revenge. The most striking sexual episodes
are thus episodes of hate. In Marco, Esther encounters a fanatical
split-off idealism. He (she finds) worships an ideal vision of purity
projected over his cousin as anima, a pure, female element split off
from himself which he narcissistically adores. Obviously for such
an individual it is a question of survival never to let this female

---

* There is almost an air of triumph, in Esther's cold-blooded presentation of her
doctor's bill: 'I was perfectly free' (p. 255). This act of 'cool' comes too at the
moment of 'cure'.

element be re-integrated within himself. The vision is split off to keep it pure. To imply that he or his cousin might really be mixed, ambivalent, human, brings an intense hate reaction.

'I am in love with my cousin.'
I felt no surprise.
'Why don't you marry her?'
'Impossible.'
'Why?'
Marco shrugged. 'She's my first cousin. She's going to be a nun.'
'Is she beautiful?'
'There's no one to touch her.'
'Does she know you love her?'
'Of course.'
I paused. The obstacle seemed unreal to me.
'If you love her,' I said, 'you'll love somebody else someday.'
Marco dashed his cigar underfoot.
The ground soared and struck me with a soft shock. Mud squirmed through my fingers.
. . .
. . . Marco's face lowered cloudily over mine. A few drops of spit struck my lips. 'Your dress is black and the dirt is black as well.'
. . .
'Slut!'
The word hissed by my ear. (p. 114)

Esther is presented as having a compulsive fascination with Marco, just as she is fascinated later by the man whose attempted suicide she reads of in the newspaper. These male imagos will become clearer in their significance when we examine the poems. They stand for the animus—the negative male dynamic. Yet Esther's remarks about love are, by contrast, characteristically feminine, too, and it is this that Marco cannot tolerate, as the author partially sees.

There is an underlying theme at this stage in the book, which is that of the discovery of femaleness and female capacities for sexuality. There is a desperation in Esther's attempts to 'find' sexuality. Of course, some of the ways in which she thinks about sex belong to normal adolescence, the adolescent interest in any experience going—and how well new experiences can be coped with: 'I was quite proud of the calm way I stared at all these grue-some things.' This latter remark is about foetuses in bottles, but it could well be about her response to Buddy Willard's genitals. Her unawakened reaction to nakedness is that of a girl who finds the whole idea ridiculous:

> undressing in front of Buddy suddenly appealed to me about as much as having my Posture Picture taken at college, where you have to stand naked in front of a camera, knowing all the time that a picture of you stark naked, both full view and side view, is going into the college gym files to be marked A B C or D depending on how straight you are. (p. 71)

Here her quirky detachment does show a capacity to satirize the American impulse to reduce the person, in the name of 'objec-tivity', to a thing.

Yet she is aware of the pain of the need for integrity in love. Esther's relationship with Buddy seems at one stage to be pro-gressing in a normal adolescent way, with competitiveness deve-loping between Joan Gilling and Esther. But then she learns of Buddy's relationship with a waitress, and is deeply hurt. She tries to take this coolly ('Buddy seemed relieved I wasn't angry', p. 72) but what stings is the double standard:

> What I couldn't stand was Buddy's pretending I was so sexy and he was so pure, when all the time he'd been having an affair with that tarty waitress and must have felt like laughing in my face. (pp. 73–4)

Buddy has, that summer, actually slept with the 'slutty waitress' thirty times, 'smack in the middle' of knowing Esther. She is offended by Buddy's insincerity and hypocrisy. His mother preached virginity for men, and both she and Buddy bring out moralistic mouthings: but Buddy 'didn't have the guts to admit it straight off to everybody and face up to it as part of his character' that he was having a sexual relationship with a woman who was nothing to him, while demonstrating an interest in Esther.

Esther cannot bear this hypocrisy of American suburban life because it is deadly to feeling. But she responds by deliberately

becoming less tender. In response to the shock, at Buddy's grossness, and the painfulness of being made to feel inexperienced,
Esther decides, in that coldly determined American way, to get
herself seduced.

> I felt so fine by the time we came to the yoghourt and straw-
> berry jam that I decided I would let Constantin seduce me.

> Ever since Buddy Willard had told me about that waitress I
> had been thinking I ought to go out and sleep with somebody
> myself. Sleeping with Buddy wouldn't count, though, because
> he would still be one person ahead of me, it would have to be
> with somebody else.
>
> . . .

> The more I thought about it the better I liked the idea of
> being seduced by a simultaneous interpreter in New York City.
>
> (pp. 81–3)

Sylvia Plath means this to satirise the stream of sex-in-the-head
consciousness of American youth ('one person ahead'). But while,
in one element of her style, she proceeds with the tale as though
she didn't care, there is another 'persona' writing the book whose
attitude persists under the 'taboo on tenderness', and who is aware
of the poignant underlying need for the 'significant other', and the
need for love. Because of this underlying gravity, the development moves on to the first act of attempted suicide in the book—
which is prompted by desperation over the relationship with
Buddy Willard. It belongs to a dull ache deep down in herself. At
the end of Chapter Seven, Esther is remembering this accident:

> Every time it rained the old leg-break seemed to remember
> itself, and what it remembered was a dull hurt.
> Then I thought, 'Buddy Willard made me break that leg.'
> Then I thought, 'No, I broke it myself. I broke it on purpose
> to pay myself back for being such a heel.' (p. 90)

—'being such a heel' is meant explicitly to imply that she was bent
on paying Buddy out for his waitress and is also reacting adversely
against his parents' respectable pressures ('I guess I'll be leaving
you two young people . . .'). But at a deeper level, the skiing

accident, which is described in the next chapter, is a suicidal manifestation of her desperation over *being a woman, unable to respond to a man*. This heel is on the black shoe of false maleness.

In a significant passage at the beginning of Chapter Seven Sylvia Plath's heroine begins to reflect on the absence in herself of the feminine element. What sets off this reflection is 'a stern muscular Russian girl with no make-up': a non-feminine girl with no mask of Western image-femininity:

> . . . I thought how strange it had never occurred to me before that I was only purely happy until I was nine years old.
>
> After that—in spite of the Girl Scouts and the piano lessons and the water-colour lessons and the dancing lessons and the sailing camp, all of which my mother scrimped to give me, and college, with crewing in the mist before breakfast and black-bottom pies and the little new firecrackers of ideas going off every day—I had never been really happy again. (p. 78)

The author does not make clear the connection between her unhappiness after the age of nine, and the Russian male-like girl interpreter. The connection belongs to her private language. It was Daddy who died when she was about nine, and the interpreter is a kind of Colossus: she wears a double-breasted suit, and is a 'doer'. In her, Esther sees a kind of identity with which she could identify in her desperate search to find what it is to be a woman. Yet she also sees that this would still be a form of pseudo-male doing, leading to yet another form of petrifaction:

> I wished with all my heart I could crawl into her and spend the rest of my life barking out one idiom after another. It mightn't make me any happier, but it would be one more little pebble of efficiency among all the other pebbles. (p. 78)

We remember other pebbles: the baby a white pebble in its mother's belly; Constantin 'a pebble': the protagonist in *Tulips* becoming a pebble. In the bewilderment of not being able to find oneself a being-woman, one solution, albeit false, is to petrify oneself, and to cope with the world by such a hardness of male doing ('barking'). The remedy is now one recommended by women's 'liberation'.

From Laing's work, and from my analysis of *Poem for a Birthday*, we can see that this desire to be petrified is a desire to shrink into an invulnerable state, to await rebirth. But this is to become insensitive, no source of honey, unfeminine and inhuman. On pages 78–9 of *The Bell Jar* Esther ruminates (as does Sylvia Plath in the poem *The Disquieting Muses*) on how she could not do any of the things other girls do normally, such as cooking and short-hand. 'The trouble was, I hated the idea of serving men in any way.' ' I was a terrible dancer'. In the poem *The Disquieting Muses* (*The Colossus*, p. 58) the darning-egg dollies prevented the prota-gonist from dancing, made her tone-deaf and defemininised her. So the failure to become feminine is linked with the failure of responsiveness, creative power, perceptiveness, and hope for a fruitful realisation of potentialities—under the influence of symbolic objects which are like 'a bundle of clubs', malignant male objects. The dread of a failure of potentialities is made clear in the novel :

I saw my life branching out before me like the green fig-tree in the story.

From the tip of every branch, like a fat purple fig, a wonderful future beckoned and winked. One fig was a husband and a happy home and children, and another fig was a famous poet and another fig was a brilliant professor, and another fig was Ee Gee, the amazing editor, and another fig was Europe and Africa and South America, and another fig was Constantin and Socrates and Attila and a pack of other lovers with queer names and off-beat professions, and another fig was an Olympic lady crew champion, and beyond and above these figs were many more figs I couldn't quite make out.

A lack of a sense of identity precludes her picking any of these fruits :

I saw myself sitting in the crotch of this fig-tree, starving to death, just because I couldn't make up my mind which of the figs I would choose. I wanted each and every one of them, but choosing one meant losing all the rest, and, as I sat there, unable to decide, the figs began to wrinkle and go black, and, one by one, they plopped to the ground at my feet. (p. 80)

Esther is made to try to turn it into a joke: she goes out to eat with Constantin, and 'It occured to me that the vision of the fig-tree and all the fat figs that withered and fell to earth might well have arisen from the profound void of an empty stomach' (p. 81). But there is a problem, not of an empty stomach but of an empty identity, of being responsive to others, a problem bound up with her capacity to feel real in a meaningful world, a capacity that should develop normally through love.

There is no love in *The Bell Jar*. Most of the relationships in the book are negative ones. Esther and Constantin find themselves on a collision-collusion path of mutual hate. Buddy separates his sensual encounter with the waitress from his desire to have a real relationship with Esther, and his other serious relationship is with Joan, who seems herself a negative of Esther, and is somewhat lesbian. Buddy is worried about his capacity to be a man to a woman. Esther is fascinated by male women, such as the 'double-breasted' interpreter, and her feelings about other women in the mental hospital are imbued with more warmth than her relationships with men. The woman she is most fond of, and most admires—Joan—hangs herself in the end, and beside her grave Esther hears her heart's brag, 'I am I am I am'.

Underlying all these unsatisfactory relationships there is the constant theme of the need to find the capacity to be. The relationships with men seem unlikely to contribute anything to this end, since Esther finds men unreliable, insignificant, and often only targets for her hate. Her hatred of man is a hatred of '*serving man*', and thus of those impulses in a woman to be complement to man—to respond to man in a womanly way. Constantin, whom she tries to encourage to seduce her, simply goes to sleep beside her.

But then, there is a quite different tone—libidinal and elated—when it comes to suicide. Here there is love and hope, para-doxically! In the skiing incident elements are revealed which are new in the novel—and which are given us in a quite different prose to anything that has gone before: it is no longer 'Esther's' rather zany prose, but a prose akin to the poetic voice of Sylvia Plath.

A small, answering point in my own body flew towards it. I felt my lungs inflate with the inrush of scenery—air, mountains, trees, people. I thought, 'This is what it is to be happy.' (p. 102)

'I have been half in love with easeful death'—something like the phrase of Keats's comes to mind. The callow youth fades into inconsequential nothingness: the problem is not that of 'sexual relationships' with Buddy. There may be a problem of relationship with 'Man', but only as part of a deeper problem of *what it is to be*. The prose becomes poetic: and yet we are aware that Esther could singularly feel no such poetry in love and sexuality. Esther (or rather, surely, 'Sylvia') glides here towards a purity of relationship with the cosmos. The sun is an 'insentient pivot'—and is, as I believe the symbolism of the poems suggests, in a sense the dead father, who, now in the world of death, is insentient. The sun here, at this moment, is like the North Wind Mother in George Macdonald's *At the Back of the North Wind*, only it is the father. In contemplation of this pivot Esther is sublimely happy—as she approaches death, which, since the ski-slope is a symbol of the birth-passage, is also a regeneration. Esther thus seeks to escape from the ambivalent, complex, mundanity of her relationship with Buddy, into a pure 'cosmic' marriage. 'I wanted to hone myself on it till I grew saintly . . .'.

Esther, like Sylvia Plath in her more psychotic poems, is thus in love with death, because 'in' death is the loved father, and his reflection offers the possibility of a new and sharp sense of being. This pure quest makes all earthly encounters ridiculous.

Moving towards the father-in-death provokes elation: turning towards the live mother prompts a loss of creative relationship with the world. These ambiguities parallel the strange confusion of sexual roles. (As Winnicott has urged, we could benefit here by talking less of sexuality, homosexuality, lesbianism in such matters, and talking instead of male and female elements in the personality.)

A crucial moment in the novel comes in Chapter Ten, during which Esther decides to stay in her mother's house, despite the dangers she recognises in the situation. It could be said that this is the moment at which Esther chooses the path which must lead her to suicide and madness. She is invited on the telephone to join some other girls for the vacation—even though her writing course hasn't come up, but she does not choose freedom:

One more morning listening to Dodo Conway's baby carriage

would drive me crazy. And I made a point of never living in the same house with my mother for more than a week.

I reached for the receiver.

My hand advanced a few inches, then retreated and fell limp. I forced it towards the receiver again, but again it stopped short, as if it had collided with a pane of glass. (p. 125)

This is the bell jar, coming down. She sends an insult to Buddy ('I did not want to give my children a hypocrite for a father')— and chooses instead the dangerous relationship with her mother.

In this, she chooses the desperate path to rebirth (at this moment it is also a choice to write a novel, itself an attempt at re-mothering). Against the glass wall of the bell jar is pressed the nose of the pickled foetus. The bell jar encloses the subject, so that she feels a sense of having a sheet of glass between herself and reality. This is the 'plate glass feeling' noted by Laing and others in schizoid patients. For instance, Guntrip (1966) writes:

A somewhat common schizoid symptom is the feeling of a plate glass wall between the patient and the world . . . A middle-aged woman patient discovered in the course of analysis that she did not need the spectacles she was wearing and discarded them. She said: 'I realise I've only worn them because I felt safer behind that screen. I could look through it at the world.' (p. 63)

The bell jar that comes down is thus not only a barrier, but a shield: and inside the jar is the regressed ego. The foetus in the bottle is the 'pristine unitary ego' waiting to be born, but shrinking from the world, virtually dead, until an opportunity for rebirth offers itself.

We meet the bell jar explicitly in Chapter Fifteen. The protagonist is leaving one hospital for another and hopes to leap to death from a bridge as the car goes over it. She feels that wherever she is the bell-jar will stand between her and reality

. . . wherever I sat—on the deck of a ship or at a street café in Paris or Bangkok—I would be sitting under the same bell jar, stewing in my own sour air. (p. 196)

While the bell jar is a symbol of being enclosed, encapsulated, dissociated from reality, its deeper symbolism as the womb becomes obvious on the following page where the jar seems rather like *not* committing suicide.

> My room was on the first floor . . . If I jumped I wouldn't even bruise my knees. The inner surface of the tall wall seemed smooth as glass. (p. 197)

The bell jar is a womb which contains the regressed libidinal ego that cannot find its way to become born:

> To the person in the bell jar, blank and stopped as a dead baby, the world itself is the bad dream. (p. 250)

> I sank back in the grey, plush seat and closed my eyes. The air of the bell jar wadded round me and I couldn't stir . . .
> (pp. 196–7)

After ECT the bell jar lifts a little: but on leaving hospital there remains the fear that it will come down again.

> How did I know that someday—at college, in Europe, some-where, anywhere,—the bell jar, with its stifling distortions, wouldn't descend again? (p. 254)

Similarly, at the end of *Poem for a Birthday* there is no real sense of being reborn after treatment. Esther is interviewed by a board of doctors who have already decided whether or not she is to leave. It is a false solution, a rebirth but without any resurrection in terms of 'being'. It is the closing bracket of a period that began with a ceremony of degradation—her committal. She is but an 'applicant': 'There ought, I thought, to be a ritual for being born twice—patched, retreaded and approved for the road . . .' (p. 257). The eyes of the doctors at the end seem to be offering her an identity merely assembled by impingement—the kind on which she pours scorn in her references elsewhere to puppets and dolls. All the hospital has offered is an irrelevant 'doing to', as far from recreating her inner being as the original inadequate handling. The only rebirth, she becomes convinced yet more strongly, lies in suicide.

The images of rebirth in *The Bell Jar* confirm the insights of Guntrip into the schizoid suicide. As I have tried to show elsewhere this interpretation can also be used to illuminate the poetry of Dylan Thomas, whose alcoholism was a form of suicide (albeit an agonisingly slow one). I was fascinated by Esther's remark that 'I had been so free I'd spent most of my time on Dylan Thomas . . .' (p. 131). Sylvia Plath understood Thomas in an uncanny way, through psychic affinity, and her sequence of poems handed in for the English Tripos at Cambridge shows how much she was influenced by him (e.g. *Lament*, published in the *Orleans Poetry Journal*, No. 52 in *Two Lovers and a Beachcomber*: 'The sting of bees took away my father . . .' The poem seems to echo *Do Not Go Gentle Into That Good Night*).

It is possible that Sylvia Plath took over from Dylan Thomas the image of a bottled foetus: it occurs quite early in her work in a poem about a glass paperweight. To be confronted with actual bottled foetuses in a medical laboratory is to Esther all too redolent of meanings evocative of the imprisoned self. Esther says early on that she likes 'looking on': she has a compulsive need to record disturbing experiences:

> If there was a road accident or a street fight or a baby pickled in a laboratory jar for me to look at, I'd stop and look so hard I'd never forget it. (p. 13)

Fairbairn (1966) says

> There are probably few 'normal' people who have never at any time in their lives experienced an unnatural state of calm and detachment in face of some serious crisis, a transient sense of 'looking on at oneself' . . . such phenomena, I venture to suggest, are essentially schizoid phenomena. (p. 8)

Sylvia Plath was one whose experience seemed often to be of this 'déjà vu' kind (as recorded in her heroine's sexual experiences). The intense feeling of 'looking on' at everything from the outside gives the uncanny 'cool' clarity to her vision.

The actual babies in bottles are shown to Esther at the opening of the scene of depersonalised birth.

> Buddy took me out into a hall where they had some big glass bottles full of babies that had died before they were born. The baby in the first bottle had a large white head bent over a tiny

curled-up body the size of a frog. The baby in the next bottle was bigger and the baby next to that one was bigger still and the baby in the last bottle was the size of a normal baby and he seemed to be looking at me and smiling a little piggy smile.

(p. 65)

Taking refuge in a light-hearted, trivialising style in this early part of her book, the author pretends that her heroine was not at all moved by the experience of such 'gruesome things' ('These cadavers were so unhuman-looking that they didn't bother me a bit'). This flip tone, however, is a defence. The way the image of the pickled foetus recurs obsessively gives the lie to this posture. The image creeps back from time to time, as when she turns to a copy of *Time* or *Life*: 'The face of Eisenhower beamed up at me, bald and blank as the face of a foetus in a bottle.' (p. 93) The image colours her feelings about babies altogether:

I leafed nervously through an issue of *Baby Talk*. The fat, bright faces of babies beamed up at me, page after page—bald babies, chocolate-coloured babies, Eisenhower-faced babies, babies rolling over for the first time . . . babies doing all the little tricky things it takes to grow up, step by step, into an anxious and unsettling world . . . (p. 234)

To an individual obsessed with the unborn self, it is obviously extremely difficult to face dealing with a baby who needs total support in developing its own identity. As Sylvia Plath discovers in *The Night Dances*, the problem arises of how one can do for one's own baby what has never been done for oneself. Whereas Esther regards dead babies with detachment, live ones repel her: yet she yearns to be feminine, too:

I smelt a mingling of Pabulum and sour milk and salt-cod-stinky diapers and felt sorrowful and tender. How easy having babies seemed to the women around me! Why was I so unmaternal and apart? Why couldn't I dream of devoting myself to baby after fat puling baby like Dodo Conway?
If I had to wait on a baby all day, I would go mad. (p. 234)

Renouncing the mother's role is renouncing the female element in oneself. Esther thinks, as she climbs on the the examination table to be fitted for a contraceptive device:

> 'I am climbing to freedom, freedom from fear, freedom from marrying the wrong person . . . just because of sex . . .'
> . . .
> I was my own woman. (p. 235)

But she is in part delighting not only in freedom from being feminine but ultimately in freedom from being human—and this as we shall see can also be a search for a certain black purity.

For those in the bell jar life is a 'bad dream': the only hope is in waking up. The foetus in the jar is in liquid which seems like the amniotic fluid. Death-by-water is a continual presence in Sylvia Plath, and when the images are studied they are often revealed as images of rebirth ('the/Water striving/To re-establish its mirror . . .', Words, Ariel, p. 86). The images of reflection symbolise the mother's eyes. Esther looks in the mirror for confirmation of her identity, after the disturbances set up in her by watching Doreen and Lenny, and finds it warped, impure. It is a symbol of failed provision for the emerging identity by the mother's 'mirror-image role':

> The mirror over my bureau seemed slightly warped and much too silver. The face in it looked like the reflection in a ball of dentist's mercury.

—such a ball might dissolve, and so might she. The bath, too, becomes a symbol of finding a new state in re-birth. Feeling like a 'dirty, scrawled over letter', after becoming aware of the sexuality of others, Esther decides to take a hot bath:

> There must be quite a few things a hot bath won't cure, but I don't know many of them. Whenever I'm sad I'm going to die, or so nervous I can't sleep, or in love with somebody I won't be seeing for a week, I slump down just so far and then I say: 'I'll go take a hot bath.' (p. 21)

It is like being in the amniotic fluid in the womb but to Esther the bath may also be a coffin:

> I remember the ceilings over every bath tub I've stretched

out in . . . I remember the tubs, too: the antique griffin-legged tubs, and the modern coffin-shaped tubs . . .
I never feel so much myself as when I'm in a hot bath.

She lies in this one for an hour

and I felt myself growing pure again. I don't believe in baptism or the waters of Jordan or anything like that, but I guess I feel about a hot bath the way those religious people feel about holy water.
I said to myself: 'Doreen is dissolving, Lenny Shepherd is dissolving . . . New York is dissolving, they are all dissolving away and none of them matter any more. I don't know them, I have never known them and I am very pure. All that liquor and those sticky kisses* I saw and the dirt that settled on my skin on the way back is turning into something pure.'
The longer I lay there in the clear hot water the purer I felt, and when I stepped out at last and wrapped myself in one of the big, soft, white hotel bath-towels I felt pure and sweet as a new baby. (pp. 21–2)

To die is the ultimate freedom from ambivalence, or 'stickiness', the mess of human emotions: its purity is an escape from humanness.
The suicide attempt on the ski slope is a quest for purity, like the bath, and the sky seems to be looking at her, reflecting:

The great, grey eye of the sky looked back at me, its mist-shrouded sun focusing all the white and silent distances that poured from every point of the compass, hill after pale hill, to stall at my feet. (p. 101)

Reality 'stalls': there is a loss of control as her impulse towards symbolic rebirth overcomes her.

The interior voice nagging me not to be a fool—to save my skin and take off my skis and walk down, camouflaged by the scrub pines bordering the slope—fled like a disconsolate mosquito. *The thought that I might kill myself formed in my mind coolly as a tree or a flower.* (p. 101, my italics)

* Cf. 'Two lovers unstick themselves', *Berck-Plage*. The stickiness is the glue of bodily experience such as is loathed by Sartre: 'bad' inner contents, *la nausée* itself. See Masud Khan above, p. 8.

As she plummets down, having recklessly flung herself into outer reality, Esther thinks, 'This is what it is to be happy'.

> People and trees receded on either hand like the dark sides of a *tunnel* as I hurtled on to the still, bright point at the end of it, *the pebble at the bottom of the well, the white sweet baby cradled in its mother's belly.* (p. 102, my italics)

This pebble-baby is pure, but there are no loving hands to receive her: there is only the harsh discovery of reality. Instead of the discovery of the breast, she is given a stone: 'My teeth crunched a gravelly mouthful. Ice water seeped down my throat.' As in *Poem for a Birthday*, to come round like this when one hoped to be born again pure and sweet is too dreadfully evocative of the experience of impingement. The attempt to subdue outer reality to the inner world fails:

> A dispassionate white sun shone at the summit of the sky. I wanted to hone myself on it till I grew saintly and thin and essential as the blade of a knife. (p. 103)

—but she is 'stuck in a cast for months' instead. The cast symbolises a false hard mould or stony identity, instead of the newborn self that should have emerged alive and warm from the matrix.

In all these perplexities Esther is shown to be poignantly aware that she is 'different'. In one episode there is an acute contrast between the normal jolly company she is in, browning hot dogs on the public grills at the beach, and her inner dissociation: anybody who looked at her with half an eye could see she didn't have a brain in her head:

> A smoke seemed to be going up from my nerves like the smoke from the grills and the sun-saturated road. The whole landscape—beach and headland and sea and rock—quavered in front of my eyes like a stage backcloth.
>
> I wondered at what point in space the silly sham blue of the sky turned black. (p. 166)

The familiar blue of our sky is a 'sham', to one whose dynamic of identity, in its dealings with external reality, has collapsed into a 'smoke'. This is the 'déjà vu' state of which Guntrip writes: it is the view from the bell jar: 'I thought drowning must be the kindest way to die . . .'—because it would be like being re-evolved, in the salt water.

> Some of those babies in the jars that Buddy Willard showed me had gills, he said. They went through a stage where they were just like fish. (p. 166)

She swims out: 'as I paddled on, my heart beat boomed like a dull motor in my ears'. Even as she tries to die, or (by her logic) to become reborn, her body declares that it is alive, 'singing in her ear' like Ted Hughes's Littleblood.

'I am I am I am.' She is: but she is not. She seeks to be, but by destroying the self in the bell jar. She tries to duck herself to death, but her tenacious hold on life defeats her:

> . . . the world was sparkling all about me like blue and green and yellow semi-precious stones . . . I knew when I was beaten . . . I turned back . . . (p. 170)

A grey rock mocks her. Later she remembers how 'the rock . . . bulged between sky and sea like a grey skull'. We meet this rock in her poetry: it is the white skull under the surface: it is an appre-hension of the real death that is not rebirth. It is the reality of the stone colossus outside the jar, for Daddy and death often merge: so, it is the stone at the heart of being. It is also the pestle of impingement, merged with Daddy's deathly grey big toe. And it is real death, for death seems the ultimate impingement, of false male doing or being-done-to. This death in reality she meets when Joan is buried:

> There would be a black, six-foot deep gap hacked in the hard ground. That shadow would marry this shadow, and the pecu-liar, yellowish soil of our locality seal the wound in the white-ness, and yet another snowfall erase the traces of newness in Joan's grave.
> I took a deep breath and listened to the old brag of my heart. I am, I am, I am. (p. 256)

'I am' is what the heart says: but the agony is being unmistake-ably alive when the I AM feeling in the identity does not complete and confirm the bodily existence.

When she tries to hang herself Esther discovers a dichotomy

4

between the impulses of the living organism and the impulses of the human identity;

> But each time I would get the cord so tight I could feel a rushing in my ears and a flush of blood in my face, my hands would weaken and let go, and I would be all right again.
> Then I saw that my body had all sorts of little tricks, such as making my hands go limp at the crucial second, which would save it, time and again, whereas if I had the whole say, I would be dead in a flash. (p. 168)

Who is the 'I'?

> I would simply have to ambush it with whatever sense I had left, or it would trap me in its stupid cage for fifty years without any sense at all. And when people found out my mind had gone, as they would have to, sooner or later, in spite of my mother's guarded tongue, they would persuade her to put me into an asylum where I could be cured.
> Only my case was incurable. (p. 168)

To find oneself in one's own body seems to her a trap: to be really human seems a loss of freedom. Esther believes (from reading paperbacks on psychology) that she is incurable and that 'The more hopeless you were, the further away they hid you' (p. 169). What she fears is that she will be removed from all hope of being reborn out of the bell jar, by society's rejection of her as 'mad'.

R. D. Laing is taken to imply by his work that those who are labelled as 'schizophrenic' are victims of the political coercions and mystifications of a mad society. This view would seem to be that adopted by critics who find that Sylvia Plath's myths speak for 'us' (e.g. A. E. Dyson's remark in a review of *Ariel* that her last poems 'are among the handful of writings by which future generations will seek to know us and give us a name').

This view seems to me, however, to be a dangerous over-simplification which should perhaps be corrected in the light of the work of Fairbairn and Winnicott. There *are* manifestations of collective psychopathology in our society, such as war and preparation for war, and there *is* insanity in the way we accept these as normal. The execution of the Rosenbergs preoccupies Sylvia Plath's heroine in *The Bell Jar* because it was an insane act committed by 'society'. She sees it as insane when the 'normal' world does not, because, as a schizoid individual, she can see into what is happening with dreadful clarity. The fashion world was promoting bile green that year. She says to one of the magazine women, 'Isn't it awful about the Rosenbergs?'

> 'Yes!' Hilda said, and at last I felt I had touched a human string . . .
> 'It's awful such people should be alive' . . . 'I'm so glad they're going to die.' (p. 105)

This paranoid hate merges with the image-promoting world and its poisonous emptiness ('bile green with nile green, its kissing cousin'). Here we would seem to find confirmation of the 'politics of experience' of R. D. Laing and his view that schizophrenia is the inevitable product of this kind of society.

But there is another problem—which is why, among all the other human beings in this society, Esther (or Sylvia Plath) should be so susceptible to breakdown? And why she should come to feel, as she did at times, that the *only* way to deal with a schizoid society is to take the path of ultimately *dehumanising oneself*? Esther's thoughts about suicide and her impulse to suicidal acts are obsessional—so obsessional that the novel becomes at times the love-story of a girl who adores suicide: but the obsession is not 'placed': it is the author's. As Andrew Brink (1968) notes in his essay, Sylvia Plath is left in the end with only one possible identity: 'she-who-commits-suicide'. The life of her protagonist is the story of one who is involved in a 'meaningless succession of mere activities to keep a self in being'. There is no other way in which she can behave: her life is all false male 'doing', and this, in the light of my phenomenological analysis, has an intrapsychic aspect. The psychiatry she experiences is no less an attempt to 'manufacture a sense of being she does not possess'.

In the novel Esther finds a nurse sewing her name on everything.

> 'Where is everybody?'
> 'Out.' The nurse was writing something over and over on little pieces of adhesive tape. I leaned across the gate of the door to see what she was writing, and it was E. Greenwood, E. Greenwood, E. Greenwood, E. Greenwood.

> 'Out where?'
> 'Oh, OT, the golf course, playing badminton.'
> I noticed a pile of clothes on a chair beside the nurse. They
> were the same clothes the nurse in the first hospital had been
> packing into the patent leather case when I broke the mirror.
> The nurse began sticking the labels on the clothes. (p. 199)

The economy of symbolism here is one with the mordant coolness of the prose. 'Everybody' is 'out': the self is a body out of the
clothes, which are not worn, but passed from hospital to hospital.
The nurse sticks the labels on to the clothes: the being recognises
neither the name, nor the clothes. Having broken the mirror in
which she fails to find her identity reflected, she passes on, like the
clothes, separated from her identity. Note that the nurse simply
does not say: 'Why, look, honey, I'm sewing your name on!'
This institutional depersonalisation is, as Jules Henry (1966) says,
an indication of how, in Western society, 'humanness is ebbing'.
Note, too, the reference to breaking the mirror, for which she is
being punished—the punishment taking the form of having one's
identity institutionalised. Instead of a coherent reflection she has
the ball of mercury which dissolves at a blow into millions of
fragments: or the implosive threat of shadows.

> I thought the most beautiful thing in the world must be
> shadow, the million moving shapes and cul-de-sacs of sha-
> dow. There was shadow in bureau drawers and closets and
> suitcases, and shadow under houses and trees and stones,
> and shadow at the back of people's eyes and smiles, and
> shadow, miles and miles and miles of it, on the night side of
> the earth. (p. 155)

Identification becomes a process not of being reflected by others
so much as desiring to become them, in a desperate search for a
sense of identity. Esther cannot decide who she is: and she refuses
to be glib about it:

> When they asked me what I wanted to be I said I didn't
> know.
> 'Oh, sure you know,' the photographer said.
> 'She wants,' said Jay Cee wittily, 'to be everything.'
> I said I wanted to be a poet. (p. 106)

So for Esther (and we may assume for Sylvia Plath) 'being a poet' was an act of asserting the *Dasein*.

> Now, lying on my back in bed, I imagined Buddy saying, 'Do you know what a poem is, Esther?'
> 'No, what?' I would say.
> 'A piece of dust.'
> Then just as he was smiling and starting to look proud, I would say, 'So are the cadavers you cut up. So are the people you think you're curing. They're dust as dust as dust. I reckon a good poem lasts a whole lot longer than a hundred of those people put together.'
> 'People were made of nothing so much as dust, and I couldn't see that doctoring all that dust was a bit better than writing poems people would remember and repeat to themselves when they were unhappy or sick and couldn't sleep. (pp. 58–9)

In this way Esther can transcend her sense of non-fruition She learned as a child how to find life in words: 'I wanted to crawl in between those black lines of print the way you crawl through a fence, and go to sleep under that beautiful big green fig-tree' (p. 57). Just as Esther wants to find an identity by crawling into the Russian woman interpreter, so she wants to crawl into her writing to find an identity there (as did Sylvia Plath herself).

But without confirmation in intersubjectivity there can be no confident identity and no creative perception; so the meticulous attention to creativity, though it could help with the *Dasein* problem, cannot cure her dissociation of personality, in the depth of the 'psychic tissue'.

Chapter Ten, in which Esther goes home, begins after she has been beaten up by Marco the woman-hater, and traces the story of her breakdown. It begins: 'The face in the mirror looked like a sick Indian.' In the train window 'A wan reflection of myself, white wings, brown ponytail and all, ghosted over the landscape.' The attack by the man in hate, the collapse of the image-world of New York bustle, the vacancy of 'fun', have exposed the empty centre of herself. What she sees in the mirror is an alien ghost, not a self reflected. She keeps a mark of blood on her face, because (she doesn't say so, but we feel it) if she can be attacked in hate, at least she is real (even though she throws the 'grey scraps' of the clothing that seems to give her an identity into the air of New York from a building). There are at least some 'inner contents' on her face, so she must exist. The moment of arriving home is deeply significant, in the light of Winnicott's insight into the mother's mirror-role.

> A summer calm laid its soothing hand over everything, like death.
> My mother was waiting by the glove-grey Chevrolet.
> 'Why lovey, what's happened to your face?' (p. 119)

This can be read as a failure to reflect. Note that Esther's mother doesn't say 'What has happened to *you*?' Esther needs the gentleness of Mary: yet this is the most dangerous thing in the world (as it is in the poem *Kindness*).

This fear of the love she needs explains why Esther is so overcome by home, and feels too trapped in suburbia:

> The grey, padded car roof closed over my head like the roof of a prison van, and the white, shining, identical clap-board houses with their interstices of well-groomed green proceeded past, one bar after another in a large but escape-proof cage.
> I had never spent a summer in the suburbs before. (p. 120)

This is a characteristic adolescent feeling. But, as we see later, Esther's hostility to her mother is horrifiyingly strong. And it is directed against the mechanical nature of her mother's routine:

> At seven I had heard my mother get up, slip into her clothes and tiptoe out of the room. Then the buzz of the orange squeezer sounded from downstairs ... Then the sink water ran from the tap and dishes clinked as my mother dried them and put them back in the cupboard.
> Then the front door opened and shut. Then the car door opened and shut, and the motor went broom-broom and, edging off with a crunch of gravel, faded into the distance. (p. 121)

Although her mother calls her 'lovey', she seems in the home to offer only mechanical 'doing'. The whole effective smooth routine of suburbia seems to Esther a threatening 'impingement', hateful.

She had hoped to escape, into a kind of creativity, in her writing course. But she receives a blow at once with her mother's announcement:

'I think I should tell you right away,' she said, and I could see bad news in the set of her neck, 'you didn't make that writing course.' (p. 120)

So, trapped in suburbia, her hate turns against all the women around her, their respectability, their prying, their creaking pram-wheels—until the idea of being in proximity with such femaleness seems stifling. The paraphernalia of domesticity, especially of feeding children, provokes Esther's crisis:

Dodo raised her six children—and would no doubt raise her seventh—on rice crispies, peanut-butter-and-marshmallow sandwiches, vanilla ice-cream and gallon upon gallon of Hood's milk. She got a special discount from the local milkman. (p. 123)

The mothering woman seems to mock her own need to be mothered, which, as she encounters it at home, seems to threaten hopelessness:

I watched Dodo wheel the youngest Conway up and down. She seemed to be doing it for my benefit.
Children make me sick.
. . .
I had nothing to look forward to. (p. 123)

Yet when she tries to lift the telephone to take action and find a way out, as we have seen, the bell jar intervenes.

As we have also seen, the mother is regarded as dangerous:
In the dim light of the streetlamp that filtered through the drawn blinds, I could see the pin curls on her head *glittering like a row of little bayonets*. (p. 129, my italics)

In her need for glittering eyes, Esther, paranoically, sees daggers. So, she feels an impulse to kill the unfortunate middle-aged woman with 'a snore ravelling from her throat' which is a 'column of skin and sinew' Esther wants to 'twist to silence'.* The language

* The 'column of skin and sinew' bears a significant resemblance to the under-lying penis-image: cf. 'I am nude as a chicken neck' (*The Bee Meeting*) and 'The

here is illuminating. 'Ravelling' for instance invokes Macbeth who had 'murdered sleep' that 'knits up the ravelled sleeve of care'. The breath that comes out of the mother only 'ravels'—entangles, knots. Esther wants to murder her in her sleep. But in the background is the bafflement I have analysed—of the father lurking within, who is also the destructive and malignant animus, even an aspect of Death. Moreover, in wanting to kill her mother she is liable to destroy her only hope of being reborn. Yet she knows that her mother cannot now provide any means of being reborn: she can only feel repulsion at the contact and proximity between them.

Psychiatry offers no mothering either. Nothing is more poignant than the account of false fathers and mothers in Esther's experience of psychiatry. When she has an insulin reaction she screams for Mrs Bannister the night nurse: 'And when Mrs Bannister held the cup to my lips, I fanned the hot milk out on my tongue as it went down, tasting it luxuriously, the way a baby tastes its mother' (p. 213). Since the time of Esther's experience insulin shock therapy has been discontinued as too dangerous and in any case, even when successful, it often left only a deadened and confused personality. It was also found that successful therapy was not the effect of the drug at all, but the effect of the *concern* expressed by the doctors and nurses *on account of the danger* of the drug. It was a kind of brutal mothering.

When we know this, it is pitiful to read of an Esther who is able to speak of her true predicament, and yet only receives from those who care for her further impingement that seems dreadfully irrelevant. Esther wants to taste her mother but all she gets is 'reactions': when she comes round from attempted suicide she hears a voice calling 'Mother'. Coming round she looks hopefully into a reflecting object, only to find it is Daddy's black shoe.

The connection between this shoe-symbol and death is clear from an incident when the girls attending the Ladies' Day 'banquet' are poisoned by crabmeat ('it was chock-full of ptomaine'). Sylvia Plath's shortest paragraph is:

Poison.

---

only thing I could think of was turkey neck' (*The Bell Jar*, p. 71). The above murderous moment seems to relate to images of castration aimed at the castrating mother (who must be castrated before she castrates Esther).

To her, 'inner contents' are fascinating. To her protagonist, 'There is nothing like puking with somebody to make you into old friends' (p. 45). As she recovers she has a vision of Doreen as the Virgin Mary:

> ... her blonde hair lit at the tips from behind like a halo of gold ... I felt a sort of expert tenderness flowing from the ends of her fingers. She might have been Betsy or my mother or a fern-scented nurse.
>
> . . .
>
> I felt purged and holy and ready for a new life.
>
> . . .
>
> 'Well, you almost died,' she said finally. (p. 49)

This rebirth is false: it is not even real death.

But when Esther first comes round:

> The next thing I had a view of was somebody's shoe.
> It was a stout shoe of cracked black leather and quite old, with tiny air holes in a scalloped pattern over the toe and a dull polish, and *it was pointed at me* ... (p. 47, my italics)

When she drops a razor on her calf:

> The blood gathered darkly, like fruit, and rolled down my ankle into the cup of my black patent leather shoe. (p. 156)

After this episode she goes to her father's grave. 'You do not do, black shoe' in *Daddy* (*Ariel*, p. 54) gives us the clue to the symbolism of these shoes.

When she loses her virginity to the mathematics professor she bleeds badly from the ruptured hymen: 'the blood trickling down my legs and oozing, stickily, into each black patent leather shoe' (p. 243). Esther's first sexual act, in the search for 'meeting' is a kind of death: so her 'inner contents' flow down into her shoes. Shoes are associated with death because Daddy died from a diseased toe. But the protagonist woman in Sylvia Plath is often 'in Daddy's shoes', because her identity is constructed around Daddy. The way in which these shiny black shoes confront Esther at deathly moments symbolises the focus of her quest for 'creative reflection': instead of the mother's eyes, she finds the black shiny shoe of the father pointed at her. She hopes to get from the father what she did not get from the mother, but what she gets is a black threat as if of hate and death. The mother seems unable to give reflection because she did not mourn. The truth would seem to be that, in life, Sylvia Plath's mother hid her grief from her child: so, by strange infant logic, she was not grieving enough, and the daughter must take on this role.

> I had a great yearning, lately, to pay my father back for all the years of neglect, and start tending his grave. I had always been my father's favourite, and it seemed fitting I should take on a mourning my mother had never bothered with. (p. 175)

This suggests an element in Sylvia Plath's predicament (culminating in *Daddy*) of not being able to relinquish the dead Daddy, however menacing he is, because mourning was incomplete. The graveyard disappoints Esther.

> The stones in the modern part were crude and cheap, and here and there a grave was rimmed with marble, like an oblong bath-tub full of dirt, and rusty metal containers stuck up about where the person's navel would be, full of plastic flowers.
> . . .
> I couldn't find my father anywhere. (p. 176)

As we have already seen, the bath-tub is to her both a coffin and a place of rebirth: so the tombs seem to have a navel linking them to the surface ('the voices just can't worm through'). The images of birth persist. Esther is dressed in a black mac she has bought that morning: she had asked the sales girl if it was water-repellant. In the background are strange feelings about 'inner contents' (tears, amniotic fluid, and perhaps 'golden rain') associated with intense emotional needs, and paranoid dread.

The episode is 'seen' as through the eyes of a child. We recall how, as Esther begins to experience her break-down, she regresses:

> That morning I had tried to write a letter to Doreen, down in West Virginia, asking whether I could come and live with her and maybe get a job at her college waiting on table or something.
> But when I took up my pen, my hand made big, jerky letters like those of a child . . . (p. 137)

This symptom meant nothing to the psychiatrist treating her who is, smooth, vain, worldly, and encapsulated in his own denial of 'being'.

By her father's tomb she regresses again, and this yields one of the most moving pieces of writing in the book.

> Then I saw my father's gravestone.
>
> It was crowded right up by another gravestone, head to head, the way people are crowded in a charity ward when there isn't enough space. The stone was of mottled pink marble, like tinned salmon, and all there was on it was my father's name and, under it, two dates, separated by a little dash. (p. 177)

The 'dash' is his life. Sylvia Plath is obsessed with decades perhaps because her own father died when she was little. What is between decades seems insubstantial and meaningless. Even the gravestone belongs to the world of mass-production, ugliness, the indifference to people in the mass which is America:

> At the root of the stone I arranged the rainy armful of azaleas I had picked from a bush at the gateway of the grave-yard. Then my legs folded under me, and I sat down in the sopping grass. I couldn't understand why I was crying so hard.
>
> Then I remembered that I had never cried for my father's death.
>
> My mother hadn't cried either. She had just smiled and said what a merciful thing it was for him he had died, because if he had lived he would have been crippled and an invalid for life and he couldn't have stood that, he would rather have died than had that happen.
>
> I laid my face to the smooth face of the marble and howled my loss into the cold salt rain. (p. 177)

It is an important moment of mourning: but it does not enable her to let Daddy go. Significantly, the next paragraph begins brusquely: 'I knew just how to go about it.'

Leaving a note ('*I am going for a long walk*') Esther attempts suicide efficiently at last—or rather only more or less efficiently, since she survives. She records her compulsive tidiness in preparing for the event, and descends to the cellar (compare the cellar and its significance in the 'bee' poems): '. . . this secret, earth-bottomed crevice . . . I . . . crouched at the mouth of the darkness, like a troll.'* The symbolism is both of an entry into her father's grave, and of an entry into the womb, too. The prose becomes lyrical with love, and with caul-symbols:

> Cobwebs touched my face with the softness of moths. Wrapping my black coat round me like my own sweet shadow, I unscrewed the bottle of pills . . . (p. 179)

In the ensuing record of sensation there are images of reptation which suggest birth again:

> . . . my head rose, feeling it [the darkness], like the head of a worm . . . I was being transported at enormous speed down a tunnel into the earth . . . a slit of light opened, like a mouth or a wound . . . I tried to roll away from the direction of light, but hands wrapped round my limbs like mummy bands, and I couldn't move . . . through the thick, warm, furry dark a voice cried, 'Mother!'

> Air breathed and played over my face.' (pp. 180–1)

The symbolism here is complex. She identifies with the libidinised internalised penis of the father ('the head of a worm') which is entering the mother's body. She is also Christ in the Tomb,† as anyone must be in this civilisation who is wrapped in bands in a hollow cave. She is a mummy. She is inside the womb ('warm, furry, dark'). She is being reborn. She is wrapped in mummy bands (navel wrappings) and is being handled as a baby at birth. She is breathing in air. Her account gains its force from the uncanny presentation of the near-death with joy, with a sense of

---

* Cf. Dylan Thomas, 'In the groin of the natural doorway/Crouched like a tailor/Sewing a shroud for a journey . . .'—a recurrent image in his work. Esther feels 'as if I were being stuffed farther and farther into a black, airless sack with no way out' (p. 136)—an image which also recurs in Dylan Thomas who spoke of the 'sad sack of the self' and who was fascinated by Houdini. See *Dylan Thomas; the Code of Night*, p. 142.

† Identification with Christ seems to be a common schizoid manifestation. I have heard of a schizophrenic patient in a mental hospital, who stabbed a fellow-patient, in order to be executed and to 'rise as Christ in four days' time.' The association in Sylvia Plath's mind between being in the cave, and being Christ who, like Lazarus, rises from the vault is clear in a number of places. In *Nick and the Candlestick* the room is a cave, he is the baby in the barn, and there are strong references to Christ, communion and resurrection. In *Tulips* the dead shut their mouths on freedom 'like a Communion tablet' and in *Mystic* she asks 'What is the remedy?/The pill of the Communion tablet, the walking beside still water?'

security and satisfaction. But the outcome is futile: later she asks 'I want to see a mirror'. What she sees offers no confirmation of a new self.

> At first I didn't see what the trouble was. It wasn't a mirror at all, but a picture.
>
> You couldn't tell whether the person in the picture was a man or a woman, because their hair was shaved off and sprouted in bristly chicken-feather tufts all over their head. One side of the person's face was purple, and bulged out in a shapeless way, shading to green along the edges, and then to a sallow yellow. The person's mouth was pale brown, with a rose-coloured sore at either corner.
>
> . . .
> I smiled.
> The mouth in the mirror cracked into a grin.
> A minute after the crash another nurse ran in. (p. 185)

The sexless image of a woman who simply fell to earth under the influence of drugs fails to confirm the hope of a new identity: a nurse snarls, 'At you-know-where they'll take care of *her*!' Because she *broke the mirror* she is to be sent to another hospital, where there is closer coercion: her mother says, 'You shouldn't have broken that mirror. Then maybe they'd have let you stay'.

The symbolism of the need for a mirror, her need for its smashing, and the needs of the soul thus expressed in the light of the fact that the mirror is a symbol of the mother's reflecting eyes, is very poignant—not least when she is told, 'You should have behaved better, then'.

> It is easy to blame the dark: the mouth of the door
> The cellar's belly . . .
> *Witch Burning, Poem for a Birthday*

What psychiatry provides for Esther is a series of false fathers and mothers, who offer forms of 'doing' which are directed towards 'curing' her, implicitly blaming her for hankering after shadows, doors and cellars. But in destroying these hankerings, they've blown her 'sparkler out', obliging her to conform and adopt a 'correct' identity that no longer seeks by 'wingy myths' to solve the problem of being. Her deeper, real self seeks something more radical. To reflect this radical need would be true care, true love. But though her mother, and Philomena Guinea, care enough to pay for her treatment, they are still felt, at the deepest level, to be false parent-figures, mystifying her.

This falsity is detected in her earliest encounter with psychiatry —in Dr Gordon. She sees how this kind of individual is protected by his egoism from understanding.

> Doctor Gordon's features were so perfect he was almost pretty.
> I hated him the minute I walked in through the door.
> I had imagined a kind, ugly, intuitive man looking up and saying 'Ah!' in an encouraging way, as if he could see something I couldn't, and then I would find words to tell him how I was so scared, as if I were being stuffed farther and farther into a black airless sack with no way out. (pp. 135–6)

Esther finds no *intuition*—none of the female element she needs— in Dr Gordon: 'I could see right away that he was conceited'. Far from telling her 'why everything people did seemed so silly, because they only died in the end', he adopts a posture which makes it obvious that he is unable to allow himself the discomfort of experiencing her ego-weakness. He cannot tolerate humanness because he cannot bear to be human. She cannot tell him she is afraid. She hallucinates as an alternative someone who is almost a Winnicott—a modest, non-pretending, reflecting analyst who is concerned with helping her find herself: capable of 'giving the patient back what he brings'. What she gets is someone who intends to *do things to her*: to *impinge*:

> 'Suppose you try and tell me what you think is wrong.'
> I turned the words over suspiciously, like round, sea-polished pebbles that might suddenly put out a claw and change into something else.
> What did I *think* was wrong? That made it sound as if nothing was *really* wrong. I only *thought* it was wrong. (p. 137)

At once he rejects her need to have her predicament existentially experienced, to have someone feel her despair, which is real enough, in the body and being.

Dr Gordon turns out to be one of those 'hidden anti-socials' of whom Winnicott speaks, who identify with authority to suppress individuality. She enters his hospital—a house of *correction*. There were people: but 'I realized that none of the people were moving.'

> I focused more closely, trying to pry some clue from their stiff postures . . . but there was a uniformity to their faces, as if they had lain for a long time on a shelf, out of the sunlight, under siftings of pale fine dust.
> Then I saw that some of the people were indeed moving, but with such small, birdlike gestures I had not at first discerned them. (p. 149)

If the schizoid person's fear is of being petrified, then Dr Gordon is the kind of psychiatrist who will petrify them. They pass a woman being dragged along: the image is one of repression, by a blindness to the meaning of madness, the blindness of violence:

> Dumpy and muscular in her smudge-fronted uniform, the wall-eyed nurse wore such thick spectacles that four eyes peered out at me from behind the round, twin panes of glass. I was trying to tell which eyes were the real eyes and which the false eyes, and which of the real eyes was the wall-eye and which the straight eye, when she brought her face up to mine with a large conspiratorial grin and hissed, as if to reassure me, 'She thinks she's going to jump out the window but she can't jump out the window because they're all barred.' (p. 150)

The preparation of Esther for ECT echoes the childbirth scene— and the execution of the Rosenbergs.

> I shut my eyes.
> There was a brief silence like an indrawn breath.
> Then something bent down and took hold of me and shook me like the end of the world. Whee-ee-ee-ee-ee, it shrilled, through an air crackling with blue light, and with each flash a great jolt drubbed me till I thought my bones would break and the sap fly out of me like a split plant.
> *I wondered what terrible thing it was that I had done.*
> (pp. 151–2, my italics)

All the puzzled self can feel is a horrible sense that in some way for which she is by no means to blame, she has committed some appalling offence. The offence has been to offer the symbolism of a 'strategy of survival': so it feels as if what *was wrong was to wish to be*, to live, to be born.

Esther finds herself remembering a violent electric shock she had received in her father's study. 'A scream was torn from my throat, for I didn't recognise it, but heard it soar and quaver in the air like a violently disembodied spirit.' One trauma recalls another: and brings back only the 'disembodied' dissociation of it. The essential needs remain unfulfilled. Dr Gordon, asking her how she feels, repeats his inane, vain, irrelevant remark about Esther's college having been a wartime station for the women's armed services, hinting at his own sexual prowess and smartness. Esther decides she is through with him. But when she does so, she finds her mother, too, thinks it is a question of 'deciding' to be 'alright'.

> My mother smiled. 'I knew my baby wasn't like that.'
> I looked at her. 'Like what?'
> 'Like those awful people. Those awful dead people at that hospital.' She paused. 'I knew you'd decide to be alright again.'
>
> (p. 154)

Mother and psychiatrists collude, to urge Esther to pull herself together—she must *decide* not to have a real identity, and not to stand out from other people in such unrespectable ways: though the mother also sees that the patients have been made dead by ECT.

Chapter Fifteen opens with Esther imprisoned in Philomena Guinea's black Cadillac, on her way to an even more expensive psychiatrist, for whom the lady novelist is now paying. Philomena Guinea, at the peak of her career, has 'taken an interest in the case' after reading about Esther in the papers, and after having been told the girl 'thinks she will never write again'. But Esther can feel no gratitude: 'I knew I should be grateful to Mrs Guinea, only I couldn't feel a thing.' She is in the bell jar 'stewing in my own sour air'. Everyone winds her into a knot (in Laing's sense of the word). Dr Nolan, a woman this time, is even more sinister than Dr Gordon: she coerces in such a *nice* way.

Esther tells her about the ECT.

> While I was telling her she went very still.

'That was a mistake,' she said then, 'It's not supposed to be like that.'

I stared at her.

'If it's done properly,' Doctor Nolan said, 'it's like going to sleep.'

'If anyone does that to me again I'll kill myself.'

Doctor Nolan said firmly, 'You won't have any shock treatments here. Or if you do,' she amended, 'I'll tell you about it beforehand, and I promise you it won't be anything like what you had before. Why,' she finished, 'some people even *like* them.' (p. 200)

Dr Nolan promises, but only to reassure her patient, and to prepare her for a gentler coercion. Her intention (Sylvia Plath sees) is not to respond to the inner dynamics of Esther's true self, but to encourage her to accept the annihilation of her existential perplexities—a form of socially acceptable self-negation. One morning Esther finds she is having no breakfast—because she is on the list for shock-therapy. Although Dr Nolan comes over at once, Esther still feels she is being 'done to', and indeed has been treated like a child, and not consulted in case it frightened her. In the meantime she has been given injections, the purpose of which she is not told: they turn out to be insulin. Esther only finds this out from another patient—a situation which exposes Dr Nolan's methods of 'dealing with' her patients. She has a disturbing reaction. Each of these incidents conveys vividly the way in which the 'patient' is treated in such a way as to undermine her value and volition as a human being, as by demonstrations of no confidence. The psychiatrists demonstrate that they conceive of their work in terms of cutting up patient's psyches as a surgeon cuts up a patient's body: they, too, are pestle-wielders, rather than sources of creative reflection.

Dr Nolan, too, is a petrifier. Valerie shows Esther her scars 'as if at some time she had started to sprout horns, but cut them off'.

'I've had a lobotomy.'

I looked at Valerie in awe, appreciating for the first time her perpetual marble calm.

Valerie's independent personality is destroyed for ever:

'I can go to town, now, or shopping or to a movie, along with a nurse.'

'What will you do when you get out?'

'Oh, I'm not leaving,' Valerie laughed. 'I like it here.' (p. 204)

She is forever reduced to total dependence. She is no longer 'angry'—because as an individual she has ceased to exist. In the physical annihilation of her 'brain' complete conformism has been obtained.

While no doubt such drastic measures may be thought necessary is some agonising cases, there are those in psychiatry who see them (as Sylvia Plath does) as forms of annihilation of the personality, of the ultimate destruction of autonomy and freedom. The dangers are discussed by Winnicott:

> The surgeon who does a leucotomy would *at first* seem to be doing what the patient asks for, that is, to be relieving the patient of mind activity, the mind having become an enemy of the psyche-soma. Nevertheless, we can see that the surgeon is caught up in the mental patient's false localization of the mind in the head, with its sequel, the equating of mind and brain.
> (1958, p. 253)

The patient really seeks 'full-functioning *in order to be able to have psyche-soma existence*' But the irreversible brain changes make this forever impossible: the only value is in 'what the operation means to the patient'. Elsewhere Winnicott calls it an insane delusion between surgeon and patient. He says

> My own personal horror of leucotomy and suspicion of ECT derives from my view of psychotic illness as a defensive organisation designed to protect the true self... (p. 287)

That is, insanity is a 'strategy of survival'—all too easily met by coercion and the failure to see the meaning of the mechanism which attempts to defend the regressed libidinal ego and give it a chance. Is such therapy an attack on the defensive organisation *because* of its individual visionary qualities, because it is a quest for 'being'?

In these circumstances, with marvellous irony, Sylvia Plath makes Esther reflect on her birthday roses. It is a birthday in which there is no rebirth. It is not to be celebrated because she feels born dead. All is waste—her mother's gift of flowers on her birthday; the pretence in hospital of bringing about rebirth; the roses which mock her no-flowering. So—to the waste-basket. 'Out of the waste-basket poked the blood-red buds of a dozen long-stemmed roses' (p. 214).

Her mother has been quizzed:

> She never scolded me, but kept begging me, with a sorrowful face, to tell her what she had done wrong. She said she was sure the doctors had thought she had done something wrong because they asked her a lot of questions about my toilet training, and I had been perfectly trained at a very early age and given her no trouble whatsoever. (p. 215)

Details of potty-training are no more relevant to this catastrophe than the guilt induced by ECT. The 'poking' buds, symbolising the sad truth of the 'mother of pestles' Esther experienced, speak plainly of the truth from the wastepaper basket. Whatever went wrong belongs to strange dynamics of love, not 'child management'.

The American psychiatry Esther experiences is blandly convinced of its own truth, built as it is into a system, with textbooks, machines, institutions and training programmes. Esther is not deceived by the hygienic niceness of it all: it may be all very knowing and pleasant. It tolerates even hate as nice, while to express hate is 'pleasing'. But the road to existential security through despair and suffering is closed by a smile. So, Sylvia Plath maintains an ironic underplay: 'What was she trying to prove? I hadn't changed. Nothing had changed...' The ECT is merely a little more cosily offered (Christian names this time) but no less violent: the patient is a frightened, beaten child:

> Through the slits of my eyes, which I didn't dare open too far, lest the full view strike me dead, I saw the high bed with its white, drumtight sheet, and the machine behind the bed, and the masked person—I couldn't tell whether it was a man or a woman...
>
> ...
>
> 'Talk to me,' I said.

> Miss Huey began to talk in a low, soothing voice, smoothing the salve on my temples and fitting the small electric buttons on either side of my head.
>
> ... she set something on my tongue and in panic I bit down, and darkness wiped me out like chalk on a blackboard (p. 226)

Esther has sought out her father ('I couldn't find my father anywhere') and has laid her cheek on the cold stone of his grave. She has sought for love, in the spirit of the line in Sylvia Plath's poem *The Moon and The Yew Tree* (*Ariel*, p. 47), 'How I would like to believe in tenderness'. But the need for love is ignored, in favour of the application of a shocking machine. A masked sexless figure wipes the 'me' out. It is all done in such a polite way, like putting down unwanted suburban cats. But it is still like the execution of the Rosenbergs—a society eradicating the dynamics of being which it paranoically fears.

After much regular ECT ('for how long?' 'That depends', Doctor Nolan said, 'on you and me'—i.e. 'Be a good girl and we will stop'), the bell-jar lifts a little. 'I felt surprisingly at peace. The bell jar hung, suspended, a few feet above my head. I was open to the circulating air' (p. 227). But what has happened is a detachment, a dissociation, rather than an engagement and enrichment.

> I took up the silver knife and cracked off the cap of my egg. Then I put down the knife and looked at it. I tried to think what I had loved knives for, but my mind slipped from the noose of the thought and swung, like a bird, in the centre of empty air. (p. 228)

It is after her 'cure' that Esther enters desperately and coldly into her horribly depersonalised sexual relationship with the mathematics professor, and nearly bleeds to death. As a 'cured' woman she sends him the doctor's bill for 'fixing' the haemorrhage from her hymen—while making it impossible for him ever to see her again! It is as if Sylvia Plath is telling us that psychotic dissociation is the product of such 'cure': this is the 'after hell' (see *Poem for a Birthday*, last section). All that her therapy achieves is symbolised by the snow in the last chapter that blankets the asylum grounds: 'the sort that snuffs out schools and offices and churches and leaves, for a day or more, a pure, blank sheet in place of memo pads, date books and calendars.'* Sylvia Plath's uncanny insight is not deceived. 'Treatment' merely freezes her.

> The heart of winter!
> Massachusetts would be sunk in a marble calm . . .
> But under the deceptively clean and level slate the topo-graphy was the same. (p. 249)

A few memories are suppressed; the landscape underneath has not changed: how could it be different?

> I remembered the cadavers and Doreen and the story of the fig-tree and Marco's diamond and the sailor on the Common and Doctor Gordon's wall-eyed nurse and the broken thermo-meters and the negro with his two kinds of beans and the twenty pound I gained on insulin and the rock that bulged between sky and sea like a grey skull.
> Maybe forgetfulness, like a kind snow, should numb and cover them.
> But they were part of me. They were my landscape. (p. 250)

She resents the forgetfulness which is all her experience of therapy has brought: it has deadened perception and suppressed aspects of her personality. Her self is *in* the symbolism of her strategies of survival. Rebirth could only come creatively from the ego involved in the defence mechanisms: other ways out are false and a death. Her way to find herself was in the life-rhythms and symbols of her madness. Her mother wants 'all this' to be for-gotten 'like a bad dream'. How impossible to forget what has at its centre the failure ever *to be*!—'blank and stopped'. When she departs, she feels politely that she *should* feel reborn.

> I had hoped, at my departure, I would feel sure and know-ledgeable about everything that lay ahead—after all, I had been 'analyzed'. Instead, all I could see were question marks.
> I kept shooting impatient glances at the closed boardroom door. My stocking seams were straight, my black shoes cracked,

---

* Cf. 'Coldness comes sitting down, layer after layer' in *Poem for a Birthday*. See above, p. 54. Both passages evoke 'Winter kept us warm, covering/Earth in forgetful snow' from *The Waste Land*. 'The heart of winter' here evokes 'The very dead of winter' from *The Journey of the Magi*.

but polished, and my red wool suit flamboyant as my plans. Something old, something new. . . . (p. 257)

She gets out, like an applicant, in the black shoes of her father, the stockings of her mother, the red suit of flamboyance as if of the flames of the witch-burning she had suffered, or as if it were her wedding day. Something of her old self: but what is new? The suit? We recall the former images of mere clothes, empty, labelled. The 'board' are so important. But all they offer is another conformity.

There is nothing fundamentally new in the situation: except that she has agreed to agree, in the city of spare parts. Yet under ECT some of the 'sap' has 'flown out of her'. In *Poem for a Birthday* 'I am as good as new' takes on a new irony. It means both 'I shall be good as gold' but also implies that the newness is that of a 'retread'.

I have dealt at length with *The Bell Jar* because, first novel as it is, I believe it to be an important record for our time. While it is important to resist giving total assent to Sylvia Plath's view of psychiatry and society, the novel displays her consistent attention to the problem conventional psychiatry fails to keep at the centre of its preoccupations: the desperate need of the schizoid individual to love and to be loved, to be understood, and to begin to be, rather than be 'done to'. The question remains, of course, how this can ever be achieved on the scale necessary for public medicine, and this raises the question of the degree to which the ordinary community fails to make its contribution to being. But in literary studies, our concern is with the phenomenological meanings and here *The Bell Jar* is a courageous record that illuminates many aspects of our schizoid civilisation.

4
The Schizoid Problem
in Creative Writing

Leslie H. Farber (1966), in his chapter 'Schizophrenia and the Mad Psychotherapist', says that schizophrenia is 'a disorder consisting of a double failure in areas that might loosely be called meaning and relation'. Sylvia Plath was not schizophrenic: her utterance is often extraordinarily clear. But because of her schizoid condition, we are driven in reading her work, as I have shown, to complete certain meanings, add interpretations, and establish certain connections—and so there are many difficulties of artistic judgement, as with many modern works. A parallel example is afforded, perhaps, by the strangely 'unfinished' paintings of Francis Bacon. If (as Winnicott has said) he is 'striving to be seen', our seeing is an attempt to complete what is incomplete. But are we, as audience, to serve the artist? Or should he enrich us? May we not in our troubled reactions be at the receiving end of a 'breakdown of meaning and relation', and so depleted? Perhaps all he has done is to make life more difficult for us? Or has he forced on us the problem of existence itself? But what regeneration does he offer us?

In our society, in any case, it is difficult enough (as is clear from *The Bell Jar*) for human beings to feel whole, and human, and able to exert their freedom and autonomy. The schizoid individual especially is tormented by these problems of becoming a person. Winnicott (1968, a) discusses this as a consequence of the failure of integration. He categorises the primary processes of development in the infant as '(1) integration (2) personalization and (3) the appreciation of time and space and other properties of reality—in short, realization' (p. 140). In normal life we take these processes for granted. The therapist works with people in whom these processes are not complete. To understand their nature we have to open our eyes to 'a great deal that had a beginning and a condition out of which it developed'. These processes of developing a self which feels real and which can perceive a real world are bound up with the development of ego-strength. Where there is ego-weakness, this has come about through a failure of ego-relatedness. This may be linked with the whole problem of seeing a meaningful world: the artist works between the need to feel whole, and the need to see the world in a meaningful way. We can learn from this.

Winnicott links the capacity to believe in a benign world with an 'ego-supportative environment' which has become 'built in to the individual's personality' so that:

> there is always someone present, someone who is equated ultimately and unconsciously with the mother, the person who in the early days and weeks, was temporarily identified with the infant, and for the time being was interested in nothing else but the care of her own infant. (1965, p. 36)

It is this ego-supportative element Sylvia Plath seeks in herself, but does not find. She lacks what Guntrip (1966) called a 'conviction', in terms of feeling, not merely in idea, of the 'reality and reliability for [herself] of good objects in the outer world'.

> This is not the same as a capacity to fantasy good objects. We must distinguish between enjoyable remembering on the basis of actual good experience, and compulsive anxious fantasying and thinking as an effort to deny actual bad experience.
>
> (pp. 226–7)

In her work in consequence there seem to be two compensatory activities at work. One is 'compulsive fantasying' intended to *deny bad experience*—as when Sylvia Plath is writing aggressively in *Lady Lazarus* or *Daddy*—proclaiming her indifference to some malignity that menaces her. Secondly, as in *The Beekeeper's Daughter*, she is engaged in 'enjoyable remembering', but in some desperation (the queen bee 'does not show herself'). So she assembles scraps of memories of Daddy ('he who keeps my being'), a 'cupboard of rubbish' divided disastrously against itself.

Having no confidence in her internal reserves, she cannot find the universe benign, and cannot see it as meaningful. So, the need for re-birth is at one with the need to experience the world: but because of the confusions I have examined, we often find her rituals are death-births. We can see this in a poem like *Face Lift* (*Crossing the Water*, p. 17):

> You bring me good news from the clinic,
> Whipping off your silk scarf, exhibiting the tight white
> Mummy-cloths, smiling: I'm all right.
> When I was nine, a lime-green anaesthetist
> Fed me banana gas . . .
>
> . . .
> Mother to myself, I wake swaddled in gauze,
> Pink and smooth as a baby.

We have here images of Daddy, of the mummy-cloths being removed (from a new baby), and of the self-mothering itself bringing a new self to birth. When she becomes hopeless this search for birth through death takes destructive paths, as in *Lady Lazarus*, which declares raucously that the big strip-tease of death must be frequently repeated, while in *Edge* (*Ariel*, p. 85), one of her last poems,* there is a bitter expression of an ultimate loss of hope that even her death can generate a creative response in the moon-mother's face:

> The moon has nothing to be sad about,
> Staring from her hood of bone.

And so she lapses into futile vengeance: and can seduce us into nihilism.

The search for integration and meaningful perception lies between these poles. Our problem of response to the art is that of trying to decide when she makes creative gains and when she promotes desperate dehumanisation. Some poems are very much in the balance.

In *Tulips* (*Ariel*, p. 20), for instance, the protagonist is lying in

---

* '*Balloons, Contusion, Kindness, Edge* and *Words* belong to the last week of her life'. (*The Art of Sylvia Plath*, p. 193.)

hospital and finds a strange joy in being depersonalised, which seems to be strongly regressive.* The nurses who tend her are faceless and anonymous, and they cannot be distinguished one from another. As Winnicott tells us, the baby at first does not know that all the experiences that happen to him are happening to the same person: thus, he does not experience himself as the same person. It takes time for him to become realised.† In *Tulips* Sylvia Plath is re-experiencing and relishing (because of the pain and fear of being operated on) her regression to the state of an infant passively experiencing 'impingement':

> The nurses pass and pass, they are no trouble,
> They pass the way gulls pass inland in their white caps
> Doing things with their hands, one just the same as another,
> So it is impossible to tell how many there are.

> My body is a pebble to them, they tend it as water
> Tends to the pebbles it must run over . . .

Being a patient in hospital under repair is like being a baby tended by a mother. But the experience is given here with such delight in detachment—as if the mothering were mechanical and had none of the elements of primary maternal preoccupation. The body is tended like a stone, impersonally as if it were petrified. The nurses 'must' tend her. Their handling of her is a form of remote doing ('Doing things with their hands'): but there is no quality of spontaneous confirming love as from one 'I' to a 'Thou' in their care, meticulous as it is: they are non-human, like gulls. The gulls here are the birds in *Poem for a Birthday*: the nurses 'pass the way gulls pass inland in their white caps . . . one just the same as another', '. . . it is impossible to tell how many there are'. Both bird images are of remote breast-symbols, tending and soothing, but not enabling the infant to piece the various experiences of handling into one 'object called mother', in relation to one self. Since the self and object remain fragmentary, perception itself is experienced as something passive: the patient's head 'has to take everything in'. The poem symbolises a relationship with an

---

* *Tulips*, Ted Hughes tells us, 'records some tulips she had in the hospital where she was recovering from an appendectomy' (ibid).
† 'Primitive Emotional Development' (1968a, p. 145).

'impinging' reality 'on a conformity basis', while perception itself is resented and relinquished. In *Tulips* we have a fundamental ambiguity at the heart of Sylvia Plath's work expressed—whether to stay in the world and suffer the pain of ego-weakness, or whether to take the path of desperate attempts to be born again. In the end, she seems to be wanting to come back despite the pain: the salt water of tears belonging to health. There is thus both a positive and negative drive in Sylvia Plath's feelings about experience. And because of the schizoid characteristics in them, her experiences are both like ours, and at the same time unlike ours, in certain vivid ways. We might, for example, feel depersonalised in hospital, as her protagonist does in *Tulips*. But we would be unlikely to feel as threatened as her protagonist by a gift of tulips which look to her like the mouth of a voracious animal— our 'mouth-ego' is not so rapacious. Nor do we normally feel so strangely divorced from our bodies, as Sylvia Plath often does. Yet there is, again, a sense in which people can become strangely divided from their bodies, and in which the sense of identity seems at times impossible to sustain, in terms of the whole body and being in the world. So, we can sympathise with her feelings of alienation, though we ought to be startled, despite her bland tone, when she speaks of her body as if it were not 'her', and of how she needs to 'ambush' it, to have the 'whole say' and be 'dead in a flash' (*The Bell Jar*, p. 168—see above, p. 88).

We perhaps never feel so divided as to see ourselves in some kind of conflict with the body, trying to outwit it in order to prevent it clinging to life—because living in the body seems intolerable. Such a degree of the sense of 'life, without feeling alive', of a failure of personalisation, of a feeling as of not being in one's own body and of *not being the same as it*, is psychopathological. Jung once told a group of students about a young woman who dreamt 'Jack Frost' had entered her bedroom and pinched her on the stomach. She woke and discovered she had pinched herself. But she was not frightened and did not react emotionally. This filled Jung with foreboding: and the girl later committed suicide with the same unfeeling hand.

A mechanical feeling about our bodies is, however, also an aspect of our thought about ourselves, in an age of 'objective' science, in which we are functioning organisms in a world which is 'matter in motion' only.

We tend to think of ourselves, other living creatures, and the world as 'nothing but' mechanical entities—much the same way as Sylvia Plath portrays a human being in *The Applicant*. Viktor Frankl reports coming across a book in which man is defined as 'nothing but a complex biochemical mechanism powered by a combustion system which energises computers with prodigious storage facilities for retaining encoded information' ('Nothing but . . .' in *The Alpbach Seminar*, ed. Koestler and Smithies). This kind of view is immanent in our thinking about ourselves. It is characteristic of our time that, in *The Bell Jar*, Esther feels as if she is in conflict with an 'internal drive' that belongs to her body and is in opposition to her mind. In *Berck-Plage* (*Ariel*, p. 30), written under the shock of death and encounter with cripples, Sylvia Plath conveys a horrified sense of human life being meaninglessly mechanical.* Esther inevitably regards her mental illness from a reductionist point of view.

> I had bought a few paperbacks on abnormal psychology at the drug store and compared my symptoms with the symptoms in the books, and sure enough, my symptoms tallied with the most hopeless cases. (*The Bell Jar*, pp. 168–9)

Cartesian dualism lies behind her absurd delusion (not unknown among neurologists and even brain surgeons) that the 'self' is in the head, together with whatever is 'wrong' with the self:

> I wanted to tell her that if only something were wrong with my body it would be fine, I would rather have anything wrong with my body than something wrong with my head . . .
>
> (p. 193)

Such a feeling both seems natural to us, since our intellectual patterns and modes are 'imprisoned in physicalism'†. But we need

---

* '. . . we had visited Berck-Plage. . . . Some sort of hospital or convalescent home for the disabled fronts the beach. It was one of her nightmares stepped into the real world. A year later—almost to the day—our next door neighbour, an old man, died . . . In this poem that visit to the beach and the death and funeral of our neighbour are combined' (Ted Hughes, *The Art of Sylvia Plath*, p. 194).

† See Ledermann, 1972. Also the work of Peter Lomas, R. D. Laing, Marjorie Grene, Frankl, and Roger Poole.

to recognise how schizoid this strange dissociation of 'self' from 'body' is. Sylvia Plath shows us how a schizoid individual may even seem at times to be detached from his body, as if 'looking down on the self', and may even feel (like Alice) that she has no authority over her members. So, the individual's 'life-world' may be bound up with the feeling, in a dehumanised urban environment, of being essentially empty and dead, disembodied and shadowy:

> Piece by piece, I fed my wardrobe to the night wind, and flutteringly, like a loved one's ashes, the grey scraps were ferried off, to settle here, there, exactly where I would never know, in the dark heart of New York. (*The Bell Jar*, p. 117)

So, the identity is 'grey scraps' (like the grey scraps of wasp-chewed paper she offers as the basis of her identity in *Poem for a Birthday*), made of knowing oneself intellectually. But in the dark heart of megalopolis she cannot 'find' herself in the realm of 'being', because there is no provision for encounter. On its part, American culture could not 'hear' her, having cut itself off so much from recognition of the intuitive, female element faculties of being.

The intellectual awareness which is dissociated from whole being and autonomy also tends to take on a dynamic of 'male analytical doing' which stands in lieu of being. It thus becomes a way of dealing with the world, as a defence against collapse. In Guntrip, Lomas, Fairbairn and Winnicott we learn of this 'false self'. It is the outer shell of bustling activity and coping, the 'mask of horn', which conceals the emptiness at the heart of our ego-weakness, the centre of the tornado. This explains the powerful and excited energy in such an individual as Sylvia Plath, whose internalised structures and imagos sometimes seem more important to her than any person 'out there' in the real world. They provided a kind of environment to live in and to feel real in: she crawls into the words that embody them.

The conflict within the self may be explained in terms of inner conflict. The hungry 'all mouth' or 'regressed libidinal ego' is subject to the 'anti-libidinal' aspect of the self. The baby at the heart of the self feels weak and so menacing: so, it is hated by the internalisation of those rejecting aspects of the mother that were sometimes turned on the child (or seemed to be). This explains the cruelty we can turn on our own needs. As Fairbairn says, we have

> a *libidinal ego* characterised by ever-active and unsatisfied desires which come to be felt in angry and sadistic ways; and the attachment to the rejecting object results in an *anti-libidinal ego* based on an identification which reproduces the hostility of the rejecting object to libidinal needs. (Quoted in Guntrip 1968, pp. 71–2)

Such divisions can lead to powerful destructive energy turned against oneself.

> Inevitably the libidinal ego is hated and persecuted by the anti-libidinal ego as well as by the rejecting object, so that the individual has now become divided against himself. This is easy to recognise in the contempt and scorn shown by many patients of their own needs to depend for help on other people or on the analyst. It is seen also in the fear and hate of weakness that is embedded in our cultural attitudes. (Ibid., p. 72)

These observations are most illuminating culturally, for they reveal that much of today's contempt, scorn and nihilism are manifestations of weakness, and a hatred of being human. Ted Hughes's play *Orghast* began 'with a baby being stamped on on a mountainside',* while Edward Bond's *Saved* contains a scene showing a baby being smeared and stoned to death: both forms of 'acting out' of the anti-libidinal ego's hatred of the regressed libidinal ego or littlesoul, whose weak existence threatens from within.

Sylvia Plath's poems display immense energy—especially towards the end. But in her later poems there is a development of a closed death-circuit resulting from this kind of conflict, and the need to escape from even more dreadful fears. Guntrip (1968) speaks of the

> closed system of the inner world of internal bad objects and the antilibidinal ego, in which is concentrated all the patient's secret and repressed hatred of his infantile dependent libidinal

---

* 'Singing a lullaby, Furorg cradles a baby in his arms, and gives it to Ussa. Instructed by both Krogons, Sheergra stamps it to death . . .' (*Orghast at Persepolis*, A. C. H. Smith, 1972).

ego, the source of his bad weakness; but also his fear that if he were to give up or escape from his bad objects, he could be left with no objects at all and be facing the ultimate, and what Winnicott calls . . . the *unthinkable* anxieties . . . (p. 202)

This shows why, bound up in the closed-circuit system, an individual can come to prefer self-destruction as a way out.

A related problem here is that, as a schizoid individual moves into such encapsulation, he may become cut off from all relationships. And this draws our attention to the fact that for this kind of person relationships in any case are based on intense identification.

> What looks deceptively like genuine feeling for another person may break into consciousness, when in fact it is based on identification with the other person and is mainly a feeeling of anxiety and pity for oneself. (Ibid., p. 38)

Guntrip here refers to a novel, Ngaio Marsh's *Enter a Murderer*, in which a character says, 'He was completely and utterly absorbed, as though apart from me he had no reality'.

> In other words, the man was swallowed up in his love-object, had no true individuality of his own, and could not exist in a state of separation from her. It was as though he had not become born out of his mother's psyche and differentiated as a separate and real person in his own right, and identification with another person remained at bottom the basis of all his personal relationships. (Ibid., p. 39)

It seems clear that Sylvia Plath's capacity for relationship was affected by impulses towards identification of the above kind—so that in a sense she could hardly exist herself in a state of separation. The intensely consuming envy of her kind of identification is evident in *Shrike* and the short story *The Wishing Box*. When she feels deserted, as in *Birthday Present*, and *Berck Plage*, she has no defences against a malignant world that threatens to close in on her, echoing the voraciousness of her own needs.

Although the schizoid individual shrinks from close relationship, and suffers terribly from such proximity, Sylvia Plath did commit herself to close relationships—and bore the pain, in hopefulness of being fulfilled. Her last poems are virtually cries of anguish at the searing and wounding effects of such relationships and the dangers in them of being swallowed up. As Guntrip says:

> Identification is a major problem in the schizoid patient's relations to the external world, because it leads to the danger of over-dependence on objects, creates the fear of absorption into them, and enforces the defence of mental detachment. Thus the original schizoid withdrawal from an unsatisfying outer world is reinforced by this further obstacle of detachment as a defence against risking dangerous relationships. One patient identified with her work as a means of maintaining her personality without risking any close personal attachment. Then she insisted that *she would have to commit suicide when she retired because she would then be nobody.* (Ibid., p. 40, my italics)

The schizoid individual thus lives in a private hell, between fear of extinction through loss of relationship, and the menace of annihilation by dangerous relationship: out of this emerges the desperation of the suicidal impulse to escape both dangers.

Robert Daly (1968) explains from his special study of schizoid states how catastrophic the experience of close relationships can be for a schizoid individual:

> Unfortunately, this warm and favourable climate of taking and being given to begins to fail almost as soon as it begins to succeed. Compassion, assistance, or treatment are also familiar names for deceit, humiliation, and depersonalised subjugation . . . near success in establishing a viable, dependent and dependable relationship with another person becomes the breeding ground of suspicion, querulousness, manipulation, procrastination and withdrawal . . . (p. 405)

So, in *Kindness* (*Ariel*, p. 83) for instance, the normal care offered by others is a sickly sugar that merely 'poultices' a deep wound:

> Sugar can cure everything, so Kindness says.
> Sugar is a necessary fluid,
>
> Its crystals a little poultice.
> O kindness, kindness
> Sweetly picking up pieces!

> My Japanese silks, desperate butterflies,
> May be pinned any minute, anaesthetized.

Even the care offered her in hospital is seen as 'depersonalised subjugation', while normal human interaction is often full of menace. Ted Hughes's *Lovesong* (*Crow*, p. 88) expresses the dangers of intense identification in several ways.

> Their heads fell apart into sleep like the two halves
> Of a lopped melon, but love is hard to stop
> In their entwined sleep they exchanged arms and legs
> In their dreams their brains took each other hostage . . .
> In the morning, they wore each other's face . . .

In an interview with John Horder (*The Guardian*, 23 March 1965) Hughes remarked that,

> There was no rivalry between us . . . in these circumstances you begin to write out of one brain . . . we were like two feet of one body . . . A working partnership, all absorbing. We just lived it. It all fitted very well . . .

Yet, at the end, in poems like *Daddy*, she seems to be rejecting this intense identification itself, because of her resentment at it. For instance in *Tulips* the 'I' of the poem, looking in hospital at the photographs of her husband and child, says

> Their smiles catch onto my skin, little smiling hooks

—while in *Three Women* (*Winter Trees*, p. 40), many deep resentments are expressed, at the claims of relationship:

> Is this my lover then? This death, this death?

Children are

> Those little sick ones that elude my arms . . .

Birth is a death:

> I should have murdered this, that murders me.

And one woman speaker feels:

> The incalculable malice of the everyday.

5

The followers of Women's Liberation movements who read Sylvia Plath from the platform are not aware, of course, that such a poem presents in some of its choruses an agonised, specifically schizoid view of female experience, love, and birth: they take it all as 'the truth' about all women's experience. To see it in perspective we only have to listen to schizoid patients quoted by Guntrip, who reveal their overdependence and the way in which relationship threatens them because of their insubstantiality of identity: '. . . I feel my destiny is bound up with theirs, and I can't get away, yet I feel they imprison me and ruin my life . . .'.

I believe it is difficult to understand the intensity of the kind of identification Sylvia Plath experienced with those near to her unless we study the way in which schizoid persons (as Laing showed) can actually feel they *are* someone else. Guntrip (1968) gives some instances:

> Another patient dreamed of being 'grafted on to another person'. The 40-year-old male patient said, 'Why should I be on bad terms with my sister? After all I am my sister,' and then started in some surprise at what he had heard himself say . . .
>
> A young married woman struggling to master a blind compulsive longing for a male relative she played with as a child, said: 'I've always felt he's me and I'm him. I felt a terrible need to fuss around him and do everything for him. I want him to be touching me all the time. I feel there is no difference between him and me . . .'. (p. 40)

As the psychotherapist comments:

> Identification is betrayed in a variety of curious ways, such as the fear of being buried alive, i.e. absorbed into another person, *a return to the womb*. This is also expressed in the suicidal urge to put one's head in a gas oven; or, again, in dressing in the clothes of another person. One patient feeling in a state of panic one night when her husband was away, felt safe when she slept in his pyjamas . . . (Ibid., p. 40)

The full horror and poignancy of the schizoid condition is indicated by Guntrip's picture of schizoid breakdown:

The schizoid repression of feeling, and retreat from emotional relationships, may, however, go much further, and produce a serious breakdown of constructive effort. Then the unhappy sufferer from incapacitating conflicts will succumb to real futility: nothing seems worth doing, interest dies, the world seems unreal, the ego feels depersonalised. Suicide may be attempted in a cold, calculated way to the accompaniment of such thoughts as 'I am useless, bad for everybody, I'll be best out of the way.' One patient who had never reached that point said, 'I feel I love people in an impersonal way: it seems a false position, hypocritical. Perhaps I don't do any loving. I'm terrified when I see young people go off and being successful and I'm at a dead bottom, absolute dereliction, excommunicate.'

(Ibid., p. 39)

While the achievement of her poetry was continually set against Sylvia Plath's feelings of futility, in it at times she expresses this encroaching despair. In *Elm* (*Ariel*, p. 25) for instance:

I know the bottom, she says. I know it with my great
    taproot:
It is what you fear.
I do not fear it: I have been there.

Is it the sea you hear in me,
Its dissatisfactions?—

. . .
I have suffered the atrocity of sunsets.

. . .
I am incapable of more knowledge . . .

One of the elements in her anguish revealed here is a deep lack of satisfaction. Robert Daly suggests that we can call someone's behaviour schizoid if his actions appear to follow a particular set of remarkable and predominating 'rules' as he pursues, or fails to pursue, a succession of goals. He has observed, for example, as one 'rule', that the schizoid individual cannot 'achieve any enduring satisfaction with his activities'. I was told of Sylvia Plath, by Mr Jim Lape, her headmaster in Boston, that her success in writing seemed to bring her no satisfaction, even when she was young. In her work she seems confused at times about what satisfactions she should be obtaining and how she should relate means to ends. In *The Night Dances* she finds encounter with her baby puzzling and cannot feel the satisfaction she knows she should feel.* In *Edge* the incapacity to relate ends and means, actions and thought, becomes acute.

Because of the schizoid individual's failure to relate ends and means, says Daly, his way

> can be likened to a series of approach—avoidance conflicts . . . Fantasies, feelings and decisions are so arranged that as one conflict-ridden goal is approached, the mounting tendency to avoid reaching that goal becomes the path to another conflict-ridden goal . . . the most general characteristic of this kind of individual is that *he is always in transition*. He never (or seldom) arrives—for long. (Op. cit., p. 401)

This is precisely Esther's predicament in *The Bell Jar*, and that of the protagonists in many of Sylvia Plath's poems. Transition is the theme of *Ariel* the poem (and *Ariel* the book); as in *Getting There* (*Ariel*, p. 43):

> How far is it?
> How far is it now?
> . . .
> Turning and turning in the middle air . . .

The ultimate goal is some rebirth, as here:

> And I, stepping from this skin
> Of old bandages, boredoms, old faces
>
> Step to you from the black car of Lethe,
> Pure as a baby.

—but there is confusion as to how to arrive at 'there'.

Daly also notes that in this condition 'anxiety, in some form, is usually high'. Many of Sylvia Plath's poems are full of deep, menacing anxiety—even in the midst of a benign environment, as in *The Bee Meeting*. But in this, as in many poems we find the following further 'rule' of Daly also exemplified: 'The well-springs of worth are in perpetual jeopardy, both from within and

* See below, p. 204ff.

without', with the result that 'self-esteem follows a jerky temperamental curve'. 'These individuals describe themselves as having been alienated early in life from the coherent and affectionate regard of others' (op. cit., p. 401). Throughout Sylvia Plath's work one finds a continual theme of being deprived by those who, she feels, have given her stones instead of bread and milk:

> I would get from these dry-papped stones
> The milk your love instilled in them . . .
> (*Point Shirley, The Colossus*, p. 24)

In *All the Dead Dears* (*The Colossus*, p. 27) mother, grandmother and great-grandmother are menacing:

> From the mercury-backed glass
> Mother, grandmother, great-grandmother
> Reach hag hands to haul me in . . .

Instead of reflecting her, these past generations rise in the mirror to drag her down into death, which is, 'The gross eating game . . .'. In *The Disquieting Muses* (*The Colossus*, p. 58). she speaks of alienation among 'Faces blank as the day I was born . . .'. In *The Moon and the Yew Tree* 'The moon is my mother' but 'The moon is no door'. In *Elm* the moon is 'merciless' and 'scathes'. In *Edge* 'she' stares unreflecting and indifferent from 'her hood of bone'. In *The Bell Jar* Esther refers to 'my mother's face anxious and sallow as a slice of lemon' (p. 13).

Sylvia Plath's poems are a combination of vision and nightmare. Daly says: 'In his efforts to escape this dilemma-ridden existence, the schizoid individual creates pretensions and dreams hopeful beyond all reason, as well as the darkest night the soul can impose on itself' (op. cit., p. 402). As we have seen, Sylvia Plath often manages to combine both dreams and nightmares in her poems— as in *Getting There*, from 'I am in agony/I cannot undo myself' to the hopeful dream of stepping out of her old skin from the black car of Lethe reborn. *Lady Lazarus* expresses the boast that she can commit suicide without damage, beyond all reason, and find the same purity. But the late poems certainly contain indications of a confusion such as Daly describes:

Intense, demanding, strident wishes for precarious unions

which require the most delicate adaptations are followed by suspicion, withdrawal, self-recrimination, criticism and repudiation of others, and despair. Apathy, illusory thoughts, self-destructive urges and murderous obsessions may at times preoccupy the sufferer . . . (Op. cit., p. 402).

Similar violent urges are evident enough in *Lady Lazarus* ('I eat men like air'), *Daddy, Edge* and *Medusa*.

We have already discussed the prevalent expression of the following 'rule' in her work: 'disliked and disliking, misunderstood and misunderstanding, doubly bound and doubly binding in his relations with others, the schizoid individual usually develops a remarkable, elaborate and complex set of relations with his body' (Daly, Op. cit., p. 402). One of the aspects of this confusion (Daly says) is the attempt to reify 'inexplicit wishes, fears and fantasies pertaining to the meaning of body parts and functions'. As we have already noticed, this is a particular aspect of Sylvia Plath's experience of her body about which she displays at times a fetishistic or even perverted fascination—for instance, it is exciting when it reveals its inside (see *Cut*). On the other hand, her very integrity in her quest is schizoid too:

> The ideationally schizoid individual quests for the *truth* in the language of ideas. He is always in the process of searching for, engaging in, or disengaging from, a doctrine, a concept, a set of terms, or a final life-giving (and occasionally life-taking) principle. *His transitions occur between being and nothingness.*
>
> (Daly, Op. cit., p. 406, my italics)

This search extends itself to her disciplined work on meaning. Behind her work lay a training in the manipulation of language 'from the outside' such as I discover and analyse as a schizoid-type activity in Dylan Thomas.* As Ted Hughes has shown:

> In her earlier poems, Sylvia Plath composed very slowly, consulting her Thesaurus and Dictionary for almost every word, putting a slow, strong ring of ink around each word that attracted her. Her obsession with intricate rhyming and metrical schemes was part of the same process. Some of those

* See *Dylan Thomas; the Code of Night*, pp. 123–36.

early inventions of hers were almost perverse, with their brist-
ling hurdles. But this is what she enjoyed . . .

(The *Poetry Book Society Bulletin*, February, 1965)

Daly says of the schizoid individual that 'he is convinced that
only the truth will save him, and he is equally certain that no
formulation of *the real* will meet his remarkable specification'. But
(as the theories of Winnicott about the origins of culture make
clear) the quest for truth is bound up with relationship: 'The bond
of human relatedness is the bond of truth-sharing and action-
making—making the truth actually true . . .' For the schizoid
individual, the difficulty is that when there has to be cooperation,
truth is compromised. Inevitably, the truth itself becomes suspect
for this reason, in time. Daly's next paragraph surely applies to the
stages of Sylvia Plath's decline as we can follow it in her poems:

> It is in a state of exhaustion and with a sense of futility that such
> individuals reach the day when no investigation is worth
> conducting, no spiritual exercise merits any effort, and no
> prophet, master, or teacher can command, inform or instruct
> the wayfarer. Action of any sort becomes more and more
> difficult to execute. Ideation may be refuted as a way of life. *But
> it now seems to have a life of its own, like unto dreams.** Conceptual
> activity becomes unbearable but endures—only now in a form
> apparently inseparable from conscious control. Fantasies clash,
> overlap, decompose, and re-emerge in twisted and bizarre
> (*often paranoid*) forms, terrifying the sufferer and creating
> confusion and uncertainty among those who attempt to cope
> with such an individual's speech and gestures. In this context,
> incessant symbolisations are sometimes stilled forever by a man
> who *knows* at last that death is the final truth, the great experi-
> ment, the only reasonable subject left for him to investigate.

(Op. cit., p. 408, my italics and note)

The fashionable acclaim for *Daddy* and *Lady Lazarus* is acclaim for
the final, terrifying, paranoid fantasies of such a sufferer, who
knew—it seems—that death was the last great experiment ('The
big strip tease'). A. Alvarez's admiration for 'creative destruction'

---

* '. . . the letters separated writhing like malevolent little black snakes across the
page in a kind of hissing, untranslateable jargon' (*The Wishing Box*).

is an endorsement of this schizoid delusion. Of a certain schizoid type, which he must have met in a woman, Daly says, after a complex discussion of her circles of self-defeat: 'Then she plays another scene which may seduce yet another audience.' The *huis clos* of moods arises essentially because 'traditional symbols of personal affection and ideational truth have no demand quality for her'.*

This is virtually what Sylvia Plath tells us in *The Couriers* (*Ariel*, p. 12):

> A ring of gold with the sun in it?
> Lies Lies and a grief . . .

Love is

> A disturbance in mirrors,
> The sea shattering its grey one—
> Love, love, my season.

Daly says of the psychological type just considered: 'It is her largely inexplicit, radically idiosyncratic, and highly differentiated and ambivalent use of affective cues that makes her actions so unpredictable and perplexing, both to herself and others' (op. cit., p. 410). Isn't this what we have in such lines as:

> The word of a snail on the plate of a leaf?
> It is not mine. Do not accept it.
>
> Acetic acid in a sealed tin?
> Do not accept it. It is not genuine.
>   (*The Couriers*)

Much of Sylvia Plath's poetry arises out of her perplexity over normal 'affective cues' and her consequent unpredictability

> Why am I given
>
> These lamps, these planets . . .
>   (*The Night Dances, Ariel*, p. 27)

Daly concludes his insightful paper with paragraphs which actually echo phrases which relate Sylvia Plath's condition phenomenologically to her poetic images. After the remarks

---

* 'Demand quality' is a phrase from German existentialism, *Aufforderungscharakter*, that which draws out potentialities (see Frankl, 1967, p. 21).

quoted above about 'seducing another audience', he says: 'The impulsively schizoid individual is often incoherent during her flight into sickness . . . this disturbed and disturbing individual is most often seen in terms of 'splits' and 'fragments' . . .' This brings to mind

> Now I break up in pieces that fly about like clubs.
> . . . I must shriek.
>
> (*Elm, Ariel*, p. 25)

But also:

> . . . she is, at times, very difficult to distinguish from those whose behaviour follows the rules which are indicated by the term 'psychotic'. The relationship of her thinking to her action is confused by nearly every known deviation from traditional means-ends schemas. The tag-ends of affects appear to be intensely and randomly displayed rage, lust, quiet incoherence, unresponsiveness, sullenness and sudden charm, just prior to desperate attempts at mutilation of herself and others.
>
> (Op. cit., p. 412)

What we can say, as readers, is that we travel the whole gamut of these moods in *Daddy* (*Ariel*, p. 54). 'Mutilation' is the impulse expressed in 'the black telephone's off at the root' and this is an impulse in fantasy to mutilate the self and others. The hope of finding encounter with Daddy in the grave is rejected: 'The voices just can't worm through.' The latter evokes an image from Marvell's *To His Coy Mistress*

> then worms shall try
> That long-preserved virginity

which is both sexual and cadaverous. She castrates him, and castrates herself, so there shall be no hope of reflecting intercourse. Our phenomenology in interpreting such meanings involves making what Daly calls 'extraordinary connections'. Only those with special experience of schizoid expression can 'guess at the specific connections that obtain among the words, gestures and moods that characterise the plight: and even they have difficulty in decoding the troubled language of the body which is often the major vehicle for communication' (op. cit., p. 412).

Daly speaks of the struggle in such a woman to 'repudiate her impulses', the alternative to which is to attempt to 'side with the negative component of her dilemma' If the struggle fails, we may have a lapse into this attachment to nihilistic circuits—such as W. R. D. Fairbairn (1958) traced in his patient Ivy, who speaks in terms which have a fury strikingly reminiscent of *Lady Lazarus* and *Daddy*:

> 'I have no words to describe how I hate you. But why can't I just hate you and get on with it? The only reason I can think of is that I need my hate for some other purpose. It's too precious to waste on you. It is vital to my internal economy not to waste hate on you. I feel I need the hate for myself. I need the hate to run myself on . . . I want my hate to keep me short-circuited. Instead of running myself on outside people and things. . . I get gratification from self-things . . . I feel I'm like a skilled finan-cier . . . Every bit of hate has to be accounted for. . . . I hate you for trying to make me stop doing this. I need to hate you to get energy for my inner persecution. I'm breathing it. I'm in an orgy of destruction. I can't wait to get my hands on myself to destroy myself . . .* This is my life— a drawn out ecstasy of slowly killing myself. That is wicked; and it's the only wickedness I can do. I want to be evil in other ways, but I can't. I've sold myself to the Devil; and this is the only way I can do it. I'm a willing Isaac. The greater the frustration outside, the greater the ecstasies inside. I want to have no inhibitions in bringing about my own destruction.
> (pp. 374 ff.)

The quest here is for a purity of total moral inversion, that is obviously bound up with a (black) purifying of inner contents:

> I dedicate my life to my bowels. I used to think I wanted to get on with life, and ordinary life is a nuisance. My inner economy is different from that of ordinary people . . . my anger to use for inner purposes . . . My aim is to sail as near the wind as I can to killing myself. My aim is to carry out Mother's and Father's wishes . . . I do it partly to please them, and partly to annoy them. I'm going as near the wind as I dare to killing

---

* This ecstasy is paralleled in *Lady Lazarus*: 'I do it so it feels real', etc.

myself. I don't confine it to sexual things . . . I extend it to my whole life . . . ordinary life is an interference with my neurosis . . . I feel my unconscious life is my true life; and it is a life of frustrated excitement, which I seem to regard as bliss. I feel I really have a strong urge to destroy myself . . . I want to see how near I can get to the edge of the cliff. There is a bit of me that keeps me alive . . . (Ibid.)

This 'bit of me that keeps me alive' is the pulse, the bloodflow, Littlesoul and Littleblood. It is 'the old brag of my heart'—'I AM, I AM' which she hears. 'Ivy' goes on in a very Lady Lazarus way:

. . . but my real purpose is directed to killing myself and frustration. I have trouble over you; for I don't want to tell you things. If I have a relationship with you, it interferes with my death-circuit . . . You interfere with my neurosis and my desire to destroy myself. You are just a nuisance. It is daft to have a relationship with you, because it just weakens my inner purpose . . . The worse I get, the better I'm pleased, because that is what I want,—which is a negation of all that is right . . . I want to devote myself to working myself up to a state of need and not having it satisfied. This is involved in my desire for self-destruction. I must accept that I frustrate myself. I expect that originally I was frustrated from outside; but now I impose frustration on myself; and that is to be my satisfaction . . . It is a terrible perversion. (Ibid.)

Fairbairn speaks here of 'an obstinate tendency on the part of the individual to keep his aggression localised within the confines of the inner world as a closed system'. We can see how the tendency to maintain an inner world, with powerful negative energies, can become a dynamic leading towards death. In Sylvia Plath this inner circuit is bound up with the way in which her identity is based on fragments of maleness that were experienced as hate. In *Daddy* she is attempting to renounce the animus which possesses her with its hate-impulses: yet, since she identifies with it, she is turned against herself: it was a 'terrible perversion'.

The word 'animus' is, of course, from Jungian psychoanalysis, and it represents the personification of male tendencies in a woman, both in its good and bad aspects. The male element in woman can be a 'hard, inexorable power', as when a 'sacred conviction' is proclaimed in a 'loud, insistent, masculine voice' (see Jung's *Man and His Symbols*, pp. 177 ff). Some of the favourite themes of the animus, says Von Franz (who completed this book after Jung's death) are 'The only thing in the world that I want is love—and he doesn't love me', and 'In this situation there are only two possibilities, and both are equally bad', themes expressed in *Daddy* for example. The animus is basically influenced by a woman's father. Very often this animus is 'a demon of death', as the animus in a man can be, telling him 'I am nothing' and luring him to suicide.

When Sylvia Plath writes a poem like *Love Letters* (*Crossing the Water*, p. 44), it sounds as if she is writing to a 'beautiful stranger': 'I knew you at once.' This is surely the Colossus who is also the animus?

> Viewed mythologically, the beautiful stranger is probably a pagan father-image or god-image, who appears . . . as king of the dead (like Hades's abduction of Persephone). But psychologically he represents a particular form of the animus that lures women away from all human relationships and especially from contacts with real men. The animus personifies all those semi-conscious, cold, destructive reflections that invade a woman in the small hours, especially when she has failed to realise some obligation of feeling . . . [nursing secret destructive attitudes . . .] A strange passivity and paralysis of all feeling, or a deep insecurity that can lead almost to a sense of nullity, may sometimes be the result of an unconscious animus opinion. In the depths of the woman, the animus whispers. 'You are hopeless. What's the use of trying? There is no point in doing anything. Life will never change for the better.'
>
> (Von Franz, Op. cit., p. 193)

Von Franz speaks of a state of possession—of which resemblances can be detected in Sylvia Plath's poems—while the spell they cast on us, as does *Edge*, is of this kind:

> Unfortunately, whenever one of the personifications of the unconscious takes possession of our mind, it seems as if we ourselves are having such thoughts and feelings. The ego

identifies with them to the point where it is unable to detach them and see them for what they are. Only after the possession has fallen away does one realise with horror that one has said and done things diametrically opposed to one's real thoughts and feelings—that one has been the prey of an alien psychic factor. (Op. cit., p. 193)

This 'alien psychic factor' humiliating the anima or animus can become a 'collective infection' in which men give way to impulses that do not belong to them. And this, as I hope to show, is why such art as Sylvia Plath's is so dangerous: her poetry seduces us, to taste of its poisoned chalice. She herself recognised such dangers. In *The Swarm* (*Winter Trees*, p. 37) she writes with great insight of the collective infection that can develop among men, if they are persuaded to give way to impulses that 'possess' them. So it is possible, in the light of her work, to see how negative false solutions may arise from the impulse to seek rebirth and a new world (Napoleon, in *The Swarm*, pursues the pink and gold domes of Russia, as if they belonged to a celestial city).*

The strangest implication of her work is that conventional psychiatry seems to accentuate the negative dynamics in the personality. From the evidence of *The Bell Jar* and *Poem for a Birthday* I believe we may suggest that ECT, for her, may even have reinforced the influence of the hostile animus itself, as a dynamic.

In Marion Milner's *The Hands of the Living God* there is a fascinating account of the effect of ECT on a schizoid patient: 'she said . . . that the patients she had seen who had had ECT looked "so peaceful—as if they had died", (p. 13). 'She also felt that the patients who were getting ECT were getting something, and if they were, why wasn't she?' It is possible that such 'treatment' may encourage the individual to 'identify with the aggressor within herself' and Mrs Milner seems to suggest that ECT destroyed her patient's soul, and 'concern'—and even her capacities for growth.

Besides this we may set Laing's observation that what the schizoid individual really believes in is his own destructiveness. Shock treatment perhaps teaches a schizoid individual that the solution to the problem of life *is* to identify with one's own aggression directed against oneself. If so, this would seem to be a

* See below, p. 231.

heavy price to pay for the conformist identity induced by conventional psychiatry of a technological kind. Does Sylvia Plath tell us that shock therapy taught her that suicide was the 'correct' solution to the need to be re-born? It is true that she spoke of this episode of shock treatment as:

> A time of darkness, despair, disillusion—so black only as the inferno of the human mind can be—symbolic death, and numb shock—then the painful agony of slow rebirth and psychic regeneration.   (Lois Ames, 'Notes towards a Biography', *The Art of Sylvia Plath*, p. 163)

Surely, in her last poems her recognition of the regressed libidinal ego and of her need to love seem to have become suppressed altogether. Love and meeting are rejected and she becomes encapsulated in falsity, involved in the cycles of hate which led her into psychotic dissociation and self-destruction. As Andrew Brink (1968) has said: 'She found herself in suspended animation, without any community into which hostility could be fed to be given back as restoring symbols.' She was thus driven back into what Laing calls the 'separate "skin-encapsulated" ego' in an ever-increasing solipsism' (1960, p. 68).

The problem of the human being who wants to begin to be is that, insofar as he becomes conscious of his need, he may not be able to bear it. Guntrip (1968) notes that: 'The main practical problem for psychotherapy is "can the patient stand the return to consciousness of his basic ego-weakness?" When it does return, he is most likely to feel "I can't stand it, I only want to die"' (pp. 183–4). There were circumstances in the life of Sylvia Plath when, it would seem, she felt she could no longer stand going on living. At times she protects herself from this pain by diminution of affect, a withdrawal from feeling. But throughout her work there is a continual theme of 'in my end is my beginning', not in the Christian sense, but in ways in which the imagery shows that death offered her a re-birth. In *Birthday Present* (*Ariel*, p. 48), Sylvia Plath says of what seems to be the imminent announcement of some dreadful end, 'Let us sit down to it, one on either side, admiring the gleam', 'Let us eat out last supper at it . . . '. The last supper is on the way to crucifixion—but also to resurrection. The veils hiding the 'message' are 'White as babies bedding . . . ', and the knife of the pain of it she would like to enter 'Pure and clean as the cry of a baby ...', This often intense, and often joyful, feeling of purity, hope and newness associated with death takes on a crazy libidinal eagerness, especially in *The Bell Jar*. It has such a clear and untroubled logic that it carries us along with it and we too become deluded and fail to see that it only makes sense if one realises that her suicide was a schizoid suicide. And so we come to the essential clue to her predicament. Guntrip (1968) makes a thorough analysis of the strange logic of the schizoid suicide:

> Schizoid suicide is not really a wish for death as such ... there is a deep unconscious secret wish that death should prove to be a pathway to rebirth ... schizoid suicide is at bottom a longing to escape from a situation one just does not feel strong enough to cope with, so as in some sense to return to the womb, and be reborn later with a second chance to live. Here is a dramatic instance of ... basic ego-weakness ... What is the mental condition which drives a human being into such a dilemma as needing to stop living while not wanting to die? (pp. 217–18)

Sylvia Plath's poetry expresses (and sometimes falsifies) this dilemma, and so did her suicide, as the ultimate false solution. Her poetry, at best, was a contest with basic ego-weakness; at times the expression of the attempt to 'escape' with a 'second chance to live'. At other times, because she was overcome by negative feelings, not least those of hopelessness and the schizoid impulse to 'give oneself up to the joys of hating', she wrote poetry that deepened her own delusions. In such moods she flew into what Andrew Brink calls 'abandonment': as he says, 'the resulting isolation is delicious ... [with] accompanying self-pity'. She was 'sucking at the paps of darkness', or 'death's mouldy tits', and taking in the milk of annihilation.

Here the very disturbing problem arises of why what was intended to redeem did not redeem: how poetry can become the 'product of naked creativity turning in a void from which there is no satisfactory release into the inner ring of health and connectedness' (Brink). How is it possible for a divided self to integrate, and to turn callously upon its very life?

Guntrip says that the unconscious infantile ego, consequent

upon a failure of ego-relatedness, is ultimately 'very clearly experienced as a fear of dying, when its threat to the stability of the personality is felt':

> when exhaustion begins to develop, as it periodically does, out of this struggle to master this internal breakdown threat, then it may be experienced as *a wish to die* . . . a longing to regress, to escape from life, to go to sleep for an indefinite period.
>
> (Ibid., p. 215).

This life-tiredness, consequent upon a failure of the true self to develop at the heart of being, can culminate in suicide. 'Whereas in depressive suicide the driving force is anger, aggression, hate and a destructive impulse aimed at the self to divert it from the hated love-object, i.e., self-murder, schizoid suicide is a longing . . . to return to the womb and be reborn later with a second chance to live' (ibid., p. 218).

Ted Hughes, her husband, wrote after her death, 'It is impossible that anyone could have been more in love with life, or more capable of happiness, than she was' (Note in *Encounter*, October, 1963). Perhaps one of the most terrible aspects of human experience is that a person can seem to be loving life, to be successful to all intents and purposes, and, to all people around her, to be alive and real—while at the heart of being still feeling dead, unreal, overcome with a sense of futility, and full of hate and nihilism. This is the schizoid tragedy.

5

Doing, Being and Being Seen

The capacity TO BE is drawn out in the child, as we have seen, according to Winnicott, by the special gifts of the mother who is able to allow her baby to make use of her in very special ways (see Winnicott 1968a passim and Guntrip 1961). This ability is associated with certain feminine qualities which are found in both men and women—but which are crucial between mother and infant in the first months of life. If we are to understand schizoid art, we need to follow Winnicott's theories here rather closely. We shall find that they illuminate the kind of problem of existence already examined in Sylvia Plath's *Poem for a Birthday* and throw light especially on the problems of meaning in her work centring around male and female, seeing and being seen, and the ability to perceive creatively and to be autonomous.

In his long experience of dealing with mothers and infants as a paediatrician and analyst, Winnicott noticed in the expectant mother an increasing identification with her child. She becomes able and willing to drain interest from her own self on to the baby. Winnicott also emphasises that by an intuitive gift the mother 'knows' what is right for her baby. By such uncanny gifts the mother enters a heightened state of sensitivity before the baby is born, and this lasts for a few weeks after the birth. So weird is this state that our recognition of it has been heavily denied, and in individuals the memory of it is suppressed. If it were not for the baby, the state a woman goes into at this time would seem like a schizoid illness, and it 'shows up as such if the baby dies'.

At first, the infant knows no difference, says Winnicott, between himself and the breast from which he feeds. He feels he 'is' because the breast 'is'. Here is the origin, he says, of 'knowing by identification'. In discussing these matters Winnicott is, in fact, employing concepts which illuminate much in poetry, in philosophy, and problems of perception. We may have observed the primary confusion ourselves sometimes, as when a baby puts his finger in the mother's mouth to feed her, as she is feeding him. The breast (or 'experience of being fed and handled') can seem to a child like something which comes and goes—but which is not taken substantially into the self.

Guntrip, taking a lead from Winnicott, argues from this that there are two ways of 'knowing'. The 'male' way of knowing reaches its highest development perhaps in objective scientific investigation. The 'female' way of knowing is, in the completest sense, the mother's intuitive knowledge of her baby, but it is also manifest in art. In the field of gynaecology, Winnicott urges all doctors and midwives to realise that while they may know all about health and disease, they do not know thereby what a baby feels like from minute to minute, 'because they are outside this area of experience': 'only the mother knows'. The very vulnerability of this female area of being is also something of which we are all afraid, and so there is a good deal of hostility to it—a tendency which itself is rationalised in the mechanisation of childbirth.

When a woman is unable to enter into the state of 'being for' her baby, she may behave in ways which leave a permanent impression on her infant. In a successful nursing, the mother lets the baby make use of her, and lets him treat her as if she were his 'subjective object'—that is, part of himself. But a mother who is unable to 'be for' the baby in this way may well try to make up for her lack of this capacity by a kind of handling that interrupts the baby's 'going-on-being'. This concept of 'going-on-being' seems important to Winnicott, who knows how tenuous the baby's sense of a continuous identity and body can be. Of course the processes are beyond conscious will. But even in her desire to do the best for her child, a mother may handle her baby in a bustling, 'external' way, and it does not feel right to him. She does not appear at the right moment and does not deal with him as he yearns to be treated.

This is a failure of communication, of 'encounter', at a very deep level. The consequence of things going wrong in this way is, as we have said, to make the infant feel he is being impinged upon. This 'impingement' is experienced not only in such a way as to produce frustration, but actually as a *threat of annihilation*. This, according to Winnicott, is a very real primitive anxiety which comes long before any anxiety 'that includes the word death in its description' (1968a, p. 303). 'The mother's failure to adapt in the earliest phase', says Winnicott, 'does not produce anything but an annihilation of the infant's self . . . Her failures are not felt as maternal failures, but they act as threats to personal self-existence.'

When a nursing process goes wrong, even the mother's attempt to give loving care to her child is felt, mysteriously, as 'impingement'. This impingement is experienced as hate and even as the dreadful threat of nothingness. There can be serious dislocation of the capacity to find and relate to the world.

It is perhaps something like this unsatisfactory experience of the mother that lies behind Sylvia Plath's symbolism: the feeling she communicates of trying to base her identity and dealings with the world on such scraps of experience as she could assemble, all being the experience of impingement, felt as the experience of hate in the psychoanalytical sense. This (in the formation of her identity) was the experience of a *male* way of being handled. When she tried to find reliable resources within herself, often all she could find was *pseudo-male doing* and a collection of impingements, her 'bundle of clubs'.

Winnicott's maxim is 'after being—doing, and being done to: but first, being'. As Guntrip (1968) remarks, 'If "being" exists, doing will follow naturally from it. If it is not there but dissociated then a forced kind of "doing" will have to do duty for both'. He quotes a speaker in a television programme, 'The Sense of Belonging', who said, 'I plunged into marriage and motherhood and tried to substitute doing for being'. Guntrip comments that this woman's personality, insofar as if sought to be female, 'remained a dissociated potentiality in the absence of which any amount of busy "doing" was like the superstructure of a house with no foundation' (p. 253). This is exactly what Sylvia Plath is telling us when she writes 'This is a dark house, very big/I made it myself . . ,' (*Poem for a Birthday*). When 'doing' is substituted for 'being', the experience of doing, as Guntrip says, 'degenerates into a meaningless succession of mere activities . . . performed. . . . as a futile effort to keep oneself in being: to manufacture a sense of being one does not possess'. This may become a 'manic or obsessional compulsive activity, for the mind cannot stop, relax or rest, because of a secret fear of collapsing into non-existence'. But this doing (often in an intellectual form) tends to be dissociated from the deeper levels of being and an individual caught in the need to exert this kind of thinking still cannot find the autonomy and authenticity of the true self.

The failure of being, and the consequent weakness of the core of 'female element being', with an inner emptiness which is compensated for by a bustling outward 'male' activity, may be related to the difference Winnicott postulates between true and false self, a theory developed by Lomas on existential lines. The manic outward bustle is something of a 'screen of frontline troops', as Guntrip puts it. The individual is not on a path of development which is personal and real: he tends to be a 'collection of reactions to impingement'—and this condition is what Sylvia Plath refers to when she talks of being married to a 'cupboard of rubbish', and describes Fido Littlesoul as finding 'A dustbin's enough for him/ The dark's his bone'. The true self, which here is a little puppy, is 'hidden behind a false self which complies with and generally wards off the world's knocks', as Winnicott puts it (1968b, p. 17).

All kinds of circumstances may affect the delicate intersubjective processes of psychic parturition—the mother's illness, or absence in hospital, or the birth of one baby soon after another, or a bereavement. There is no clear 'reason'. In normal parturition the mother recovers her self-interest 'at the rate at which the infant can allow her to'. As the child finds the mother as his 'objective object', that is, finds her as a real separate not-me creature, so she recovers from her strange preoccupation (in which she has been feeling that she *is* the baby). This is 'psychic weaning', and it is a normal process of 'letting the infant go', towards becoming himself. But the mother who is experienced as unreflecting cannot wean her baby in this way. The infant has 'never had her', so for him weaning has no point. The mother may become over-dependent on her infant: or she may wean him too suddenly: 'without regard for the gradually developing need of the infant to be weaned' (Winnicott, ibid., pp. 15-16).

Normal weaning is a necessary 'disillusioning' process, that is, it is a way of gradually allowing the child to discover a meaningful world that exists beyond himself. As we have seen, such processes are his path to 'belief in a benign environment', through various stages from absolute dependence, towards independence, so that he sees his whole world by apperception, by being involved in its meanings—and does not simply, blankly, perceive it.

It was this successful psychic weaning, as the source of the core of being, that Sylvia Plath seems never to have fully experienced, for whatever reason. Her poetry can be read as an attempt to re-experience it: she must mother herself.

We have seen many of the bodily feelings which arise from this need to be mothered, but one of the most illuminating insights here is her *need to be seen*. In many of Sylvia Plath's poems we are aware of the impulse to be experienced in this way, and to feel something.

> There are long stretches of time in a normal infant's life in which a baby does not mind whether he is many bits or one whole being, or whether he lives in his mother's face, or his own body, provided that from time to time he comes together and feels something. (Winnicott, 1968a, p. 150)

In a paper on 'Alice and the Red King, a psycho-analytical View of Existence' an American psychoanalyst discusses the kind of need in human beings expressed in the text 'Thou God seest me'. Dr Solomon quotes a patient's dream:

> There is a giant lying on the grass. There is a big circle above him indicating that he is dreaming (like in the comic strips). I'm in the dream just doing ordinary things. I get the idea that I exist only in his dream. It is important for him to stay asleep, because if he wakes up, I will disappear. This is a tremendous fear. (1963, p. 63)

This obviously recalls the situation in *Through the Looking Glass*, an evident schizoid fantasy.

Sylvia Plath, is continually seeking to be seen in this way: in mirrors, in water, in eyes, she seeks for some reflection. Often, however, she finds nothing but a stony gaze. The most substantial element in her mythology is the cracked Colossus, who sees nothing with eyes in which she is buried: 'The bald, white tumuli of your eyes.' Something like this Solomon found to be the predicament of his patient who existed only in the *mind of her Colossus*:

> Xenia . . . projected a good image of herself into the mind of the father, as demonstrated by her dream. *It also became evident that she reintroduced the male image of her father into herself. This led to her acquiring his masculinity as a spurious identity. She also displaced and projected her hostility to her mother on to her father, fortifying her own fears of his actual power over her.* Defensively, her helplessness was also projected outwardly, allowing her to feel powerful and bossy over other people. This form of tyranny over the assumed helplessness of others gave her a reason for her existence and created a form of temporary ego mastery.
>
> (Ibid., my italics)

This could be taken as a diagnosis of Sylvia Plath's relationship with the internalised father.

The development of the infant's perception of the 'not-me' is bound up with a sense of the *meaning* of the seen world. The mother has to allow him, at first, to believe that he is creating his world, and gradually as he creates it he finds it and perceives it as meaningful. This is her way of 'being for' him, allowing him to make use of her.

Winnicott thus comes to see that in his psychic interaction with the 'breast' the infant is discovering not only the world but himself. When he says 'breast', of course, he means all those aspects of being attended to and fed which appear in the baby's vision: 'Now, at some point the baby takes a look round. Perhaps a baby at the breast does not look at the breast. Looking at the face is more likely to be a feature. What does the baby see there?' (1971a, p. 112). From his experience of psychoanalysis Winnicott answers that 'what the baby sees is himself or herself': 'In other words, the mother is looking at the baby and what she looks like is related to what she sees there. All this is too easily taken for granted' (p. 112).

If there is a long experience of 'not getting back what they are giving', babies who 'look and do not see themselves' suffer a deep dissociation of the capacity to see. 'Firstly, their creative capacity begins to atrophy, and in some way they look round for other ways of getting something back from the environment . . . Secondly, the baby gets settled in to the idea that when he or she looks, what is seen is the mother's face' (p. 112). Our reaction to the second point is perhaps, 'but the baby is looking at the mother's face'. But if that face is not a reflecting one, then it can convey something like a de-creation of oneself, that destroys one's capacity to see a meaningful world. It is such a blank moon-mother's face that stares from Sylvia Plath's poems, as we have seen.

To see a meaningful world is to see it with all one's being: this is apperception. Where the mother's face does not reflect, 'perception takes the place of apperception, takes the place of what might have been a significant exchange with the world, a two-way process in which self-enrichment alternates with the discovery of meaning in the world of seen things' (Winnicott, ibid., p. 113). What Keats called 'a greeting of the spirit' in our capacity to perceive the world in a meaningful way, depends, therefore, upon the degree to which the mother, by responding to us in her face, makes us feel real and alive, and able to get back from the world what we give of ourselves, by confirming us, and bringing out in us the capacity for 'creative looking'. To Sylvia Plath it seems that if the mother's face can be mollified, all will be well. But non-reflection can bring

a threat of chaos, and the baby will organise withdrawal, or will not look except to perceive, as a defence. A baby so treated will grow up puzzled about mirrors and what the mirror has to offer. If the mother's face is unresponsive, then the mirror is a thing to be looked at but not looked into . . . (Ibid., p. 113)

Sylvia Plath wrote:

Mirrors can kill and talk; they are terrible rooms
In which a torture goes on one can only watch.
The face that lived in this mirror is the face of a dead man.

Do not worry about the eyes.
(*The Courage of Shutting Up, Winter Trees*, p. 20)

Unresponsive looking differs from the normal process: 'when the average girl studies her face in the mirror she is reassuring herself that the mother-image is there and that the mother can see her and that the mother is in rapport with her . . .' (Winnicott, ibid., p. 113).

Winnicott postulates a historical process in the individual, which depends upon being seen:

When I look I am seen, so I exist.
I can now afford to look and see.
I now look creatively and what I apperceive I also perceive.
In fact I take care not to see what is not there to be seen (unless I am tired).

From this he deduces that psychotherapy itself should be 'giving the patient back what the patient brings': that is, supplying a mirror-role which is a creative way of enabling the patient to find his or her own self.

One of the patients Winnicott quotes remarked that it would be awful if the child looked into the mirror and saw nothing! Another 'had to be her own mother'. Sylvia Plath's problems of perception arise because she could never really feel that 'When I look I am seen, so I exist'. Her uncanny and acute visual perception was yet another way perhaps of 'getting something of herself back from the environment'.

Sometimes, for her, the mirror seemed to threaten that it would eat her, as in *All the Dead Dears*. In a poem called *Mirror* (*Crossing the Water*, p. 52) the mirror speaks, and speaks of how it eats away the life of the woman who gazes into it.

The mirror is 'silver' but although it is felt to be valuable, it is not warm and creative: it gives back only an 'exact' reflection, to which nothing creative is contributed. It is perception, unenrichened by apperception.

> I am not cruel, only truthful—
> The eye of a little god, four-cornered.

It is also voracious:

> Whatever I see I swallow immediately
> Just as it is, unmisted by love or dislike.

The mirror is non-human, and cannot invest the world with human meaning.

Most of the time I meditate on the opposite wall.
It is pink, with speckles. I have looked at it so long
I think it is part of my heart. But it flickers.
Faces and darkness separate us over and over.

A woman appears, trying to find herself in the mirror reflection, and we see her as Magritte, the surealist painter, might portray her —desperately trying to see the real self but instead seeing only a mechanical reflection which has no meaning:

Now I am a lake. A woman bends over me,
Searching my reaches for what she really is.
Then she turns back to those liars, the candles or the moon.

The candles and the moon are those sources of light which cast a glow over the truth, that she is ageing. But there is no confidence in their 'natural' reflection: they are liars. 'Faithful' reflection is the mirror's realism—which is reflection without meaning. This faithfulness is rewarded by despair:

She rewards me with tears and an agitation of hands.

The mirror's attitude, we realise gradually, is one of hate: its faithfulness is that of a hate which has the intensity of love.

I am important to her. She comes and goes.
Each morning it is her face that replaces the darkness.

The poem is written as if by a mirror seeking reflection. As in *All the Dead Dears*, the mirror represents the mother, while the woman 'searching my reaches for what she really is' is the self. But the mirror-mother eats the woman-self. By her intense search for 'what she really is' the young woman virtually commits suicide in the mirror, and an old woman rises triumphant in her place:

In me she has drowned a young girl, and in me an old woman
Rises toward her day after day, like a terrible fish.

This fish is old, scaly, and an ugly 'O-gape': the consuming mother who eats rather than creatively reflects. While the mirror seems predatory, the seen world may seem blank, because it cannot be invested with meaning. In the short story,

The Wishing Box, the protagonist kills herself because she could not bear going on seeing the world by perception, unredeemed by apperception.

> The utterly self-sufficient, unchanging reality of the *things* surrounding her began to depress Agnes . . . She felt choked, smothered by these objects whose bulky pragmatic existence somehow threatened the deepest, most secret roots of her own ephemeral being . . .

She seeks to hallucinate . . .

> Anything to prove that her shaping imaginative powers were not irretrievably lost; that her eye was not merely an open camera lens which recorded surrounding phenomena and left it at that.

The 'vistas of the world' are here not endorsed, when captured, by any confidence that meaning may be thrown over them. As a mother herself, Sylvia Plath wants her children to see a meaningful world. In *Child* (*Winter Trees*, p. 12) she wants to fill the child's perception with joy and interest, because the window of its soul is so beautiful

> Your clear eye is the one absolutely beautiful thing.
> I want to fill it with colour and ducks,
> The zoo of the new . . .

The child's eye is a pool 'in which images/Should be grand and classical'. She does not want the child to see the world as

> . . . this troublous
> Wringing of hands, this dark
> Ceiling without a star.

—which is her world. The 'dark ceiling without a star' is the sky seen as Sylvia Plath often sees it. It echoes 'the gaping void in her own head' (*The Wishing Box*). In the short story, Agnes has to keep staring at all kinds of printed matter:

> reading kept her mind full of pictures. Seized by a kind of ravenous hysteria, she raced through novels, women's magazines, newspapers, and even the anecdotes in her *Joy of Cooking*;

she read travel brochures, home appliance circulars, the Sears Roebuck Catalogue, the instructions on soap-flake boxes, the blurbs on the backs of record jackets—anything to keep from facing the gaping void in her own head . . . But as soon as she lifted her eyes from the printed matter at hand, it was as if a protecting world had been extinguished.

At last her fear becomes explicit:

> Finally, a bleak, clear, awareness of what was happening broke upon her: the curtains of sleep, of refreshing, forgetful darkness dividing each day from the day before it and the day after it, were lifted for Agnes eternally, irrevocably. She saw an intolerable prospect of wakeful, visionless days, and nights stretching unbroken ahead of her, her mind *condemned to perfect vacancy, without a single image of its own to ward off the crushing assault of smug, autonomous tables and chairs.* (my italics)

So the environment is not only unreliable and not benign: it is also meaningless, and blank, while the self perceives it unwillingly. Sylvia Plath discusses this in *Tulips* and elsewhere. In *Insomniac* (*Crossing the Water*, p. 21), the sky seems a black screen over the light of death:

> The night sky is only a sort of carbon paper,
> Blueblack, with the much-poked periods of stars
> Letting in the light, peephole after peephole—
> A bonewhite light, like death, behind all things.

This kind of blankness may be associated with dreadful images in Sylvia Plath of 'bald eyes', or of bald figures: 'She may be bald, she may have no eyes . . .' (*The Tour, Crossing the Water*, p. 61). What is this eyeless, pink, inhuman ghost that lurks about Sylvia Plath's environment?

> Dead men leave eyes for others.
> Love is the uniform of my bald nurse.
>
> Love is the bone and sinew of my curse.
> (*Poem for a Birthday*)

The words 'dead', 'eyes' and 'bald' are often juxtaposed in Sylvia Plath. What she is saying here is something like this:

Here in hospital I am being handled by a bald male nurse in an impersonal uniform.

This is like being handled by a male-like mother in infancy, with a bald face. This 'dead' handling left me with dead sight, just as dead men (like my Daddy) leave (dead) eyes for others (for me).

But my curse (madness) is fixed in my psychic tissue, and I cannot see my world, except as a dead world. His eyes are tombs.

The connection between eyes, baldness and the mother's face is made clear elsewhere. For instance in *A Life* (*Crossing the Water*, p. 54):

> Touch it: it won't shrink like an eye-ball,
> This egg-shaped bailiwick
> A woman is dragging her shadow in a circle
> About a bald, hospital saucer.
> It resembles the moon, or a sheet of blank paper.
> . . .
> She lives quietly
> . . . like a foetus in a bottle
> > . . . a drowned man . . .
> Crawls up out of the sea.

In *The Moon and the Yew Tree* (*Ariel*, p. 47) she says 'The moon is my mother'. So, we may reasonably assert that the 'bald nurse' whose face resembles the moon symbolises the mother who (she feels) handled her 'blankly', the mother of pestles, who is mingled in her imagery with the 'old man' shrunk to a doll.

Yet there is an urgent desire to soften this blankness, because, while she has a face like bone,

> The moon is no door.

She is separated from her 'house' by a row of headstones: that is, she is separated from 'coming into her own' by death, and the moon-mother offers no 'way through'. What she wanted of the mother was a reflecting assurance that she was loved in her own right.

> How I would like to believe in tenderness
> The face of the effigy, gentled by candles,
> Bending, on me in particular, its mild eyes.

But, when the saints float about the church:

> The moon sees nothing of this. She is bald and wild.

A note emerges here which is important for us: the feeling that candles could mollify the mother. This is struck again in *Candles* (*Crossing the Water*, p. 41):

> These little globes of light are sweet as pears.
> Kindly with invalids and mawkish women,
>
> They mollify the bald moon.

Here there is a deep underlying feeling that the mother could have been, should have been, 'gentled' or 'mollified' or made 'kindly' by little globes of light (as sweet as pears)—by candles. Of course the candles suggest a phallic interpretation, and so the father's mollification of the mother by sexual love. But perhaps we can reach beyond Freudian interpretations and see them as lights of meaning which could have come from the father's benign influence, had he lived: 'Upside down hearts of light tipping wax fingers'. From *Poem for a Birthday* and *The Bee Meeting* we remember 'The fingers of wisdom'. The hearts at the tips of the wax fingers are the love and spiritual wisdom coming from Daddy's milk:

> And the fingers, taken in by their own haloes,
> Grown milky, almost clear like the bodies of saints.

In *Poem for a Birthday* the 'birds made milk'. Here the milky candles are the love- and meaning-dispensing tears she takes in from the father (in lieu of the mother's breast). But he died, and so her mother was not mollified.

These candles *plumb the deeps of her eye*: so, their love-light enters her eyes as if entering a sexual organ. Here, under the surface, is the desire to develop the capacity to see with vision by taking in a loving reflection ('They are the last romantics . . .').

> It is touching, the way they'll ignore
>
> A whole family of prominent objects
> Simply to plumb the deeps of an eye
> In its hollow of shadows, its fringe of reeds,
> And the owner past thirty, no beauty at all.
>
> (Ibid., p.41)

They seem archaic because they represent 'the private point of view'. This is a strange phrase. It has, of course, an explicit meaning: in daylight, everything would be seen equally (the *whole family* of prominent objects). But this meaning does not make much sense. What does make sense is to read the poem as meaning 'It is *touching* . . . and the exertion of a *private point of view* for Daddy to pick me out (although I am thirty and not very beautiful) and pay me *sexual* attention'. The word 'private' has an undercurrent (as in 'hairy as privates' in *Berck-Plage*) and *point* has a phallic emphasis, while 'view' means looking at in a sexual way, the thrusting of the phallic light into the eye as a sexual organ, and bringing the illumination that comes from loving and being loved.

It is important to note that the eye has a 'hollow of shadows' and is a pool (which 'fringe of reeds' makes it—the reeds being lashes). At the end of the poem are further significant images. The candles, although they mollify the bald moon-mother, are

> Nun-souled, they burn heavenward and never marry.

They are thus the female aspect of Daddy and she wants to keep them pure, ideal, and for herself. The candles are standing over her own baby (in *Morning Song* she says 'we stand round blankly as walls': in *Magi* blank pure faces surround a baby). They are like guests at a christening. What are they telling her?

> The eyes of the child I nurse are scarcely open.
> In twenty years I shall be retrograde
> As these draughty ephemerids.

When she is fifty, the child will find her as archaic as she now finds the candles: this will be when her baby's eyes are open to what she is, bald like the moon perhaps.

> I watch their spilt tears cloud and dull to pearls.

The candles are eyes now: their tears cloud and dull. It is as if the promise of yielding vision fades. She goes on

> How shall I tell anything at all
> To this infant still in a birth-drowse?

There is a 'mild light' and she sees there is love and care in it. But she does not know what to tell her child, while the candles' tears merely cloud and dull to pearls. The clue to the deep underlying meaning is

> Those are pearls that were his eyes . . .

What dulls in the candles are the eyes, or pools of semen, in which she hoped to see herself.

We saw above that the moon's (mother's) face was like a blank sheet of paper. The poems are an attempt to soften that blankness. But so too are the candles, and later we shall explore further strange phallic images associated with the father's love. Somehow, perhaps, the father can be made to reflect. The perplexity is evident in *Words* (*Ariel*, p. 86), where again we have a characteristic Plath topography. There is a pool, in which the water is striving to 're-establish its mirror over the rock'. But the rock 'drops and turns'—like the grey seal, and the rock elsewhere. It is that dead petrified relic of Daddy that seems a toe, or a foot, coming up from 'where the daft father went down'. Here it drops and turns

> A white skull,
> Eaten by weedy greens . . .

'Those are pearls that were his eyes', so to speak. But

> From the bottom of the pool, fixed stars
> Govern a life.

The circumstances of her infant experience of non-reflection and her father's death are now an ineradicable deterministic influence on her existence, like the influence of the stars in horoscopes. Words are 'echoes travelling off from the centre like horses' and

> Years later I
> Encounter them on the road—
> Words dry and riderless,
> The indefatigable hoof-taps.

There is no connection made between the water and the sap welling like tears, trying to re-establish the mirror in which she can reflect herself, and the word-echoes travelling off from the centre like horses, dry and riderless. They seem, in this poem to be desperate male-element attempts to find the possibilities of reflection, even through tears, which might form a pool in which she could be seen. (This poem was written in the last week of her life.)

In *Small Hours* (*Crossing the Water*, p. 46) she describes herself in cold, empty, stony terms, like an empty museum:

In my courtyard a fountain leaps and sinks back into itself.

Meanwhile,

> The moon lays a hand on my Forehead,
> Blankfaced and mum as a nurse.

Again, we have the narcissistic fountain, 'nun-hearted and blind to the world': in the next chapter we shall find an even more bizarre version of this, which in one sense is her well-spring.

6

The Fabrication of False Selves and Daddy

Mixed up with the impulse to be reflected was a tendency to make false selves, out of fragments, scraps and shadows.

> I am nobody . . .   (*Tulips*)

> . . . they stuck me together with glue.
>   (*Daddy*)

> I see myself as a shadow, neither man nor woman . . .
>   (*Three Women*)

Ariel (the poem) (*Ariel*, p. 36) is a poem of the identity 'thawing and resolving itself into a dew'. In fact it is about riding her favourite horse. But as Alvarez points out, the horse is hardly there at all (*Art of Sylvia Plath*, p. 61). She becomes 'one' with the horse: he rapes her away, like the bull Europa: 'Hauls me through the air'. She is 'White/Godiva'—'I unpeel': all the attention of the poem is on an inner joy at losing herself in the excitement of a morning ride. Yet this assertion of vitality, characteristically, is expressed in terms of a movement towards death.

> The child's cry
>
> Melts in the wall.
> And I
> Am the arrow,
>
> The dew that flies
> Suicidal, at one with the drive

Into the red

Eye, the cauldron of morning.

She becomes the dew and the dew is involved in a 'drive into' this cauldron. It 'flies suicidal'—a strange way of regarding the normal morning experience of dew evaporating, as if it were a loss. Note that the rising of the sun, which in normal experience is symbolic re-birth and beginning, is to Sylvia Plath a threat—the sun is an incorporative and glowering 'red/Eye', heating a 'cauldron' (a word which suggests witches' brew or sinister alchemy).*

There are recurrent images in Sylvia Plath of a swarm or pack, with related images of eating and stinging; identities are screened or disguised by gloves or veils; there are recurrent images of losing the contents of one's 'inside', or having harm thrust into one, against which implosion some protection needs to be worn. There are also images of vulnerability, and images of coverings within which there is nothing, or masks which disguise. Often she exploits the problem of not being able to piece the self together, in relation to the problem of not being able to put the object together, and this leads to a complex problem of getting the proportions right (as in *The Colossus* and *The Swarm*). The problem of proportion seems to become acute over her images of the male object. He is Napoleon, the bees, Daddy, the man with asbestos gloves, the concentration camp doctor: she is a grain of rice or a pebble, a bundle of violent clubs, confused with her plaster cast.

We can sum all these images up by using the word 'depersonalization'. Laing (1960) uses this term about his schizoid patients and his words could be applied to Sylvia Plath's use of, and attitude to, many of her figures:

The people in focus here tend to feel themselves as more or less depersonalized and tend to depersonalize others; they are constantly afraid of being depersonalized by others. The act of turning him into a thing is, *for him*, actually petrifying. In the

* In this way images which are usually benign become hostile or malignant: 'the atrocity of sunsets', 'The moon . . . is merciless . . . Her radiance scathes me . .' 'The moon . . . her blacks crackle and drag . . .', 'the moon/Dragged its blood bag, sick/Animal/Up over the harbour lights . . .' Compare R. D. Laing's patient Julie, who was 'born under a black sun'—and whose mother is the black sun (*The Divided Self*, last chapter). Gerard de Nerval was haunted by a black spot and a black sun.

face of being treated as an 'it', his own subjectivity drains away from him like blood from the face. Basically he requires constant confirmation from others of his own existence as a person.
(p. 48)

Schizoid persons have a dread of 'being turned, from a live person into a dead thing, into a stone, into a robot, an automaton, without personal autonomy of action, an *it* without subjectivity' (ibid, p. 49). Laing quotes several patients who suffer such problems. One felt he was only 'a cork floating on the ocean'. He reproached his mother for this failure: 'I was merely her emblem. She never recognised my identity'.

Laing quotes Medard Boss, who recounts a woman's dream:

> She was afire in the stables. Around her, the fire, an ever larger crust of lava was forming. Half from the outside and half from the inside her own body she could see how the fire was slowly becoming choked by this crust. Suddenly she was entirely outside this fire and, as if possessed, she beat the fire with a club to break the crust and let some air in. (Ibid., p. 52)

Laing then gives an account of how a girl dreams of turning herself into stone in order to avoid being turned into stone by someone else. 'It seems to be a general law that at some point those very dangers most dreaded can themselves be encompassed to forestall their actual occurrence . . . To consume onself by one's own love prevents the possibility of being consumed by another' (p. 54). This illuminates both Sylvia Plath's impulse to suicide and her search for purity, as through fire in *Lady Lazarus*. The origins of these impulses, as Laing sees, are in 'a failure to sustain a sense of one's own being without the presence of other people. It is a failure *to be* by oneself, a failure to exist alone'. An individual who depends so desperately upon identification cannot exist alone: an immediate rebirth must be sought if the object of identification is lost, and this explains how deprivation can be followed by desperate acts (as in *A Birthday Present*).

Often, in criticism of Sylvia Plath, the contempt she shows for 'appearances' is taken to show her strength. But this assumes too easily that she could judge these from her own secure self. Her contempt for conventional gestures is also a kind of contempt for the false self in herself—for the mechanical modes, the inauthentic responses which are attempts to establish a self in the world. A good deal of her scathing irony is directed at the conformity of the false self, which is being-for-others (cf. Esterson, 1970, pp. 57–8). It is this false self we see pieced together at the end of *Poem for a Birthday*: it is The Applicant: it is in *An Appearance* (*Crossing the Water*, p. 23):

> The stars are flashing like terrible numerals.
> ABC, her eyelids say.

This woman's morality is only whitewashing:

> It is Monday in her mind: morals
> Launder and present themselves.

In *Totem* (*Ariel*, p. 76), the mortal remains of Plato or Christ are seen thus:

> Their round eyes, their teeth, their grimaces
> On a stick that rattles and clicks, a counterfeit snake . . .

In the journey of the soul there is no terminus,

>   . . . only suitcases
> Out of which the same self unfolds like a suit
> Bald and shiny, with pockets of wishes,
>
> Notions and tickets, short circuits and folding mirrors.
> I am mad, calls the spider, waving its many arms.

The 'wishes, notions and tickets' however, are not the common delusions and aspirations of 'society', treated (as in *The Applicant*) with scalding satire. They are the pathetic scraps and oddments by which the schizoid individual tries to assemble some kind of self.

It will not thus do to see Sylvia Plath as a woman 'speaking for all women', when she is expressing the impossibility of being a woman. Nor will it do to say that she 'uncovers that central core and cause of dissatisfaction that can exist particularly in marriage', such as is 'exposed by Simone de Beauvoir in *The Second Sex*', as Mrs Connie Richmond (1973) declares in her study. Sylvia Plath does not speak for all women, unless we are to suppose all women schizoid. Nor is she speaking of 'the subjection of women':

she is speaking, rather, of how terrible it is for a woman to have to pretend to be a woman, when she cannot find herself to be one. And she is rejecting the mere trappings of femininity, or of being a wife, thrust upon a person, by social coercion, when she does not naturally find her way into them.

The problem is discussed in *Three Women*. A false identity seems to have been thrust upon one protagonist almost by a Leda-like rape, by coercion:

> Stars and showers of gold—conceptions, conceptions.
> . . .
> And the great swan . . .
> . . .
> . . . his eye had a black meaning.
> I saw the world in it—small, mean and black,
> Every little word hooked to every little word, and act to act.
> (Three Women, Winter Trees, pp. 41–2)

This Third Voice is a very terrifying one, that cries 'What did I miss?'—and it sounds to me closest to Sylvia Plath's own soul. We sense in the above lines a deep resentment, at being raped by some male form when 'I wasn't ready'. But this must be seen in the light of Sylvia Plath's feelings about 'impingement'.

The terrible inward conflict of grappling with one's maleness, as an incorporation of one's experience of identifying with the father and others in their maleness, can be seen in the same dream which Laing quotes from Boss, to which I referred above:

> . . . a girl of twenty-five years dreamt that she had cooked dinner for her family of five. She had just served it and she now called her parents and her brothers and sisters to dinner. Nobody replied. Only her voice returned as if it were an echo from a deep cave. She found the sudden emptiness of the house uncanny. She rushed upstairs to look for her family. In the first bedroom, she could see her two sisters sitting on two beds. In spite of her impatient calls they remained in an unnaturally rigid position and did not even answer her. She went up to her sisters and wanted to shake them. Suddenly she noticed that they were stone statues. She escaped in horror and rushed into her mother's room. Her mother too had turned into stone and

was sitting inertly in her armchair staring into the air with glazed eyes. The dreamer escaped into the room of her father. He stood in the middle of it. In her despair she rushed up to him, and, desiring his protection, she threw her arms round his neck. But he too was made of stone and, to her utter horror, he turned into sand when she embraced him . . . (p. 54)

After this dream, repeated four times, the girl herself became 'petrified' physically. The sand, the glazed eyes, the stone, are all found in Sylvia Plath's poems—even Daddy cracks and crumbles. But the mother, as a source of femininity, is stony too and she finds horrifying gulfs and shifting shadows where she should be. If any female element appears, it is red, voracious, and malignant (*Purdah, Stings, Lady Lazarus*). In *Three Women* Mother Earth is the vampire of us all, her mouth is red, 'old winter-face, old barren one, old time bomb'. In *Three Women* from which these phrases come, the Third Voice sees her baby as 'my red, terrible girl': her cries are hooks through the glass. Encounter between female element beings is always like this in her work.

Winnicott says, 'being comes first: doing later'. But since being has not come first to Sylvia Plath there can be no security in the effort of putting a self together by doing. She cannot get Daddy together as the focus of identity. In *The Colossus* (*The Colossus*, p. 20) we read:

> I shall never get you put together entirely,
> Pieced, glued, and properly jointed.

'Daddy' cannot 'speak' her. All she has are the strange noises of father when she was an infant, and she associates these with puzzling, as she did then, about what he makes of her:

> Mule-bray,* pig-grunt and bawdy cackles
> Proceed from your great lips.
> It's worse than a barn-yard.
>
> Perhaps you consider yourself an oracle,
> Mouthpiece of the dead, or of some god or other.
> Thirty years now I have laboured
> To dredge the silt from your throat.

* Interestingly enough this word echoes Dylan Thomas's 'mule-bray' lament for the dead Ann Jones, whom he seeks to restore to life by incantation.

He is like a great drowned statue: all her growing life she has tried to open his mouth, so he could give his confirmation of her identity, and give tongue. She cannot get from him the spiritual wisdom of the animus:

> I am none the wiser.

She has to try to make him (with a desperate sense that if he cannot be brought to life, she cannot survive):

> Scaling little ladders with gluepots and pails of lysol
> I crawl like an ant in mourning . . .

Glue is to mend the doll: lysol is to prevent his decay, and to purify him:

> Over the weedy acres of your brow . . .

—he is the world, which is his overgrown grave:

> To mend the immense skull-plates and clear
> The bald, white tumuli of your eyes.

His eyes are 'tumuli' not only because they are the huge tombs of the earth-object in which he is buried. She too is buried in them: his looking at her might have confirmed her existence. Since he does not reflect her, she fears she cannot exist.

She is in Greece and opens her lunch: the landscape of ruined artefacts seems like the 'old anarchy' of her petrified and scattered father:

> It would take more than a lightning-stroke
> To create such a ruin.

The catastrophe which has scattered her colossus and with him her hope of integration is immense.

So, she shelters as if in one ear, which she feels perhaps can hear something of her existence (as a 'cornucopia' it has the shape of life's riches), and offers shelter:

> Nights, I squat in the cornucopia
> Of your left ear, out of the wind,
>
> Counting the red stars and those of plum-colour.
> The sun rises under the pillar of your tongue.

—but she still cannot hear the riddle of this sphinx. She is a bride of nothing,

> My hours are married to shadow . . .

And she is no longer hopeful of his live arrival, recreated as her awaited God or hero:

> No longer do I listen for the scrape of a keel
> On the blank stones of the landing.

In the direction of *doing* ('You do not do') there was no hope. The world remains blank, without meaning, 'A world of bald white days in a shadeless socket' (*The Hanging Man, Ariel*, p. 70).

She has had great difficulty in keeping hold on Daddy's memory, both for purposes of identifying, and also for mourning: she cannot let him go, but yet she cannot hold on to him. He keeps turning up, as the man with asbestos hands, or as a bee-keeper. It seems at times as if someone—a malignant animus, a Nazi, or Devil—has taken over the 'good' Daddy. Daddy is 'bad' because he let her down by dying. With childish contempt she calls him the 'daft father' for dying.

But Daddy has become the core of the self, and so is bound up with her collection of stolen male objects and her collection of experiences of impingement. 'Daddy' is thus a bundle of tools, clubs, etc. all feeling like bones:

> At twenty I tried to die
> And get back, back, back to you.
> I thought even the bones would do.
> (*Daddy, Ariel*, p. 55)

She wants to get back to find a living relationship in love, that could give her substance, and help her see the world in a real way, not in fear of total neutrality. Yet she cries, 'I simply cannot see where there is to get to'. Looking at the graveyard in *The Moon and the Yew Tree* she seems to be seeking a path into another world. But, 'The message of the yew tree is blackness—blackness and silence . . .'.

A related hopelessness pervades *The Munich Mannequins* (*Ariel*, p. 74). It is as if the poetess looks at a landscape that should be meaningful—but only succeeds in evoking her hopelessness about relationship as a source of meaning. The mannequins are both yew-trees and idealised woman figures, or idols: they resemble the stone muses. The yew trees are, ironically, called the tree of life. They 'release' their 'moons'—it is as if they have a menstrual flow which is sterile. They are perfect, in sterility:

Perfection is terrible, it cannot have children.
Cold as snow breath, it tamps the womb

Where the yew trees blow like hydras,
The tree of life and the tree of life

Unloosing their moons, month after month, to no purpose.
The blood flow is the flood of love,

The absolute sacrifice.
It means: no more idols but me,

Me and you.

To love is like a menstrual flow, a loss of inner contents. The self and the object (husband, father) are idols. Yet, as Andrew Brink (1968) says: 'Natural acceptance of the large impersonal cycles of life is denied by the pain of relationships made too easily inter-changeable; remembering the father, confrontation of the you and me turns into impasse and immobilised idols can do nothing to advance life's possibilities' (p. 57). The father is present again as the 'black shoes' in the hotel:

... In the hotels
Hands will be opening doors and setting

Down shoes for a polish of carbon
Into which broad toes will go tomorrow ...

The daily routine of life is meaningless and threatening. The black telephones stay on their hooks, 'glittering'. But they are 'digesting' 'voicelessness'. In *Daddy* she rejects the black telephone, because 'the voices just can't worm through'. Here she expresses her frus-tration that the 'thick Germans' are slumbering, while their black telephones lie fattening as it were on the unspeakable. It is as if she is expecting a call that does not come, and is stamping her foot at the failure of Daddy to emerge and communicate. The mother images are 'naked and bald' ... intolerable, without mind: dead dummies. There is no mirror-glitter in which it might be possible to be seen and find meaning: 'The snow has no voice.'

In *Little Fugue* (*Ariel*, p. 71), the father is a 'dark funnel', down back through the memory, merging into death. It is there the father is: she cannot get to him because he has faded in her memory. If she could get back to him she would recapture the sense of knowing what a man was; just as she was beginning to find out death took him.

> I remember a blue eye,
> A briefcase of tangerines.
> This was a man, then!
> Death opened, like a black tree, blackly.

Little Fugue is about the total failure of communication, especially with the dead father, and the way in which this failure makes the world and oneself black:

> So the deaf and dumb
> Signal the blind, and are ignored.
>
> I like black statements
> The featurelessness of that cloud, now!
> White as an eye all over!

Because of the bald tumuli of the eyes of the Colossus, the world is stripped of those meanings which apperception might give it, blind. In *Little Fugue*, the white cloud reminds her of the eye of a blind pianist on a ship, who felt for his food: again, this pianist is 'Daddy':

> His fingers had the noses of weasels.
> I couldn't stop looking.

While he could hear the 'horrid complications' of Beethoven, at the table there is a blankness.

> Empty and silly as plates,
> So the blind smile.

By contrast with this unbearable meaninglessness she prefers the 'big noises', the *Grosse Fugue*. This music-memory becomes a black yew hedge. And it takes her down a 'dark funnel' to the memory of her father's voice:

> A yew hedge of orders,
> Gothic and barbarous, pure German,
> Dead men cry from it.
> I am guilty of nothing.

The feelings she has about the pianist's fingers are full of guilt because she once had an urge to castrate Daddy and steal his penis;* so, Electral feelings surge to the surface:

> The yew my Christ, then.
> Is it not as tortured?

She recalls an image of her father

> And you, during the Great War
> In the Californian delicatessen
>
> Lopping the sausages!
> They colour my sleep,
> Red, mottled, like cut necks
> There was a silence!
> Great silence of another order.

In desperation, she sought to castrate her father. By the infant's talion logic, he (in fantasy) might turn on her to castrate her. How can a girl be castrated? The answer is that she is composed of the very male elements she has stolen: so, as we shall see, in *The Bee Meeting*, the self is identified with a penis that is like a neck that can be cut, as chicken necks can be chopped (see p. 215). When necks are cut there is a silence.

But then there was the big silence—of his actual death: did her castration fantasies kill him?

> I was seven, I knew nothing.
> The world occurred.

She can't be blamed, because she was in the latency period and 'knew nothing':

> You had one leg, and a Prussian mind.

---

* The connection between finger and penis is evident in the poem *Cut*, which has undertones of castration: 'Your turkey wattle/Carpet' echoing the 'turkey neck' image of Buddy Willard's penis in *The Bell Jar*.

> Now similar clouds
> Are spreading their vacuous sheets
> Do you say nothing?
> I am lame in the memory.

The Prussian with one leg is a partial memory: she is 'lame' in trying to remember him. When he died, the world went blank. Now, when the pianist reminds her of her father, more blankness threatens because she cannot remember him, and he does not communicate. The failure of memory makes her actions and her perceptions seems utterly meaningless. Because she cannot find the father to mourn, when her memories are stirred by the blind pianist, 'similar clouds are opening their vacuous sheets' as when he died.

> I survive the while,
> Arranging my morning.
> These are my fingers, this my baby.
> The clouds are a marriage dress, of that pallor.

In *Poem for A Birthday* we hear with some clarity and poignancy about the failure of fathering and mothering, but without rage, blame, and malice. What happened to turn her love (as we find it in the love-poem *The Beekeeper*) into the hate of *Daddy*? Was it, as *A Birthday Present* perhaps suggests, the breaking up of her marriage? Yet, in that she says, ironically, 'I am sure it is just what I want'—and this is true in a sense, because behind the veil of estrangement is the death for which she yearns.

'Failure in relationship with the father-husband', says Brink, 'propels thinking into lethally repetitive patterns, calling up subconscious material as in the indictments of *Daddy* . . .'. He says that this is a kind of existential reconstruction, but it is a reconstruction based on hate and has no positive direction. Brink quotes Laing relevantly on the schizoid individual:

> An exile from the scene of being as we know it, [she] is an alien, a stranger, signalling to us from the void in which [she] is foundering, a void which may be peopled by presences that we do not even dream of . . .

As we have seen in *Little Fugue*, Sylvia Plath was well aware of the way in which there could be signals from a void, and the failure of communication is centred on Daddy. From despair of ever making connection, she flies into negative dynamics. From her *Poem for a Birthday* onwards we have all the agony of what Laing (1960) calls 'negative therapeutic reaction', if therapy for her was the writing of poetry. In any case, the schizoid individual, as he says, erects a tremendous resistance against understanding, which manifests a threat: 'To be understood correctly is to be engulfed, to be enclosed, swallowed up, drowned, eaten up, smothered, stifled in or by another person's supposed all-embracing comprehension' (p. 46).

In this, I believe, we have the clue to Sylvia Plath's increasing encapsulation. Although her poetry became increasingly clear, it also increasingly crackled to itself on the top of an Alp—enclosed in its psychotic logic. After deciding 'I am incapable of more knowledge' in *Elm*, she clung to isolation: 'It is lonely and painful to be always misunderstood, but there is at least from this point of view a measure of safety in isolation', as Laing puts it. In her 'terrible autonomy', Sylvia Plath retreated from 'relationship and community'—from all hope of normal (manic-depressive) satisfactions (which are indulged in by 'tame-flower-nibblers')—to battle with the 'presences' of her encapsulated schizoid-paranoid exile. (The words quoted are from Laing.) She gives way to 'giving herself up to the joys of hatred', culminating in *Daddy*, a suicidal attack on her own false-self male structure.

We can see the enormous destructive energy behind this hate in poems in which she reveals feelings which belong to the infant's primitive feeling of envy—of wanting to 'empty' the other, out of fear that the other may empty her. In an early poem, *The Shrike*, Sylvia Plath's protagonist envies her husband's dreams while she lies awake, confined to her own thoughts:

> Shaking in her skull's cage . . .

In her hunger she becomes a bird of prey that thirsts to empty him:

> So hungered, she must wait in rage
> Until bird-racketing dawn
> When her shrike face
> Leans to peck open those locked lids, to eat
> Crowns, palace, all

That nightlong stole her mate,
And with red beak
Spike and suck out
Last blood-drop of that truant heart.
(*Shrike*, in poems submitted for the
English Tripos Examination,
Cambridge, p. 7.)

So close is her identification that his desertion into realms of fancy
is felt to be a dangerous deprivation. In order to forestall the
other's independence she seeks to empty his mind voraciously,
even to take his blood into herself. This is both frightening, but yet
exciting. That is, her envy is directed at trying to steal the capacity
to see a meaningful world. In despair of this, the fury is turned on
herself.

The Shrike is not a very interesting poem, but it gives us clues
to the origins of many of her later images. *Lady Lazarus*, for instance, expresses the same intense envy and hatred, and urge to
consume the insides out of others:

Out of the ash
I rise with my red hair
And I eat men like air.

The (mother) earth of the Second Voice in *Three Women* is a
vampire: 'Men have used her meanly. She will eat them. Eat them,
eat them, eat them in the end'. In *Death & Co.* she sees the same
shrike reflected in an aspect of death, who seems as if he intends to
do to her what she has often wanted to do to others in envy:

I am red meat. His beak
Claps sideways: I am not his yet.

This beak is surely yet another 'mouth', and it, too, is within her.
Death is (in one of his aspects) the mouth-ego—'All mouth', who

licks up the bushes
And the pots of meat.
(*Poem for a Birthday*)

Death, who eats us all, echoes also the hungry regressed libidinal
ego directed against it. The dreadful hunger she sees everywhere

round her is in her—conflicting voraciousnesses of her inner world.

Death & Co. (*Ariel*, p. 38) is one of Sylvia Plath's most macabre poems. It may have reference to an actual occasion, in which some American visitors upset Sylvia Plath by talking about how babies look in the morgue. But what this occasion set off in the poet is a deeply disturbed fantasy of a multiple and deathly animus (the visitors being, significantly, a homosexual writer and his companion). In order to understand it, as arising from this inward fantasy rather than any outward incident, we need to allow ourselves to go mad, and to make a mad response to a mad poem. If we do, we shall see a 'double exposure' such as Masud Khan reports, in his response to a schizoid woman patient (see above p. 42 note).

The two figures of the poem then become not only symbols of two aspects of death, but also two aspects of an identity built on death. Both Death 1 and Death 2 are 'in' Sylvia Plath herself. Death 1 seems female. He concentrates on how the children would look in their cot—but it isn't a cot—it is a hospital ice-box. So, Death 1 is an anti-mother. He does not reflect, but 'tells me how badly I photograph'. He never looks up, and his eyes are 'lidded and balled'—like Blake's deathmask. That is, his eyes are like the eyes of the Colossus, 'bald tumuli', or those of the moon who is 'bald and wild'. He shows birthmarks—scars which do not speak of his giving birth, but of the wounds given in birth, the scars of scalding, the poisonous effects of predatory hate. The lines here become hallucinatory:

> The nude
> Verdigris of the condor.

The fantasy which was aroused by the 'boy-friend' homosexual visitor who is male but who plays the part of female is that of a predatory animus, whose malice and envy are directed at creativity, and her babies. He, the castrating man-mother, has a beak, and she is 'red meat'—a body, alive but not feeling alive, which is but carrion for Death. He is simply wiping his beak, clapping it menacingly: 'I am not his yet'. What she finds echoed is the 'savage god' which lures her towards suicide and infanticide. He says the babies would look 'sweet' dead: he 'does not smile or smoke'. He offers no encounter except a predatory one; no love, but hate. And his menacing hate is fantasied as a cruel and consuming oral symbol—a bloody beak. His is the envious beak of the shrike: her envy.

This beaked fantasy figure is a key phantom, in the work of both Sylvia Plath and her husband. The 'condor' here is echoed in 'Krogon', in *Orghast*, who, in turn, is a version of Crow. (See also the drawings by Baskin in the limited edition of *Crow*.) The beaked figure is actually drawn for us by Ted Hughes, in a sketch of the physiology of Orghast in *Orghast in Persepolis*: of this figure A. C. H. Smith says:

> The "birdlike" figure of Krogon is kin to Crow (and Chronos), the terrifying creation in his book of the same name published and broadcast in 1970, which itself stemmed from the 'sleek, attent thrushes' in his earliest work, and was largely set in 'the early world'. The female principle of Moa haunts his writing. That the father of the new baby feels threatened and, instead of acting as the intermediary of light, may seek to dispossess the sun, imprison the son, is the dark side of the stories and poems he has written for children . . . the sequence in which a man (Krogon, he became, not Agoluz) 'kills his wife and children thinking they are evil birds', he adapted from a tale which, although Japanese, he sees as 'central to the whole Christian-Manichean area': it had already occurred in *Crow*.
>
> (*Orghast in Persepolis*, pp. 97–8)

At the same place, Smith quotes Hughes again as saying, 'the interior mythology of the play is of a piece with my early writing', and 'at the level of generalisation, on which this myth works, the writings of most poets are one system and the same'. It is certain, then, that these fantasy figures are common to those poets whom he said, 'wrote poetry as if from the same brain'. The beaked predator in *Crow*, in the story referred to above, in the poem *Crow's Account of St George*, *is* the protagonist's wife and children:

> A bell-ball of hair, with crab-legs, eyeless,
> Jabs its pincers into his face,
> Its belly opens—a horrible oven of fangs.

When the scientist attacks it, '. . . his wife and children lie in their blood' (*Crow*, p. 31).

This paranoid-schizoid fantasy, then, is both the envy which threatens the female element (Moa) and the creativity of the womb: but also the threat which comes from one's own creativity itself, the threat offered by love (see *Lovesong*, in *Crow*). To be strong, one must direct one's attack at this source of attack, in order to anticipate its menaces:

> Through slits of iron, his eyes have found the helm
> of the enemy, the grail,
> The womb-wall of the dream that crouches there,
> greedier than a foetus,
> Sucking at the root-blood of the origins, the salt-milk
> drag of the mothers.
>
> (*Gog, Wodwo*, p. 152)

Again, as here, normal creative existence is despised in favour of the 'armouring' of the 'iron horseman'. In these symbols we have a mythology that may, of course, be found in myth and fairy-tales. But also in the work of Sylvia Plath and Ted Hughes, there is this common symbolism of a menacing beak-like figure, associated with the female element, and threatening from the heart of encounter and creativity: indeed, there is a sense in which this is what *Orghast* is all about: the terrible fact that the father can be an enemy to his child, while *Gog* and *Crow* are heavy with guilt that a father can be an enemy to the creative femaleness of the mother, and must assault it. No wonder the beaked predatory figure, with male genitals, appears in the drawing by Baskin on the jacket of *Crow*!

This is one aspect of Death in *Death and Co.*, and is one nihilistic aspect of Sylvia Plath's personality. The other, Death 2, seems more relaxed. He smiles and smokes. But he, too, is pseudo-female: his hair is long and 'plausive'.* He is a 'bastard'—

---

* The word is not in the modern dictionary. But it occurs in *Hamlet*, in a most significant passage. The ubiquitous presence of the father's ghost generates a feeling of *Hamlet* in Sylvia Plath. I believe the following lines lay in the background of her memory behind her anguished musings on the predicament of being threatened with the breakdown of reason:
> So, oft it chances in particular men,
> That, for some vicious mole of nature in them,

that is, he is a mock-up, not a real element of the identity. 'He wants to be loved'—a recognition of the schizoid need, deep down, to love and be loved. He is 'Masturbating a glitter'. This is perhaps the most perplexing phrase in all Sylvia Plath's poetry— but the one, I believe, that takes us most deeply into her problem. Just as Death 1 is non-reflecting in many of his/her aspects, Death 2 is, at least, making an effort. But the effort is solipsistic, yet an attempt to establish creative reflection by male means.

The word 'glitter' recurs in Sylvia Plath, and is often used of the shiny black shoe in which she tries to see her reflection. This glitter is the 'spark' that reassures that one is alive ('the dew makes a star'; 'they've blown my sparkler out'). But the word has another more astonishing symbolism: the glitter as I have suggested relates to eyes, and eyes to mirrors. The image is that of a pool of semen in which she cannot find herself reflected, because she cannot hope to find herself reflected by the mother. The logic of infantile thinking here is simple: if I cannot get a sense of my substantiality from the mother's breast, how can I get it from the father's penis? But, alas, the father is dead. The clue to this symbolism is in *Gigolo* (*Winter Trees*, p. 14), a poem about a sexual athlete. In this the protagonist will 'mill a litter of breasts like jellyfish', and has a way of 'turning Bitches to ripples of silver . . .'—by giving them orgasms. But the end is significant:

I
Glitter like Fontainebleau
Gratified,

As, in their birth—wherein they are not guilty,
Since nature cannot choose his origin,—
By the o'ergrowth of some complexion,
Oft breaking down the pales and forts of reason;
Or by some habit, that too much o'er-leavens
The form of plausive manners;—that these men—
Carrying, I say, the stamp of one defect,
Being nature's livery, or fortune's star,—
His virtues else—be they as pure as grace,
As infinite as man may undergo—
Shall in the general censure take corruption
From that particular fault; the dram of evil
Doth all the noble substance often doubt
To his own scandal . . .

I, iv. 23–38

All the fall of water an eye
Over whose pool I tenderly
Lean and see me.

At this point I feel it will be useful to invoke an astonishing case-history, and its equally astonishing interpretation, both of which illuminate Sylvia Plath's problem in a bizarre and disturbing way. This is the phenomenological interpretation of the case of one 'Rudolph' by Roland Kuhn, in May (1958). Rudolph was a butcher's boy in Zurich who shot at a prostitute in 1939. A phenomenological investigation suggests that Rudolph shot the prostitute because he wanted to get into the 'other world' where his dead mother was.

The only relevance to the poetry of Sylvia Plath is the phenomenological interpretation of certain of 'Rudolph's' obsessions which provide a clue to her phrase 'masturbating a glitter' in relation to death:

> He [Rudolph] masturbated a great deal, partly applying perverse procedures such as the use of coins, ladies silk stockings, silk handkerchiefs, and parts of animal intestines . . . for years he kept hidden a box filled with buttons, splinters of glass, and pieces of cloth. He said that from early childhood he had searched for such objects, and, whenever he found one, would seize upon it, enjoy it hugely, and cherish it like a treasure. He also derived a great pleasure from glittering coins. In early years he had masturbated with the help of buttons and coins and he had carried small change in his mouth. This fancy could be traced to the time after his mother's death when he searched the entire house and occasionally from the window saw something glitter out in the fields. He would then go out and comb the fields for the object . . . (p. 384)

These objects symbolised for him reflecting eyes *which he had seen closed in death as an infant.* When his father died, Rudolph went to see his body, and then he behaved quite crazily: 'Again and again he opened and closed his father's eyes' (p. 373). When he was about three and a half his mother died in childbirth. Rudolph followed the bloodstains to her body and climbed up on a chair to the corpse. He knelt on it and touched the face with his hands, saying, 'You aren't dead, Mother, are you? Mary says you are . . . You are asleep, aren't you?' Rudolph's mother died just before Carnival time and her funeral was mingled with riotous fun-making. Later Rudolph stole money and bought fireworks—and made himself conspicuous by letting too many off. As soon as he had been found out, he came home, masturbated in the lavatory and threw his fireworks out into the manure pit.

So, Sylvia Plath's 'glitter' can be related to death. Because Rudolph had suicidal fantasies we can also relate it to suicide. The gleam of eyes responding to one may be associated with the aura of relationship and the 'path of love'. If existential meaning is lost the 'light goes out of the world'. The 'sparkler' goes out. Rudolph was on one occasion cured of a suicidal plan by seeing the Virgin and child: 'The image of the Virgin and child had shown a strange shimmer and looked as though it were alive . . . This took place on the anniversary of his mother's death'* (p. 386).

Masturbation is an act in which the child exerts a manic sense of aliveness, and in some ways connects himself, by projection and fantasy, with the parental sexual acts, and so with vitality. Masturbating with glittering objects may have been a way of feeling alive by 'bringing the mother's eyes alive', just as the sparkling fireworks would invoke the manic carnival that occurred at the time of his mother's death (when caught out with them he threw them away and masturbated). Rudolph was saved from suicide by seeming to see the Mother of Christ shimmer, on the anniversary of his mother's death. As Kuhn says:

> a church picture of the Virgin Mary came to life for him as her eyes assumed an extraordinary lustre. The kind of smile which the picture showed must have been related to the smile so strikingly characteristic of Rudolph himself— which, we may assume, is likewise linked with his mother's facial expression.
>
> (p. 423)

In this case-history we find phenomenological clues in the sphere of what Kuhn calls 'somatic experience': a disturbed relationship

* Cf.　　The face of the effigy, gentled by candles,
　　　　Bending, on me in particular, its mild eyes.
　　　　　　The Moon and the Yew Tree

to one's own body. That Sylvia Plath had some kind of schizoid disturbance of relationship to her own body is I hope evident from my comments above.

One of the central symbols in Sylvia Plath's poetry is the shiny black shoe, and Rudolph's case casts light on this too. He was a shoe-and-stocking fetishist, as well as being attached to glittering objects. Sylvia Plath combines both fascinations in her black shoe: *Daddy* is the 'black shoe in which I have lived'. Rudolph shot at the prostitute because when he saw her naked her genital seemed the door to the other world of death. When he 'felt sexual sensations . . . he looked upon his glossy shoes and touched them fondly' (p. 389). Rudolph, Kuhn believes, actually expressed love for his mother through this fetish 'and felt hampered in the realisation of her image by the fetish-carriers. Killing, then, would mean not only removing the annoying object from this world but also, by turning it into a corpse, making it similar to the original beloved image who is also dead' (p. 390) So, in *Death & Co.*, there is a powerful ambiguity. Sylvia Plath is full of fear of death, but is also in love with death: there is an admixture of necrophilia and necrophobia. There is a powerful undercurrent or sex-as-eating—annihilation ('His beak/Claps sidewise: I am not his yet': Cf. 'A fruit that's death to taste'). There is a mixture of dismay and resignation to the logic of her delusions: 'Somebody's done for . . .' An identity has been annihilated (by 'doing') so that it is a state of 'life but not feeling alive': and some *body* has been 'done for', that is, is to be made into a corpse. A glitter hovers over the children, in Death 1's image of them, in an 'icebox'. But they are also stone, with a simple 'frill at the neck' and 'flutings' to their gowns.

Here, as Kuhn says, 'It is the realisation of those dream-and-fantasy contents which is feared' (p. 423). That is, *Death & Co.* is stark with horror at the impending possibility that her dreams and fantasies would come true. Yet, if we follow Kuhn's phenomenological analysis, which becomes very complex at this point, we can see such poems as *a kind of mourning*. Rudolph's desperation arose out of a need to mourn, retaining both the body and being of his dead mother in his mind. Sylvia Plath shows the same desperation, in trying to complete her mourning for 'Daddy'. To her blank experience of the mother is added a terrible feeling that she did not mourn enough for her husband: so, she feels cut off from both. Rudolph searched for 'the lost and forgotten in the periphery of the body, namely in the lustre of eyes and garments'. Sylvia Plath does the same, in her obsession with glittering objects, which might offer a new vitality—but might also lure her to death. At the moment when he saw the 'glitter' in the Virgin Mary's face and it resembled his mother's smile, Rudolph found being and body fused into a unit again 'and the path toward love was open to him'. He was released from the impulse towards suicide which had impelled his crime. Sylvia Plath, by contrast, unable to bring together the two aspects of her lost one, represented by the two aspects of Death, could not find this path—and so she took the desperate paths of hate. Kuhn also links *forgetting* and *killing*—a conjunction which is evident in *Daddy*, in which her attempt to forget ['bury'] 'Daddy' are indivisible from attempts to destroy him. From this point of view her anguish and suicide were the consequence of an inability to complete the process of mourning. Kuhn quotes Rilke: 'Killing is one of the forms of our wandering mourning . . .'. Trying to unite the disparate elements of her identity, all she can find in herself is two death-male-elements, neither man with a female component, nor female with a male component. (And this apparently makes her ideal for Women's Liberation!) Nothing could be more terrible. The situation presents a logic from which there is no escape but the perfection of becoming 'theirs'. In *Death & Co.*, she proclaims ' I am not his yet' to one and 'I do not stir' to the other. She stands between them in dreadful stasis. She hopes that 'The frost makes a flower'—and it does, but only on the cold windowpane: outside it kills the flower. 'The dew makes a star'—only insofar as it reflects a star, or the sun's light. Behind these images is a tender, naive hopefulness—the hopefulness of being reborn, and finding meaning. But 'a glittering button is not a being' as Kuhn says. We may compare the images in *Death & Co.*, with the delicate image in Ted Hughes's *Full Moon and Little Frieda*, in which, in the eyes of the child, the surface of water in a bucket 'tempts a first star to a tremor'. In that poem perception is creatively intentional. In *Death & Co.*, a dull tocsin takes over: 'The dead bell', and the poem ends with an ironic resignation. After this poem it was not long before she became 'theirs'. At the end of the poem we have a feeling as of the presence of a corpse: 'Somebody's done for': the final 'doing'.

The word 'do' links the 'somebody's done for' with the 'you will not do' of *Daddy*: both poems belong to a final desperate realisation that the false male identity based on the dead father is no good. So, she turns her hate on her own animus. As we have seen, Fairbairn found a tendency in the schizoid to 'maintain the inner world as a closed system' and to 'keep his aggression localised within the confines of the inner world', often displaying intense joy in this terrible indulgence, as was the case with 'Ivy'. Sylvia Plath's withdrawal into this closed system of aggression culminates in *Daddy* (*Ariel*, p. 54). The structure and rhythm of the verse is that of a child's insolent rhyme.

> I was ten when they buried you.
> At twenty I tried to die
> And get back, back, back to you.
> I thought even the bones would do.
>
> But they pulled me out of the sack,
> And they stuck me together with glue.
> And then I knew what to do.
> I made a model of you,
> A man in black with the Meinkampf look
>
> And a love of the rack and the screw.

We may compare the lilt, and the oral sadism, with children's sadistic abuse-rhymes:

> I didn't see anyone
> As ugly as you . . .
> Your feet stink
> And so do you . . .
> A bird came near
> And pooed on you . . .
> One look at you
> And I think I'll spew . . .
> With a face like that
> You belong to the zoo.

The regression to childhood anger is symptomatic. In one sense she is 'blaming' Daddy for dying, when she was eight.* So, she speaks in the voice of a small girl, who wants to 'marry Daddy'. Insofar as she is married to a man (who is Daddy to her children), whom she feels has failed her too, he seems like Daddy who died too soon. But the poem's Daddy is within the false self structure on which her hate is now turned.

The poem is a love-hate poem which seeks with great excitement to castrate the stolen male penis which is her last insecure communication with the buried father in the world of death: 'The black telephone's off at the root'. Consequently there are dreadful fears of talion vengeance, which the frenzy of hate is an attempt to hold off. Moreover we need to bear in mind the displacement of the hatred of the mother. 'Daddy' is partly composed of the mother's male-element-doing, the penis which has been castrated and stolen is partly the *mother's*, and for this an even more terrible vengeance is feared. To hold off this fear, she has 'identified with the aggressor', and this yields a false strength. On schizoid guilt, R. D. Laing (1960) has this to say:

> The final seal on the self-enclosure of the self is applied by its own guilt. In the schizoid individual guilt has the same paradoxical quality about it that was encountered in his omnipotence and impotence, his freedom and his slavery, his self being anyone in fantasy and nothing in reality . . . *If there is anything the schizoid individual is likely to believe in, it is his own destructiveness.* He is unable to believe that he can fill his own emptiness without reducing what is there to nothing. (p. 98, my italics)

This is what *Daddy* is about. The poet is hopeless about ever solving her paradoxes. She must reduce everything to nothing. Yet she is still in love with Daddy, and wants to hold on to him, to complete her mourning, even though she resents this.

What such a person may then do, says Laing, is to 'destroy "in his mind" the image of anyone or anything he may be in danger of being fond of, out of a desire to safeguard that person or thing in reality from being destroyed' (ibid., p. 99). She is trying to destroy Daddy in her mind, to protect him. If there were nothing to want, nothing to envy, nothing to love, says Laing, there would

---

* Or seven ('I was seven'—see above p. 161); or nine, whatever the actual number of years: the figure varies, in various fantasies.

be nothing to reduce to nothing. The logic is strange: but it belongs to a 'strategy of survival'. The morality is powerful, if deluded, and the object is to save being, by dissolution: 'In the last resort, he sets about murdering his "self"— . . . he descends into a vortex of non-being, but also to preserve being from himself.'

In *Daddy* she tries to reject Daddy's black shoe, the symbolism of which we have seen, as an adequate basis for herself:

> You do not do, you do not do
> Any more, black shoe
> In which I have lived like a foot
> For thirty years, poor and white,
> Barely daring to breathe or Achoo.
>
> Daddy I have had to kill you.

In *The Bell Jar* and *Poem for a Birthday*, being revived from suicide is resented. Once again she is forced to undergo ramshackle conformity of the false self. This pseudo-male structure is made up, as we have seen, of impingement, of hate, of doing, and 'bad inner contents'. The 'black telephone' which is 'cut off at the root' and stolen from Daddy is (in Kleinian terms) in the infantile primitive mind not only his penis, but also something which belongs to the inner stuff of the lower body: what has been stolen is also a lump of excreta.*

The rhymes from childhood on which *Daddy* is based are full of such impulses to expel bad stuff at others—'poo' being the implicit rhyming word. Here there are startling parallels with Susan, Marion Milner's schizoid patient in *In The Hands of the Living God*. In her fantasies the 'walking stick' faecal mass she did in her pot merges with the father's penis she had taken into herself. Marion Milner says in a note on pp. 50-1, 'in part of her mind, people were equated with faeces, so that to let them go is at one and the same time both a loving and hating act—a kind of murder, since it is only when they are inside that they are felt to be alive—but also a loving act since only by being let go can they be allowed a free separate existence'. 'Do', 'worm through', 'root' and the 'poo' rhyme all seem to indicate this faecal undercurrent

---

* Above, the black telephones in *The Munich Mannequins* were 'digesting' voicelessness.

to the symbolism in *Daddy*: Sylvia Plath is rejecting the 'bad inner contents' basis of her identity, by excreting Daddy, in an act which, as we have seen, is both loving (to preserve him) and hating.

The sensual intensity of her relationship with the dead father's penis is evident too. The words 'screw . . . I do, I do . . . the black telephone . . . at the root . . . worm through' all suggest genital body-movements and feelings, of a primitive kind.

By this coition with the father, she, a patched-up identity, identifies with the model she puts together of him, which is sadistic, and based on hate:

> And I said I do, I do.
> So daddy, I'm finally through.
> The black telephone's off at the root,
> The voices just can't worm through.

She sees this relationship as a kind of marriage forced on her ('I do'). She has married her father, bridegroom, in the winter of his year: a fruit that was death to taste. 'Finally through', however, is ambiguous. It means 'I have finished with this false-self conformity to your model which they have forced on me'. But it also means 'I have at last got through to you, into the realm of death and I find that your death was terminal'. So, the voices can't *worm* through. In the light of her phrase 'eelish delvings' and other images it can also mean 'at last I have passed you—stool—out of my body and have finished with you as bad inner contents'. In a sense this is a desperate end to mourning: but it is also the end, in that she has nothing left to base her identity on.

There is an implicit reference to her psychiatric treatment so that, as elsewhere, she implies that ECT was like being raped by a sadistic father. By what the therapists call transference she projected her feelings for her father over the doctor who *did* to her in that way.

But, she declares, Daddy was always cruel, even when he made her fall in love with him and more so when he seduced her into the grave. But 'being done to', though it had the aim of rescuing her from such suicide attempts to get into the 'other' world where Daddy is, has the effect of making her feel hopeless, merely, about anything Daddy could do for her. When she says 'You do not do', she means she has come to feel that she can sustain herself by his male doing no longer. The struggle to build a self by identifying with the dead father who was kind and tender to her cannot be sustained, since Herr Doktor (the father-figures in hospital whom she trusted) has betrayed her and subjected her to hate. ECT has taught her that Lucifer is only driven out by a devil-woman, hate is necessary to exert against hate, and so the only path to salvation is through the ultimate self-hate which is Death. 'Punishment' has thus reinforced the hatred in her, already directed against the need to love, so that her quest for love seems the most harmful thing of all, and it becomes more admirable to 'identify with the aggressor'.

We have seen how the poet 'would like to believe in tenderness': *The Moon and the Yew Tree* (*Ariel*, p. 47). But she has never seen the female face, 'Bending, on me in particular, its mild eyes'. So, she never found a 'significant exchange' and 'self enrichment' alternating with the 'discovery of meaning in the world of seen things'. Her mirrors and seas and people do not confirm her: even psychiatric care tends to say to her 'I will give you an identity— take that!'

So she was driven to the ultimate renunciation of all relationship in *Daddy*. The recklessness of her hopeless and final abandonment to hate is manifest in the rhythm of *Daddy*, something between children's ritual rhymes and *My Heart Belongs to Daddy*. Here we may compare the 'bride' theme expressed by Laing's patient Julie who talks of her fear of being 'married' to another who would then invade or supplant her. But if Daddy is rejected, what is left? For these reasons the poem can be no more than a defiant antic, and makes no real gain in the direction of genuine independence. It is merely a false denial of dependence:

> If I've killed one man, I've killed two
> The vampire who said he was you
> And drank my blood for a year,
> Seven years, if you want to know.
> Daddy, you can lie back now.

The exorcism, however, is mere manic denial: the insights are too glib ('the vampire who said he was you'). The magic belongs to infantile omnipotence and magic, like a child driving nails into a doll in primitive hate ritual:

> There's a stake in your fat black heart
> And the villagers never liked you.
> They are dancing and stamping on you.
> They always *knew* it was you.
> Daddy, daddy, you bastard, I'm through.

Although she seems to be declaring her independence, the energy of her hate is but a tribute to her need to go on hating. Andrew Brink (1968), using the Jungian term, points out that this attack on the male element moves towards negation with damaging power in *Daddy*:

> ... her fullest rejection of the terrible animus force within, which only tightens its grip with each succeeding description. As Jung has pointed out, the dogmatic, argumentative and domineering animus can rise to dominate the psyche as a whole, even cripple its integrating and restoring functions, and that is what happens here ... All natural circulation and reinforcement of creative feeling stops and that leaves only one avenue of escape, into oblivion. (p. 53)

In Sylvia Plath her false maleness, the animus on which she had to base her identity, comes into conflict with the obvious fact (which she knew from her body) that she was a woman.

Inside herself, Sylvia Plath finds an aggressive male projectile: 'white Nike' (*Small Hours, Crossing the Water*, p. 46). As we see when she identifies with the Gigolo, she sometimes displays an aggressive attitiude towards other women, and a castrating, devouring attitude towards men. In either case, the driving force is the need to be 'found', defended against by the displaced hostility to the mother and the rage directed against her spurious male identity.

In *Gigolo* (*Winter Trees*, p. 14), she derides normal confirmation in the family. The gigolo wants to have his sex in total solipsism.

> A palace of velvet
> With windows of mirrors.
> There one is safe,
> There are no family photographs,
> No rings through the nose ...

One can see how Sylvia Plath appeals to the women's liberators—
since she presents the claims of the family as a humiliation, as
'rings through the nose'.

> Bright fish hooks, the smiles of women
> Gulp at my bulk . . .

The women's smiles are bright fish-hooks which mouth (like fish)
at his big sexual parts, elsewhere described as 'my engine'.

At a National Poetry Festival Germaine Greer claimed that
Sylvia Plath was the most 'arrogantly feminine' poetess who ever
wrote. A phenomenological analysis suggests that, while knowing
well outwardly that she was a woman,* Sylvia Plath could scarcely
find within herself anything that was feminine at all. She is,
perhaps, the most masculine poetess who ever wrote, yet, since
masculinity requires the inclusion of the anima, she is not that
either: she is sadly pseudo-male, like many of her cultists.

In one of the bee poems (*Stings*) she says, 'I have a self to
recover': and yet she fears that this 'queen bee', when found, will
be malignant, as we shall see. Not knowing her femininity, and
not having had a father on whom to exercise it during adolescence,
Sylvia Plath was unconsciously terrified of how her female
element, if rediscovered, might behave. The problem is similar to
that of bringing the dead father to life: if one brings him back,
may he not be malevolent? It is similar to the problem explored
by those who have lost their mothers, and seek to recover them
from the other world of Death—like C. S. Lewis and George
Macdonald. D. W. Winnicott tells us that infants have terrible
fears of a ruthless mother imago: this fantasy mother is much more
terrible than any human being would ever be—she threatens to
'get out of hand'. The child, as it continues to experience the real
mother, 'humanizes' this imago, and is reassured of the limits of
human evil. But, from time to time, this ruthless female figure
turns up, in myth and legend, and in our dreams.

Sylvia Plath, as we have seen, had to build her sense of
femaleness, as far as she could, round whatever she could
take in of 'being' from the father. But since Daddy is dead,
to recover this female element might be to recover a malignant
predator:

* 'I am a woman. I love my little lares and penates', she said, in an interview.

> . . .
> Where has she been,
> With her lion-red body, her wings of glass?
>
> Now she is flying
> More terrible than she ever was, red
> Scar in the sky, red comet . . .
>
> *(Stings, Ariel,* p. 65)

In *Purdah* (*Winter Trees*, p. 17), the protagonist threatens to unloose on 'him',

> From the small jewelled
> Doll he guards like a heart—
>
> The lionness,
> The shriek in the bath,
> The cloak of holes.

The reader who takes Sylvia Plath's position to be one of opposition to conventional marriage will see this as a threat to destroy a husband who has made his wife into a doll. But it is rather the expression of the secret of the schizoid woman, who has within her an impulse to annihilate the male—the animus which becomes malevolent because it cannot find itself 'female-element-being' quality. In *Widow* (*Crossing the Water*, p. 38), she writes:

> The moth-face of her husband, moonwhite and ill,
> Circles her like a prey she'd love to kill . . .

In such images we glimpse the underlying hatred which the hostile dynamic in Sylvia Plath directs at the animus. So, too, in *The Courage of Shutting Up* (*Winter Trees*, p. 20) there is an undercurrent of rage at 'Bastardies, usages, desertions and doubleness'. In this poem the male element Colossus-Daddy figure is engaged in pricking over the images of sexuality, which are 'blue grievances':

> A great surgeon, now a tattooist,
>
> Tattooing over and over the same blue grievances,
> The snakes, the babies, the tits
> On mermaids and two-legged dream girls.
> The surgeon is quiet, he does not speak.
> He has seen too much death, his hands are full of it.

So, in Sylvia Plath's inner world there are two figures—the malevolent animus and the negative anima, at their deathly work: in fact Death & Co.

The 'I' that may be recovered in the name of femininity rises with hair of flame and threatens to 'eat men like air'. She is a kind of flying vagina ('red scar') which has male characteristics ('lion-red body'). This body-mouth is hungry, and it lies under the surface in *Poppies in July* (*Ariel*, p. 82):

> A mouth just bloodied
> Little bloody skirts.

In *Berck-Plage* and *Three Women*, Mother Earth has a red mouth, which is the grave—and her vagina. This predatory vagina also eats men, and bears a resemblance to the vagina in Ted Hughes's *Crow's First Lesson* (*Crow*, p. 16):

> And Crow retched again, before God could stop him.
> And woman's vulva dropped over man's neck and tightened.

This aggressive vagina belongs to the negative anima which is thrust before us continually in our culture today.

On the other hand, the animus exerts its negative force. In places, Sylvia Plath feels that she 'is' a penis. Therefore, she wants to use this penis, aggressively, on other women. Because of these sexual feelings, she is guilty, too, and this increases her resentment.

This aggression directed against femininity is clear in *The Applicant* (*Ariel*, p. 14), which is basically a poem about the schizoid uncertainty of being human at all. But when it comes to the genitals, all she finds is a scar, wound or gash. There aren't even stitches to show that something is missing (we are here in the perplexities of an infant girl over her own lack of a penis). So, 'How can we give you a thing?'—that is, how can we give you a penis, since you can't prove you've lost one? (see below, pp. 262ff). In *Leaving Early* (*Crossing the Water*, p. 33), she writes about a protagonist who is seemingly slipping away after a sexual encounter with a woman. It apparently arose from an incident in the flat above, the occupant of which Sylvia Plath disliked for her grubbiness. Here the imagery is full of sadistic sexuality. Seeing the geraniums, she says,

> The red geraniums I know.
> Friends, friends. They stink of armpits
> And the involved maladies of autumn,
> Musky as a lovebed the morning after.
> My nostrils prickle with nostalgia.
> Henna hags: cloth of your cloth.
> They toe old water thick as fog.

As in *Tulips*, the flowers remind her of bodily hunger, and here love seems an unpalatable, musty, bodily impulse (a toeing). She is disturbed by confusions of perception (old water thick as fog) and by an image of reflection: the milky berries in a pot

> Bow down, a local constellation
> Towards their admirers in the tabletop:
> Mobs of eyeballs looking up.

The woman has 'paired' these with 'ovals of silver tissue' (mirrors): behind the woman's flowers which disgust her (because they speak of love or 'friendship') lurks the castrating mother: she even has the father's dead toe.

The other woman is described in terms very similar to those used to describe the mother in *The Bell Jar*, as if the protagonist were itching to burst her and destroy her

> The roses in the Toby jug
> Gave up the ghost last night. High time.
> Their yellow corsets were ready to split,
> You snored, and I heard the petals unlatch,
> Tapping and tickling like nervous fingers.*

We may compare the horrifying moment in the novel, at which Esther wants to strangle her mother. The same impulse with its cästratory undertones lurks behind the images in *Leaving Early*

> ... Now I'm stared at
> By chrysanthemums the size
> Of Holofernes' head, dipped in the same
> Magenta as this fubsy sofa.

---

* Her rival is 'here', 'ticking your fingers on the marble table' in *The Rival*, *Ariel*, p. 53.

Behind this poem of dislike of a neighbour their lurks a hatred of parental sexuality (the primal scene). She uses the term 'make it', meaning, how did we get up to the attic? But under the surface lurks the ambiguity of the sexual use of the term.

> How did we make it up to your attic?
> You handed me gin in a glass bud vase.
> We slept like stones. Lady, what am I doing
> With a lung full of dust and a tongue of wood,
> Knee-deep in the cold and swamped by flowers?

The phrases, 'slept like stones', 'what am I doing' suggest sexual undercurrents, and 'Holofernes' suggests sadistic impulses turned against maleness. The physical sensations are those of a hangover: but yet of a wooden or stony encounter, full of threats ('cold', 'swamped'). And there are characteristically aggressive undertones in

> Lady, your room is *lousy* with flowers.
> When you *kick me out*, that's what I'll remember,
> Me, sitting here bored as a *leopard*
> In your *jungle* of wine-bottle lamps,
> Velvet pillows the colour of *blood pudding* . . .
>
> (my italics)

Often, Sylvia Plath writes as if she were a savage animal among the chintzes, so to speak, waiting to spring and devour, with 'tigery stripes', or a lioness. The association between this hatred of woman and her suicide is evident in the virulent poem *The Tour* (*Crossing the Water*, p. 61) directed against 'Auntie',

> It simply exploded one night,
> It went up in smoke.
> And that's why I have no hair, auntie, that's why I choke
>
> Off and on, as if I just had to retch.
> Coal gas is ghastly stuff.

Her fridge bites: her furnace explodes, her Morning Glory Pool boils, hurts and destroys people. In this bizarre landscape of home there is a 'bald nurse':

> She can bring the dead to life . . .

That is, here is a 'midwife', who is a female dehumanised figure, who can carry out a schizoid suicide, 'for a very small fee' (in *Lady Lazarus*, 'There is a charge'). This deranged poem reveals the impulse, behind her aggressiveness and her suicidal savagery, to 'pay out' Auntie, who is the mother, and who is to be made into a 'sorry mother'. It may be linked with the aggressiveness which is clear in *Lesbos* (*Winter Trees*, p. 34):

> Viciousness in the kitchen!
> The potatoes hiss.

No doubt the Women's Liberation fanatics see this, too, as a protest against the sordidness of what they call 'shit work'. However, it is difficult to know who is speaking, and how we are to respond to the protagonist. Some critics have suggested that Sylvia Plath is talking to an *alter ego*. But I believe we are to take the 'voices', as we do those of *The Waste Land*, or *Gerontion*, as representative fragmentary imagos of 'modern woman'. One of these says, 'my child' is an 'unstrung puppet',

> Why she is schizophrenic . . .
> . . .
> She'll cut her throat at ten if she's mad at two.

Lady Lazarus 'does it' every ten years: here the same mythology of periodic suicide is applied to this woman's child as a prognosis. The waspish woman in Sylvia Plath's poems is evidently here, with her tiger stripes and her hate. And there seems no doubt that she identifies to some degree with this woman. In the background here there seems to be a memory of a lesbian affair, associated with the appearance of a bloody moon. The lesbian moment was a valuable moment:

> O jewel! O valuable!

But memory of it is full of guilty images of the castrating, cold-male-doing, moon-mother:

> That night the moon
> Dragged its blood bag, sick
> Animal
> Up over the harbour lights.

And then grew normal,
Hard and apart and white.
The scale-sheen on the sand scared me to death.
We kept picking up handfuls, loving it,
Working it like dough, a mulatto body,
The silk grits.
A dog picked up your doggy husband. He went on.

The moon mother appears as a sick, bloody, animal, who later becomes hard, apart and white. The image is of woman's blood-bag body, which later becomes distant and male. 'She' becomes Lamia, rejoicing in the 'scale-sheen' of the sand against her hands and its fetishistic glittering quality.

But the encounter turns to hate:

Now I am silent, hate
Up to my neck,
Thick, thick.

. . .

O vase of acid,
It is love you are full of. You know who you hate.
He is hugging his ball and chain . . .

'She' has (presumably) gone back to her man.

That is that. That is that.
You peer from the door,
Sad hag. 'Every woman's a whore.
I can't communicate.'

As with the woman in *Leaving Early*, her contempt and scorn for the unfulfilled encounter focusses on the décor:

I see your cute décor
Close on you like the fist of a baby

. . .

I am still raw,
I say I may be back.
You know what lies are for.

Even in your Zen heaven we shan't meet . . .

Sylvia Plath is fascinated with the hate she finds in the lesbian

woman, and her combination of domestic hopefulness, rejection
of her own femininity, and the 'liberation' that has simply dehumanised her in the name of 'Zen'—leaving only 'viciousness in
the kitchen'. But she can give as much as she gets: so, they are
'two venomous opposites'. Such bitter encounters between
herself and women are yet another version of 'false male doing',
in lieu of being or *becoming*: a manifestation of the malignant
animus.

7
Mother and Children

On the other hand, there are poems in which Sylvia Plath fulfils her femininity, and justifies her assertion, 'I am a woman'. After all, she had children, and, as in *The Night Dances*, knew she could not but get satisfactions from them. When she had a baby, we are told, she hoped it would reinforce her identity—an enormous burden to place on the child. We may see the enormousness of this need in *Nick and the Candlestick* (*Ariel*, p. 40), a poem about her little boy, the second baby.

She is insomniac, and the night is nightmarish with malignancy. It is a womb in the earth, and she is digging down into it, as if into the mother's inside, which is also the tomb of death, where the father's penis is, the long-dead father, of whose resurrection she has now lost all hope.

> I am a miner. The light burns blue.

—the air is full of poison.

> Waxy stalactites
> Drip and thicken, tears
>
> The earthern womb
> Exudes from its dead boredom.

The womb is bored with containing this candle-phallus and the tears coming from it, standing for the potential love to be obtained from the father—the hope of reflection—yield nothing but boredom, because she has now become indifferent, as the hope of a new existence fades. The darkness in this cave of night seems predatory:

> Black bat airs
>
> Wrap me, raggy shawls,
> Cold homicides.
> They weld to me like plums.

In 'encounter', as Martin Buber says, the human being develops a 'mansion of consciousness' in which to exist: 'from man to man the heavenly bread of self-being is passed'. When this process fails, all that comes from the death of encounter, from the cave of psychic petrifaction, as here, is an emanation that wraps her in death: not in a shawl like a new-born baby, but in rags, while the air feels like a horrible death-skin, welded to her like the skin on a plum.

The old petrified cave is familiar to her, with its calcium icicles, or remnants of Daddy: in there the echoes are to be heard—the words galloping off like echoes from the centre, as in *Words*, in her poetic quest. But there is no life there—even the newts are white. They are 'holy Joes' because they have become bereft of all live qualities and colour, in their cavernous purity, all ambiguity forsaken for piety. But their whiteness (despite the reference to holiness) is the purity of hate: so, too, with the fish:

> And the fish, the fish——
> Christ! they are panes of ice,
>
> A vice of knives,
> A piranha
> Religion, drinking
>
> Its first communion out of my live toes.

Sylvia Plath retains, as we have seen, the strange logic of the infant in her psyche. Otto Plath died from an infection which started in his toe. This toe was also, by displacement, his penis, which she has internalised, and which was also (dead) inside the mother. In this cave of death (which is a night in which she is suffering some deep anguish) there is a bundle of dead penises, which are all that is left of the dead father. The child thinks of parental sex as a form of mutual eating, sometimes like aggressive envy, and so the penis inside the mother is predatory—not least because it is a dead penis. There is a central problem for the individual who seeks to resurrect a dead loved one. Since their mourning

has to do with guilt, this centres around the hatred they have felt
at times for the 'bad' side of the deceased. The whole problem of
grieving has to do with the problem of enabling this bad, black
side of the dead person to rest, and of coming to terms with the
'bad' feelings one has had for the person—because by the same
infant logic, one's hostility may have contributed to their death.
So, there is always a possibility that if one resurrects the dead
object, it may turn out to be hostile and malignant.

So, in this cave of death, the internalised penises of the father
may be malevolent—and, since they are also his gangrenous toes,
they may well start in, like piranha fish, on her toes. Their 'piety'
is that of total pure hate, and their religion that of knives, of taking
the inner contents out of others—so the first communion with the
dead father in there may be a vampire communion, of these fragments of dead male aggressiveness sucking her blood.

But, in the midst of this nightmare, there is a miracle:

> The candle
> Gulps and recovers it small altitude,
>
> Its yellows hearten.

So far in the poem we have been pursuing psychotic phantoms
which are in a sense projections of her own shrike-like hate. But
suddenly the atmosphere is transformed by love. She catches sight of
the baby. The candle flickers, and it is as if she 'gulps', and recovers
her sanity. The candle is not a vast phallic menace, but only a candle,
and its mollifying power can hearten her, just as elsewhere the
candles can light up the eyes of the Virgin and create in them something of the mother's soft reflecting power. The colours 'hearten':

> Its yellows hearten.
> O love, how did you get here?
> O embryo
>
> Remembering, even in sleep,
> Your crossed position.
> The blood blooms clean
>
> In you, ruby.
> The pain
> You wake to is not yours.

How did the baby get into that cave of ice and death? The 'cave' now is not the fantasy cave, but the home, struck with some icy catastrophe of object-loss. Of course, she had hoped to find a baby in there—herself unborn, the regressed libidinal ego, her embryo. This baby-self has been 'crossed' (a word which recurs in Dylan Thomas for the blocked embryonic self). But this baby is Nick: and yet he is also Christ (as is the unborn self in Dylan Thomas), who remembers his crossed position in the cave from which He was resurrected.

Nick is thus the focus of a hope of rebirth, and in him there is the promise of a new start. His blood is not liable to be emptied, as 'inner contents', by hate, but has the value of a 'ruby'. He does not have to wake to her pain ('This troublous/Wringing of hands, this dark/Ceiling without a star', *Child*, *Winter Trees*, p. 12). He is not her: so through him she knows out-going love, not based on desperate identification:

> Love, love
> I have hung our cave with roses,
> With soft rugs——

> The last of Victoriana.

As a modern woman, she feels that all that Victorian emphasis on the family, on good feeling, on love, is out-of-date: but nevertheless, she promises the last remnant to Nick: for his existence redeems her universe. The universe, she believes, is that of modern science—mere unintelligible matter in motion doomed by the laws of entropy: let it go:

> Let the stars
> Plummet to their dark address,

> Let the mercuric
> Atoms that cripple drip
> Into the terrible well,

Everything goes into nothingness: all matter has become malignant and poisonous in her world. What is there to set against the nothingness of a world in which she can find nothing but blankness, hate and poison? The answer is the *Dasein* of her baby's existence:

> You are the one
> Solid the spaces lean on, envious.
> You are the baby in the barn.

Nick is the new-born Christ: and as such is the pivot of the universe, since his existence as the focus of her love, gives meaning to life. In the first part of the poem we have the spectacle of a world wrecked because it is bereft of love-objects, so that no reparation can be made to them. Reparation is urgently necessary here, as it is the only way to overcome the problem of the guilt, bound up with mourning; the only way to let the dead father go (with all the biting elements of envy that focus on him) is to make reparation, to restore wholeness to him, and to make sure his ghost is not predatory. In *Daddy* of course she tries to drive a stake into his heart to lay him. But hate cannot achieve reparation: so, the internal womb or cave in which the dead Daddy has been persistently sought, until exasperation overcomes her, even in *Nick and the Candlestick* threatens to overwhelm her whole world. Except for where her baby sleeps—and from that focus of love it seems that the world can be redeemed. Or, at least it can be relinquished, and let go, because of this one 'solid'. But then, she sees, the 'spaces' are envious of this love: so, as with the new-born Christ, the future is still ominous.

The achievement of this poem may well have contributed to the most important gain in Sylvia Plath's whole life: her recognition of the separate existence of her children, so that she did not merge them into her own death, a possibility more than hinted at when she wrote *Edge*. The *Nick* poem is a triumph of love, pursued with great courage—and how unpalatable its meaning should be to the nihilistic avant-garde, for it demolishes all their fanatical immoralism.

Her ultimate agony between the two poles of acceptance and rejection of love can be imagined. In *For a Fatherless Son* (*Winter Trees*, p. 33), she shows she knows what it must be like for a child who is fatherless: 'You will be aware of an absence'—as she was. His sky is 'like a pig's backside', blank, showing 'an utter lack of attention'. Did she realise what it would be like, for her own children to be motherless?

> One day you may touch what's wrong
> The small skulls, the smashed blue hills, the godawful hush.

In orphaning her own children she risked depriving their world of meaning.

The new existentialism and psychoanalysis have established a connection between love, encounter, and the capacity to perceive. Sylvia Plath is poignantly aware that it is the failure of love that has left her world blank. In giving birth, she hoped in some way to complete the birth processes, such as are normally completed in infancy, in herself.

This hope pervades the long dramatic poem *Three Women* (*Winter Trees*, pp. 40–52). Although divided between voices, and between characters, this is essentially a poem about birth, as an experience of Sylvia Plath herself. For instance, the girl secretary declares

> As a child I loved a lichen-bitten name.
> Is this the one sin then, this old dead love of death?
>
> (p. 41)

—surely a reference to Sylvia Plath's libidinal attachment to her dead father, and her guilt at this?

In *Three Women*, it is as if she hoped that the experience of birth would, at last, produce a sympathetic response in the mother— softening her face, and thus offering the opportunity of creative reflection. This, in its turn, would open up the possibility of meaningful perception (or full apperception). So, it is a cosmic response to her birth she seeks—a change in the face of the moon, and in the earth itself: Mother Earth—

> She is the vampire of us all. So she supports us,
> Fattens us, is kind. Her mouth is red.
> I know her. I know her intimately—
> Old winter-face, old barren one, old time bomb.
> Men have used her meanly. She will eat them.
> Eat them, eat them, eat them in the end.
> The sun is down. I die. I make a death.
>
> (p. 45)

So, to give birth is to die, in that one is making a new life which is another life to die: the ambiguity in her mind between death and birth is clear here. She identifies with Mother Earth, who is but an ultimate form of predatory femaleness. The Earth is only like her, devoted to a love of death

... And now the world conceives
Its end and runs towards it, arms held out in love.
It is a love of death that sickens everything.

(p. 45)

In the connection she makes between feelings about death and
birth, and about the whole world we exist in, we can see how her
problems relate to those of human survival.

Three Women opens with a statement of the indifference of the
universe: here, the moon, who is elsewhere said to display an
'O-gape'. Woman here is *abandonée*:

Is she sorry for what will happen? I do not think so.
She is simply astonished at fertility.

(p. 40)

Sylvia Plath's universe (like that of Ted Hughes in *Crow*) is a
dead, passive and inert one—which, because of its sheer indifference, seems to be without benignity.

So, she is in conflict, between being obliged to see life and yet
seeing all processes as only leading towards death, as if by universal entropy. The 'red seep' of a 'show' which indicates to the
woman that she is pregnant reveals to her the life-process (which
is also a death process). By contrast, from this feminine body-
reality, she sees the men as 'flat':

There was something about them like cardboard,
    and now I had caught it,
That flat, flat, flatness from which ideas, destructions,
Bulldozers, guillotines, white chambers of shrieks proceed,
Endlessly proceed—and the cold angels, the abstractions.

(p. 40)

This is the world of 'male doing', our schizoid world. Her work
at the typewriter seems 'mechanical echoes' (and we cannot fail to
connect this with Sylvia Plath's view of her own poetry as 'Echoes
travelling off from the centre . . . dry . . . indefatigable . . .'). So,
the woman is 'found wanting', between her womanly creativity,
and the 'abstractions'.

... Am I a pulse
That wanes and wanes, facing the cold angel?

> Is this my lover then? This death, this death?
>
> (p. 41)

This (second) woman feels that her social function is a death: she is one-dimensional woman.

> I am dying as I sit. I lose a dimension.

The trains that roar in her ears are, like those in the schizoid fantasy of the bees in *Swarm*, the triumph of 'the world of outcomes'—making life meaningless:

> The silver track of time empties into the distance,
> The white sky empties of its promise, like a cup.
>
> (p. 41)

In the modern world, 'fertility' is an event by which (as with the first woman) the universe is merely astonished. Male doing is a mere 'pulse' among the deathliness of the triumphant world of the I-It. To the third woman conception is an imposition of life, which feels like suffering the attentions of the swan who raped Leda. She is forced to reflect the identity of another

> I remember the minute when I knew for sure.
> . . .
> The face in the pool was beautiful, but not mine
> . . .
> And all I could see was dangers: doves and words,
> Stars and showers of gold—conceptions, conceptions!
>
> (p. 41)

The 'showers of gold' are the rains of semen which fall on the girl in *The Beekeeper's Daughter*. They are full of talion dangers. But also they are the semen falling on Danae, transcendence. So, the submission to male impregnation is full of fear as well as blessing. In *Winter Trees* (the poem, p. 11), the doves are *pietas* which 'ease nothing'—presumably the 'dove descending', as a manifestation of the Holy Ghost, the Word. Instead in *Three Women*:

> I remember a white, cold wing
> And the great swan, with its terrible look
> Coming at me . . .
> There is a snake in swans.

> He glided by: his eye had a black meaning.
> I saw the world in it—small, mean and black . . .
>
> (pp. 41–2)

Here we have something not far away from the black snake, which 'worms through', the black telephone, the black shiny shoe in which she tried to see herself. That is, this third woman speaks of male doing, which is a black phallus, in which perhaps one may find creative reflection. But she was not ready: yet

> . . . the face
> Went on shaping itself with love, as if I was ready.

Here we have something like a face in a Francis Bacon painting, trying to be seen. Each woman finds the emergence of the new identity a terrible shock. To the second, the white sheets in the maternity hospital are 'bald and impossible, like the faces of my children' (p. 42). She speaks of 'the little emptinesses I carry', which are 'life' which has been 'stitched . . . into me like a rare organ'. This woman has tried to lapse into the realm of 'female element being':

> . . . I have tried to be natural.
> I have tried to be blind in love, like other women,
> Blind in my bed, with my own dear blind sweet one,
> Not looking, through the thick dark, for the face of another.
>
> (p. 42)

The word 'thick' here gives us a clue: 'through the thick, warm furry dark, a voice cried, 'Mother!' (*The Bell Jar*). This again is Sylvia Plath saying that, as she tried to respond to her baby, there is an intrusion of the need for 'the faces of the dead'—of Daddy, of the mother.

Even to the 'calm' first woman, in hospital 'The sheets, the faces, are white and stopped, like clocks' (p. 43). The clock face is a face which is blank, with 'hieroglyphs' and 'secrets' where there should be meaningful response. This woman is the woman of *Tulips*, depersonalized in hospital ('swabbed and lurid with disinfectants') and the good mother of *The Moon and the Yew Tree* (*Ariel*, p. 47):

> The moon is my mother. She is not sweet like Mary.

Her blue garments . . .

Dusk hoods me in blue now, like a Mary.
(*Winter Trees*, p. 43)

She awaits her 'cargo of agony' resignedly.
The third woman fears death: 'And what if two lives leaked between my thighs'? (p. 44). The first experiences the cruel miracle of birth.

There is no miracle more cruel than this.
I am dragged by the horses, the iron hooves . . .
. . .
Dark tunnel, through which hurtle the visitations . . .

Again, this is the dark tunnel of the suicide attempt in *The Bell Jar*.
But birth is the creation of agonies, rather than joys:

FIRST VOICE:
I am the centre of an atrocity.
What pains, what sorrows must I be mothering?

Can such innocence kill and kill? It milks my life.
The trees wither in the street.
(p. 44)

To be born is to be born with one's deadly faults in the psychic tissue. Inevitably the verse recalls *Elm* (*Ariel*, p. 26):

Its snaky acids hiss.
It petrifies the will. These are the isolate, slow faults
That kill, that kill, that kill.

The mother fills the infant with poisonous milk that destroys her: the child destroys the mother by the agony of birth and by emptying her of her milk. Out of this comes disintegration of the identity, and the nothingness of the world:

I am breaking apart like the world . . .
. . .
My eyes are squeezed by this blackness.
I see nothing.
(*Three Women*, p. 45)

Here, loss of inner content and depersonalised bodily feelings are linked with the feeling of being no-one: and 'who is he, this blue, furious boy . . .?'

> A red lotus opens in its bowl of blood;
> They are stitching me up with silk, as if I were a material.
>
> (p. 45)

But this first woman finds love in her response to her baby, while her perception becomes 'clear'.

> What did my fingers do before they held him?
> What did my heart do, with its love?
> I have never seen a thing so clear.
>
> (p. 46)

The second woman, by contrast, feels she is a creator of corpses. Of the moon's light she says

> I feel it enter me, cold, alien, like an instrument.
> And that mad, hard face at the end of it, that O-mouth
> Open in its gape of perpetual grieving.
> It is she that drags the blood-black sea around
> Month after month . . .
>
> (p. 46)

The moon-mother who created her femininity and who governs femininity by her 'string', as by governing the menstrual tides in women, has left her, because of its irresponsive blankness,

> . . . a shadow, neither man nor woman,
> Neither a woman, happy to be like a man, nor a man
> Blunt and flat enough to feel no lack. I feel a lack . . .
> . . .
> . . . I cannot contain my life.
>
> (p. 46)

The stars merely 'rivet' abysses in place: and here we have again a statement of Sylvia Plath's predicament. She cannot relate as a person to a real universe because she is neither a woman who is really a man and content to be that, nor a man who is content to be made of 'male doing'. She feels a lack of being and so she cannot hold on to life.

The third woman sees her girl infant as Sylvia Plath might see her potentially new-born female self:

> . . . my red, terrible girl.
> . . .
> Her cries are hooks . . .
> . . .
>   Her mouth . . .
> It utters such dark sounds it cannot be good.
>   (p. 47)

The first woman sees the babies in their ward as 'made of water'. They have no expression, but they are also 'these miraculous ones'. She, speaking of all Sylvia Plath's positive feelings about being a mother and woman, is satisfied to be 'a river of milk'. Winnicott speaks of how, after the intense preoccupation of the confinement, a woman 'recovers her self-interest'. That is what is happening here:

> The mirror gives back a woman without deformity.
> The nurses give back my clothes, and an identity.
> . . .
> . . . Here is my lipstick.
>
> I draw on the old mouth.
>
>   (p. 48)

She feels (as The Applicant might feel) that in giving birth she has in some way lost a limb: her body is lost inner contents. The third woman is 'like a wound walking out of hospital':

> . . . There is an emptiness.
> I am so vulnerable suddenly.
>   (p. 49)

She is a woman suffering the vulnerability of primary maternal preoccupation.

The second voice recovers and declares

> It is I. It is I
> Tasting the bitterness between my teeth.
> The incalculable malice of the everyday.
>   (p. 49)

The first feels exposed in this state, and protects herself with a 'screen of front-line troops' or a 'mask of horn':

> ... it is as if my heart
> Put on a face and walked into the world.
>
> (p. 50)

The third feels

> It was a dream, and did not mean a thing.
>
> (p. 50)

Sylvia Plath's poetic explorations of the special states experienced by women in childbirth are valuable and important for their insights. For instance, she shows here how the memory of birth dread is soon suppressed. But we must remember she is rendering an abnormal experience of this state. For one thing there is a serious deficiency of genuinely felt satisfactions in the poem, while to her everyday life is full of incalculable malice. To give birth is not felt to be an achievement, while play and body response to the infant bring few rewards. There is also much bewilderment. She surrounded Nick with pinned up roses, a gesture towards love. In *Three Women* one character says:

> I have papered his room with big roses,
> I have painted little hearts on everything.
>
> (p. 51)

—which is very different because she is evidently only going through the motions of love. 'Normality' is associated by Sylvia Plath with gestures which still seem to her meaningless, although one makes them. Each woman expresses schizoid feelings:

> Parts, bits, cogs, the shining multiples.
>
> (p. 41)
> The face in the pool was beautiful, but not mine
>
> (p. 41)
> ... I have tried and tried
> I have stitched life into me like a rare organ ...
> I have tried not to think too hard. I have tried to be natural.
>
> (p. 42)

Birth for Sylvia Plath was the focus of anxieties about the loss of inner contents, of love as emptying, of feeling a mechanical organism at the mercy of immense forces.

I am dragged by the horses, the iron hooves . . .*

(p. 44)

It leads only to the failure of reflection, and still more formlessness and meaninglessness in consequence.

She has unusual insights into the special state of the mother. But, in her awareness, these insights are so disturbed by her schizoid perspectives that what she largely conveys is a fear and hatred of female creativity. This is why women's liberationists applaud her, because what they want to be liberated from is being female and being human.

Even the first woman hears 'The swifts . . . shrieking like paper rockets' (p. 50)—her world is full of terrors, while her positive feelings are almost caricatured:

. . . I hear the moo of cows.
. . .
I am reassured. I am reassured.
These are the clear bright colours of the nursery,
The talking ducks, the happy lambs.
I am simple again.

(p. 51)

Like Heidegger, Sylvia Plath sometimes despises all that is ordinary, and here her caricature of the 'cow' kind of woman smacks of that 'schizoid superiority' which is exercised against those normal satisfactions of love the schizoid cannot understand, but really envies. Though one woman says

I shall meditate upon normality . . .

(p. 51)

it is as if she is going through the motions of love, without really knowing what it is.

* See Ted Hughes, *Gog*:
  The rider of iron, on the horse shod with vaginas of iron
  Gallops over the womb that makes no claim, that is of stone
  (*Wodwo*, p. 153)

I do not will him to be exceptional.
It is the exception that interests the devil.
It is the exception that climbs the sorrowful hill
Or sits in the desert and hurts his mother's heart.
I will him to be common,
To love me as I love him,
And to marry what he wants and where he will.

(p. 51)

This woman does not want her child to be Christ. The love child is equated with the common and unexceptional person: by contrast, the schizoid individual is superior, but suffers. Sylvia Plath seems not to be willing to admit that even the loved child is driven (because he too is human) to ask the existential questions—though he may ask them with less desperation.

The third woman is aware of a loss:

... What is it I miss?
Shall I ever find it, whatever it is?

(p. 51)

The swans have gone from her life: she is no longer Leda. Yet while Sylvia Plath seems to feel that domesticity is a loss, after the big dramas of birth, the whole poem ends on a surprising note of hopefulness and life, despite insecurity.

The streets may turn to paper suddenly, but I recover
From the long fall, and find myself in bed,
Safe on the mattress, hands braced, as for a fall.
I find myself again. I am no shadow
Though there is a shadow starting from my feet. I am a wife.
The city waits and aches. The little grasses
Crack through stone, and they are green with life.

(p. 52)

The image of the grass is the same symbol as that in *Das Lied von der Erde*: a symbol of continuity of life. She is not a shadow. The shadow has attached itself to her body and continues to speak of death, but also of her body-existence. She has recovered her self-interest, as each woman has, being to some extent confirmed by the existence of the child, the real experience of birth that filled their emptiness with substance, which then came forth to respond to them: and so teaches love, 'a tenderness that did not tire, something healing', she is aware of the primacy of love, even for one who sees other lovers 'Black and flat as shadows'—because she finds it so hard to understand this emotion.

Her babies aroused in Sylvia Plath deep feelings of love, but also puzzlements about the nature of created life and bafflements about how to respond. In *Morning Song (Ariel*, p. 11), the baby is like a watch 'set going' by love—love seeming a mechanical act, as in *The Applicant, Berck-plage* and elsewhere. Its 'bald cry' seems inhuman and it 'takes its place among the *elements*'. At the same time the baby feels human to her, and she calls it 'You' and teases it playfully as 'fat'. Of course, in a sense the poet is registering the normal response by which we all find a new baby primitive and, as yet, less than a person. She is recording the kind of (schizoid) disturbances experienced by every gravid woman. But the especial vividness of her poem arises from her feeling of schizoid detachment from her baby who seems, now he has left her body, to be isolated in space, unrelated, and terrifyingly separate. That the baby is separate arouses in her all the schizoid fear of the loss of confirmation of the identity when a baby is not creatively reflected by the mother:

> We stand round blankly as walls.

Since the baby, as 'inner contents', was distilled from her it mirrors her. Yet in the child she sees her own self dissolve. Her inner contents being born out of her, she loses the sense that she is the baby's mother: the image is one of non-reflection that is the basis of effacement.

> I'm no more your mother
> Than the cloud that distils a mirror to reflect its own slow
> Effacement at the wind's hand.

One would expect the emergence of the child as a separate being to deepen the feelings of being a mother by the new reality of relationship. But her interest in the child seems to evaporate because it is no longer 'her', filling her inner space with something real.

From her deep feelings of insecurity of existence however come the beautiful images in *Morning Song* of evanescence evoked (as in

all of us) by the presence of a new baby: 'All night your moth-
breath Flickers...' The rest of the poem is a deeply sensitive
account of the feelings of a mother about her new child, given with
great control and economy, the images of transience persisting:

> Your clear vowels rise like balloons.

Balloons are symbols of evanescence which always fascinate children, because they belong to coming and going—along with
fluff, rainbows and bubbles. They are full of breath: you can see
through them: they are empty, except of air. *Balloons* (*Ariel*,
p. 80), reveals her own characteristic fascination with them. To
her the Christmas balloons are 'soul-animals'. They seem like
things with life, but are full of nothing but the invisible air that
comes from one's inside. As Winnicott points out the child's concept of 'spirit, soul, anima' derives from its fascination with bubbles and breath, and 'whether it comes primarily from within or
without' ('Primitive Emotional Development' in 1968a, p. 154).

Though they are capable of delighting the heart 'like wishes',
balloons can also vanish like breath or identities. Significantly,
they vanish by an act of desire—when they are bitten:

> Your small
>
> Brother is making
> His balloon squeal like a cat.
> Seeming to see
> A funny pink world he might eat on the other side of it,
> He bites,
>
> Then sits
> Back, fat jug
> Contemplating a world clear as water.
> A red
> Shred in his little fist.

Balloons does many things in its small compass and with controlled
economy. Sylvia Plath makes the poem out of her characteristic
intuition that a baby wants to eat the world he sees, out of desire
for it. The lines themselves enact the baby's movements. The word
'jug' gives us the child's podgy shape, his incorporative (empty
jug) feeling and also the inside-out feeling one has when a balloon

bursts and the expectation of floating on it is frustrated: is the clear water in the jug, or is the jug in the water? Something that expected to be filled, at any rate, is not. Having bitten, his world becomes 'clear as water'. The internal rhyme 'red/shred' enacts the child's astonished look at the scrap of rubber in his hand, and echoes the little explosion of the bursting of the balloon, which is only now heard, as an echo, so great is his astonishment. The 'red shred' seems like a scrap of torn flesh in the grip of a child who feels that the extinction of his world has occurred because he has somehow vented his oral cannibalistic impulses on it. Sylvia Plath often writes out of her existential insecurity as if she expected the world to pop at any minute and become no more than a 'red shred' in one's fist, as it often seems likely to do, to an infant. The astonishing truth seems to be that this creative and playful poem about evanescence was written in the last week of her life. One of the most beautiful and yet most disturbing of Sylvia Plath's poems is also about a baby—*The Night Dances* (*Ariel*, p. 27). It seems significant to me that for a long time I often read this poem and never brought it into focus. It meant hardly anything to me until I read a remark by Andrew Brink that it dealt with 'childhood innocence'. Even so, it was some time before I could grasp the poem at all. This experience seems to me now an important part of the poem's effect.

It is perhaps relevant to record the kind of discussion I have found this poem generate in seminars. Students are aware that someone is smiling at someone else and that intense feelings are involved. But they cannot at first be sure who the persons are. They feel there is perhaps a sexual meaning, implied by the words 'night dances', 'hot petals', and the references to 'warm and human gestures'. They see that there is dread and a kind of repulsion behind the words 'bleeding and peeling'. Yet they cannot bring into focus two human beings relating to one another. It is only when they are obliged to consider more thoroughly the implications of 'your small breath' and 'the drenched grass/Smell of your sleeps' that they begin to see that the poem is about, or to, a baby. Even then, they find it difficult to decide whether the baby is yet born or not: the 'leaps and spirals' seem like the circular movements of the foetus in the womb, yet to make 'gestures' it must surely be outside the mother?

At the same time, students are troubled by the lack of hopefulness in the poem. They feel one should feel hopeful about a baby.
Yet terrible stretches of void seem to lie behind it:

> The comets
> Have such a space to cross
>
> Such coldness, forgetfulness.
> . . .
> Through the black amnesias of heaven.

and the poem ends, dreadfully, 'Nowhere'.

Recognition of the strange moods of preoccupation in women
and men, in relation to babies and infants, is rare in literature.
There are moments in Tolstoy, and in D. H. Lawrence. Coleridge,
in pondering over the cradle in *Frost at Midnight* enters into the
developing life of his baby. It is as if he follows the development
of the mother in relationship to her infant. At first he, the infant
and the flame merge: in Winnicott's language he allows the infant
to make him into the 'subjective object'. Or shall we say, he
experiences what the mother feels in relation to a child, which is
to 'forfeit her self-interest' and to allow the infant to believe, to all
intents and purposes, that he 'is' the mother, which, psychically
speaking, he still is. But, as he progresses through this state in
imagination, he gradually 'finds' the baby as a separate person. He
also 'finds' himself:

> I was reared
> In the great city, pent mid cloisters dim
> . . .
> But *thou* . . .

And he wishes for the baby that God shall form his identity by his
creative reflection:

> He shall mould
> Thy spirit, and by giving make it ask.

The effect of this is to enable Coleridge to 'find' for his child a
future in which there is an intense and vital relationship between
the new being and the outer world: apperception. At the same
time Coleridge himself 'recovers his self-interest'. The difference
between the *me* and the *not-me* is celebrated as a process of joy in

being alive while the universe is felt to be benign—an environment that fosters growth throughout the seasons, and a rich sense of being alive. Though the existential dread is still there under the surface ('Heard only in the trances of the blast'), there could be no deeper realisation of the feeling of being real and alive, in a universe in which one is at home.*

This kind of existential security is exactly what Sylvia Plath cannot feel. The effect of the baby's presence on her identity and her sense of existence is to dissolve them into vast voids, and into a placelessness of non-being. Yet both poems begin with the kind of insight recorded by D. W. Winnicott when he says that 'the mother must be able to allow her baby to treat her as the "subjective object" or to let her baby believe *she* is *him*' (1968a, p. 99). Entering into Sylvia Plath's experience, however, opens up for us something akin to Winnicott's experience when he first began to realise that 'there is no such thing as a baby', before the emerging human person is created: there is only a 'nursing couple'. Sylvia Plath is holding her baby—she is aware that it is breathing and is warm and human, and also has a smell. Yet what puzzles her is the relationship between herself and the new being, as an identity. What does this consist of? The situation, where she is concerned, is bedevilled by her own ability to receive what is being offered: 'why am I given . . .?'

As Winnicott points out, there is no individual at the beginning: there is only a 'set-up': there is only a complexity of gestures offered and gestures received—in terms of handling, response, and contact in other ways which eventually establishes the 'kernel' or psychic baby. Moreover, 'The beginning is potentially terrible because of the anxieties I have mentioned and because of the paranoid state that follows closely on the baby's first integration, and also on the first instinctual movements, bringing to the baby, as they do, a quite new meaning to object relationships' (ibid.). Sylvia Plath is aware of these dangers—because she herself seems not to have experienced a mothering which could prevent feelings of disintegration or overcome the dread of external persecutions. In consequence she is all too aware of the terrible aspects of the stage and its potentialities for disaster. She is left with the paranoid

---

* A fuller discussion of this poem is given in the present author's *Dylan Thomas; the Code of Night*, p. 7.

state of this moment in infancy. This evokes in her feelings of disintegration and loss of contact, which in *The Night Dances* throw up the chief symbols of the poem:

> A smile fell in the grass
> Irretrievable!
>
> . . .
>
> So your gestures flake off——
> Warm and human, then their pink light
> Bleeding and peeling
>
> Through the black amnesias of heaven.
> Why am I given
>
> These lamps, these planets
> Falling like blessings, like flakes
>
> Six-sided, white
> On my eyes, my lips, my hair
>
> Touching and melting.
> Nowhere.

In these lines she expresses universal existential truths. Yet at the same time they are presented in the desperate perspectives of the schizoid individual. The truth is that all relationship and identity are based on gestures the poem describes—signs which are no more than an expression or signal launched by the individual into space. When they are received and interpreted they become a language which has meaning for both beings. But if they are not received they can indeed soar away into space for ever, meaningless and futile, like the gestures of a dying spaceman lost from a rocket ship. This sense of the essential isolation of beings in space is often evoked in us all by an infant.

Sylvia Plath also sees, although she cannot grasp it, that there is a phenomenological meaning in the child's movements which is an expression of its own self-directed freedom, as well as being something that belongs to 'encounter' with the mother. Here some observations by the Dutch phenomenologist and biologist, F. J. J. Buytendijk on the nature of play seem relevant. He sees the 'spontaneous drive to movement in the youthful organism' as a 'drive to freedom'. Marjorie Grene (1968) gives an account of his views thus:

> Play movements are goalless, undirected. They are circular, capable or repetition, and hence rhythmical. We can see this in the rhythmical movements of infants, which are produced in circumstances of boredom, impatience, or pain—whenever there is a situation of confinement, or 'unfreedom'. What is in question here, Buytendijk argues, is a spontaneous drive to movement in the youthful organism: in the last analysis, a drive to freedom . . . In the consequent rhythm of tension and relaxation, the sense of 'a promise that's kept', we get the essential dynamic of play. (p. 156)

Sylvia Plath shows herself intuitively aware of the meaning of her baby's circular movements, which express a claim for a kind of 'freedom'. She relates them to her own desire for freedom— freedom from non-being and isolation. Yet she cannot quite make the link, and ends only on that dreadful empty note, 'Nowhere'.

Her poem is written out of the experience of a mother who does not know (in her 'being') how to reflect in this creative way, to 'give the baby back what he brings' (and return a 'promise that's kept'). His gifts are tragically lost, being only 'movements without an end in view'. She herself is preoccupied with the horror of not being creatively reflected. So she imagines the terror of an unreflected baby, and feels deep pity for it. But then, the pity establishes a bridge.

As Winnicott says, the consequences of non-reflection are terrible. If things go right, there is 'the beginning of a significant exchange with the world, a two-way process in which self-enrichment alternates with the discovery of meaning in the world of seen things'. But if things go wrong perception takes the place of apperception.* Sylvia Plath cannot find this self-enrichment in herself, in relationship to her baby, though she dimly sees that it might be there:

> . . . I shall not entirely
> Sit emptied of beauties, the gift

---

* Coleridge knew of this problem and conveys it in his *Dejection: an Ode*. In this, in relation to problems of love, he looks at the thin clouds and stars, but cries, 'I see, not feel, how beautiful they are'.

> Of your small breath . . .
> Why am I given
>
> These lamps . . .

Instead of a 'significant exchange with the world' she sees the
infant's gestures as 'irretrievable' givings out of 'inner contents',
which, like the thin abstractions of mathematics, may as well disappear into the vacant universe for ever:

> And how will your night dances
> Lose themselves. In mathematics?
>
> Such pure leaps and spirals——
> Surely they travel
>
> The world forever . . .

'Movements without an end in view' as Buytendijk calls the play
movements of the youthful organism, go off into endless infinity.

She can see that, in making gestures, the infant is seeking the
response that will enable him to find a rich mutual reationship
with the world, such as Coleridge could enjoy wishing on his
baby in *Frost at Midnight*. She sees that this impulse is like the
growth of lilies, fulfilling themselves as lilies, arum or tiger, fulfilling their nature from energies within themselves:

> Their flesh bears no relation.
> Cold folds of ego, the calla,
>
> And the tiger, embellishing itself—
> Spots, and a spread of hot petals.
>
> The comets
> Have such a space to cross,
>
> Such coldness, forgetfulness.
> So your gestures flake off—

The baby is present: she can smell him in his cot, and his sleeps and
his excretions (that make the baby-smell). She recognises these as
gifts for her. They are her lilies: yet lilies, while symbols of purity
and innocence, are also associated with death. Here we may recall
the terrifying *Edge* where she speaks of the 'sweet deep throats of

the night flower'. In this poem is a subdued imagery of a lily of death, white and stiff, by contrast with the roses of the children's cheeks, which, like a mouth, it is consuming.

'Their flesh bears no relation' here means that 'the growing flesh of the lily is quite different from the growing self of the baby'. Also, 'the growing flesh of the lily has to *bear* no problem of relationship', by ambiguity. The lily, she says, does not have the problems you have in fulfilling itself as a being. The lily's growth is cold and egoistic. It simply becomes itself. By contrast, the baby's self-realisation depends upon the mother's capacity for 'relation', and the brave signals the child sends across the void, like comets. This is quite different, and dreadful, because it depends upon the capacity to receive—and so this dependency may not 'work'.*

The calla is one kind of lily, and the tiger lily another: both are impersonal stuff, molecular structures and energies determining whether the thing shall become one kind of flower or another, with spots, or merely 'a spread of hot petals'. Yet in the image there is something of a terror of the mysterious energies of life, by which a baby grows as lilies grow: of life itself spreading and un-folding. The lilies 'spread' and the child's movements speak both of ever-going-out dynamics of functional cycles and the 'drive to freedom'.

For the baby's self-realisation is something which belongs not only to the growth of tissue, but also to the realm of personality. Yet this can never be more than the flaking off of gestures in space, like the distant signals made by a comet's fire. The human identity forms on the verge of non-existence. In normal processes, accord-ing to Winnicott, there is a development: 'When I look, I am seen, so I exist . . .' Sylvia Plath cannot hope for such confidences in her baby, because she does not have such confidence herself. The gestures that should establish that he is seen become snow-flakes dissolving and melting into nowhere:

> Six-sided, white
> On my eyes, my lips, my hair

* Marion Milner (1969), in discussing her patient Susan's symbolism in draw-ings, sees one, of an imp walking down the stalk of a lily as 'herself being born out of a state of fusion with me, represented by the dark-centred lily, a real lily, because she was once really fused with her mother's body' (pp. 326 ff.).

Touching and melting.
Nowhere.

'We all go into the dark', as T. S. Eliot said: but here the recognisably human and warm baby seems to dissolve into the vacant interstellar spaces, before he has begun to be. The meaning she begins to utter dissolve like 'forgetful snow' into the 'black amnesias' of heaven before there is anyone to receive them. Two comments from a student discussion of this poem seem relevant here: first, an exasperated remark from a girl that the mother *should* have received what was offered. There is something disastrously wrong when a woman cannot, and we feel angry about it. The other was a perceptive remark from a man—that there is no suggestion here of backing from a husband or anyone else. Mother and infant are terribly alone in their enigma.

8
Be(e)ing

'The sting of bees took away my father.' As we have seen, at the age of eight or thereabouts, Sylvia Plath felt that her source of being had been taken away. In one series of poems she makes a poignant, positive search for being: the 'bee' poems.

These poems were written during the period when she was living in a Devon village and was trying to enter into a normal relationship with the community and the natural world. Yet that world is coloured intensely by her strange subjective life, so that, for instance, in *The Bee Meeting*, a procedure for manipulating bees, a quite commonplace event in rural life, seems to her like a nightmare ritual, an atrocity. The symbols belong to her private world which we have already examined: the queen bee is 'female element being', while the swarm represents her kind of identity—composed of fragments of 'male doing', which is 'the mind of the hive', can be manipulated, and threatens to implode. It is an eminently schizoid-paranoid image. Straw hives are breasts or mausoleums; wooden ones, or bee-boxes, are unopened gifts or coffins. Her bee-hives excite her because they seem to contain the secrets of maleness and femaleness, of love, hate (stings) and substance (honey): but, since they come from Daddy, who is dead, they are also very threatening.

The 'bee' poems in *Ariel* and elsewhere are among her most successful. They are records of a sensitive perception of the world in terror, apprehension, strange joy, and hope, and in them she encounters ambivalence—the mixture of love and hate which is humanness. In *The Beekeeper's Daughter* (*The Colossus*, p. 75), the child investigates a bumblebee's solitary burrow:

> ... Kneeling down
> I set my eye to a hole-mouth and meet an eye
> Round, green, disconsolate as a tear.

The hole she is looking in is not the entrance to the hive, but to a 'solitary' bee's house. Here the child is looking for reflection. But she does not look in the eye of the hive which is a breast (and so the mother's body). She peers in instead at a solitary 'house' in the grass: a bumblebee's (mouth-) hole. Daddy, the expert on bumblebees, the maestro with his baton, has perhaps hidden the secret in the ground? Her eye meets an eye—actually the 'Easter egg' in which the queen bee is going to winter. But, in that she finds her eye reflected, it is also her femininity. The image expresses the child's intense desire to mate with her father and to find herself in him:

> Father, bridegroom, in this Easter egg
> Under the coronal of sugar roses
>
> The queen bee marries the winter of your year.

The bumblebee's tunnel is an 'Easter egg' because the possibility of resurrection lies for Sylvia Plath in her union with the father. The Easter egg is perhaps a memory of the continental kind made of a hollow sugar shell, containing a panorama into which you can look from one end. The child is looking into the bumblebee's tunnel, which she feels is like that kind of sugar egg. The sugar egg is decorated with sugar roses, which are a bride's garland to her hopes. The father is associated with winter because he is dead. The roses in the garden, the roses on the sugar peepshow and the roses on Daddy's grave are lying on the ground over his bumblebee's tunnel, in which her hopes are buried.

This seasonal element gives the bee poems what Andrew Brink calls 'the pull of nature's regenerative cycle'. And yet even her experience of natural living patterns is full of dread. In the first bee poem in *Ariel*, *The Bee Meeting* (p. 60), a group of individuals are coming to meet her. They are coming to ensure the cohesion of a swarm by removing all the queens except one. This is a quite normal rural event, in North Tawton, but to Sylvia Plath it is an exhausting trial of the identity, involving deep threats of death:

> Whose is that long white box in the grove ...

She can survive the incident only by magic and by being brave
enough to stand petrified, and withdrawn enough, to be untouched
by the knives she feels to be flying: 'I am the magician's girl who
does not flinch . . .' The bees represent sweetness, the honey she
cannot feel to be in herself, but deeply desires: 'I am no source of
honey . . .' The queen bee holds the swarm together: she is the
queen pin to the identity. Bees delight in freedom, and in continuity: 'The bees are flying. They taste the spring.' They compose
an identity (the swarm) which is composed of a seeming infinity
of individual impersonal creatures. But bees can also be malignant,
and can penetrate in an uncanny way, like a cloud or emanation.
In a host they are black and obey strange laws of instinct as a
group: they seem to have a 'mind'—and so they could be a cloud
of invading thought, to threaten her thoughts.

Bees fascinate Sylvia Plath, therefore, because they symbolise
dissociation of identity and yet a vitality and unity of being she
desires but deeply fears. They may be the verb 'to be' but are
dispersed as a swarm of doing. So, from the beginning, the 'agent
for bees' brings both a hope and a threat. The poem opens with an
ordinary rustic scene:

> Who are these people at the bridge to meet me? They are
> the villagers—
> The rector, the midwife, the sexton, the agent for bees.

Is 'the agent for bees' in apposition to the sexton? Is 'the sexton,
the agent for bees'? If so, perhaps be(e)ing is in death where
Daddy is? Those coming to meet her—over the bridge, as if from
one world to another—are the rector (who is concerned with the
soul, the inner life), the midwife (concerned with birth), the sexton
and the 'agent' who might also be the sexton:

> In my sleeveless summery dress I have no protection,
> And they are all gloved and covered, why did nobody tell me?
> They are smiling and taking out veils tacked to ancient hats.

By contrast with normal people she feels exposed to dangers
against which they are 'gloved' and 'covered' by the normal
armour of identity. Their smiling seems to her to show an
enviable familiarity, or perhaps a conspiracy against her—there is
a paranoid note in her panics: 'why did nobody tell me?'. . . 'does

nobody love me?' The hats are 'ancient', showing that the others are experienced in dealing with this vital force that threatens her, a girl in her sleeveless summer dress—'summery' as if she expects joy and relaxation (honey)—but yet fears it:

I am nude as a chicken neck, does nobody love me?

Why a *chicken neck*? She does not say 'a chicken's neck'. The neck is not attached to the chicken—it is a depersonalised object with which she identifies herself, goosepimpled like the neck of a plucked chicken. The 'chicken neck' has been chopped off. That which most resembles a 'chicken neck' is thus a penis, which has the same goosepimpled skin. Standing there in fear at her exposed state she feels like a castrated penis, exposed. (When Esther is first confronted with a man's genitals in *The Bell Jar*, she 'can think of nothing but turkey neck'.)

Here the fear of implosion (the bees emerging from a box threatening to enter into the inside of her identity) makes her feel in her 'sleeveless' dress that, while the others are covered up, her internalised penis (which she has stolen) makes her especially vulnerable. Since she identifies herself with the father's penis, she feels that if this is attacked (castrated), her whole identity will suffer. The castration fear is related to her Electral feelings of excitement, directed sexually at father's bees: at a deeper level castration is feared at the hands of the mother (the queen bee seeking talion revenge).

Interestingly, the phrase 'does nobody love me?' suggests that whoever did love her would protect her, rather than invade her (which is what she most fears). So, when the 'secretary of bees' protects her, she feels this is love: the woman buttons 'the slit from my neck to my knees'. Even in such a simple phrase there is a schizoid element, evoking the feeling in a schizoid person that the smock she enters is, like her identity, 'slit' from top to bottom, 'slit' being a word here with a violent undercurrent (Cf. the cant word for the female genital, 'gash'). It is a female identity which is very vulnerable (a woman has a 'slit' rather than a penis).

Now I am milkweed silk, the bees will not notice.
They will not smell my fear, my fear, my fear.

She now looks like a silky weed: the real woman (with breasts)
8

has become 'milkweed silk': so the bees which seem to be hunting out her vulnerable human femininity will be deceived. She has become depersonalised, and so, safe. Her fear (so insistently repeated, as though with the throbbing of her heart) is that of 'being found', and imploded.

Whenever she becomes excited by the intense sexuality that surrounds bees and flowers, she withdraws into petrified depersonalisation—as in *Tulips*, and *The Beekeeper*. Here she is fascinated by the fact that everyone is becoming depersonalised: becoming protected not only from the bees, but from recognition (to her, from dangerous 'meeting'). They lose their identities ('their smiles and their voices are changing'):

> Which is the rector now, is it that man in black?
> Which is the midwife, is that her blue coat?
> Everybody is nodding a square black head, they are knights
> in visors,
> Breastplates of cheesecloth knotted under the armpits.
> Their smiles and their voices are changing. I am led through
> a beanfield.

How secure is one in this armour? She is *led* as though blind. The *breastplates* are only *cheesecloth*. Everyone is becoming an automaton. Her observation is uncanny, excited as her perception is by a horrible expectancy: the tinfoil strips to scare the birds seem like people winking; the flowers have black eyes; the leaves are like 'bored hearts' (that is, identities pierced by implosion). The tendrils seem to be *dragging blood clots*—inner contents drawn out of the bored heart—up strings. The ordinary rural allotment becomes a place of sacrificial horror. This fear of violation seems to belong to an intense fantasy of having been ravished by the father, such as Freud found in many patients. (Later analysts came to believe this to be a fantasy of talion retribution for incestuous urges.)

Her identity becomes one with the villagers—who have, however, lost their identities in the process. Her veil moulds to her face—like a death-mask. The villagers are being kind to her: they give her a hat fit for a pretty girl. But the black veil is like a widow's veil, and she is terrified by its effect of blurring the boundaries between *me* and *not me*. Making her one of them in their kindness seems a threat to her existence rather than a confirmation of identity by social contact.

> Now they are giving me a fashionable white straw Italian hat
> And a black veil that moulds to my face, they are making me
>   one of them.

Inclusion in the group fills her with deeper terror: the grove is 'shorn', the circle of hives makes her feel that her sacrifice is imminent.

Behind the poem there seems to be the kind of fear found in children by Melanie Klein's analysis of their fantasies, of parental retribution, and symbolised in myths such as that of Abraham and Isaac: are they to sacrifice her as the 'shorn' lamb?

> They are leading me to the shorn grove, the circle of hives.
> Is it the hawthorn that smells so sick?
> The barren body of hawthorn, etherising its children.

Hawthorn has a sickly smell. It bears haws so it is not strictly 'barren': but to her it seems as if the 'sick' smell is an anaesthetic which the tree is employing on the insects which come to its blossoms (breasts).* For a long time I could not see why she should call the hawthorn's a 'barren body'. Then a teacher in Australia pointed out that hawthorn is called 'mother-die' by children and according to superstition must not be taken home as this could bring the death of a member of the family. It is avoided by bees and butterflies, perhaps because of its 'decayed fish' smell, and is pollinated by flies.

So, the barren hawthorn 'etherising' its children is yet another symbol of the blank-faced mother. The smell in her anxiety ('smell my fear') perhaps evoked memories of being given shock treatment in hospital, which felt like a parental punishment.

In the next stanzas her fears deepen, because of the disguised impersonal figures, the blankness (white suit, white hive), and the loss of distinguishing characteristics. ('Is it . . . someone I know?') Her terror makes her want to run. The gorse has 'yellow purses' (containing golden inner contents, like honey) and 'spiky armoury' (reflecting her own urgent need to defend her identity): so, it 'hurts her' by its intensity of impingement on her non-existence. She feels paralysed, as in a nightmare:

---

* Cf. 'the death-stench of a hawthorn', *Whitsun* (*Crossing the Water*, p. 60).

> I cannot run, I am rooted, and the gorse hurts me
> With its yellow purses, its spiky armoury.
> I could not run without having to run forever.

If she tried to escape it could only be to such a freedom as was utter dissipation (like a dissipated swarm of bees): an ultimate loss of existence. The image has beneath it the 'vacuum' which implosion threatens. Yet, in striking contrast with the vacuum at the heart of the self, is the composite *swarm* identity. And somewhere within the hive (which is herself) is the Queen Bee with which she yearns to identify.

> The white hive is snug as a virgin,
> Sealing off her brood cells, her honey, and quietly humming.

This hive identity is 'snug' only as long as it is undisturbed: the virgin is one who has been able to keep her inner contents 'snug'.* When the smoke rolls it seems the end of everything: the situation parallels her fear of implosion in reverse:

> Smoke rolls and scarves in the grove.
> The mind of the hive thinks this is the end of everything.
> Here they come, the outriders, on their hysterical elastics.
> If I stand very still, they will think I am cow parsley,
> A gullible head untouched by their animosity . . .

She is fascinated by the way the swarm can behave like a mind, sending out single outrider bees like tentacles (on 'hysterical elastics'). While she can outwit these by being unresponsive (and witty), the devotees are hunting for the queen. We have three problems of identity symbolised: the collective bee-identity, which fears annihilation by smoke; the poet who opposes gullibility to animosity; the queen who is hiding, eating honey, is 'very clever', and 'old, old, old'. Sylvia Plath identifies with this queen (who is perhaps her true self, who 'must live another year'). She feels threatened by the new virgins, who would (if not removed) destroy the old queen or take off sections of the swarm with them. And she puts this in a characteristically ironic way: 'The upflight of the murderess into a heaven that loves her.'

---

* As Brink points out, in *Stings* she writes of having 'a self to recover, a queen./ Is she dead, is she sleeping?'—when the whole weight of the poem is against making any such recovery.

When a new queen soars into the air in the bride flight she is pursued by drones seeking to mate with her. The bee which succeeds is torn to pieces—castrated and annihilated. To a schizoid individual this murder-love would obviously be fascinating, and would symbolise deep feelings about relationship—and thus also elements within the self. What fascinates Sylvia Plath here is the symbolism of her search for the female element, the 'false male doing' of the swarm, and the threats of break up of the collective identity by the bride-flights which the villagers seek to prevent. Yet their very desire to avoid chaos and preserve unity seems a threat. The old queen seems almost unwilling to live another year: the old queen (the weary true self?) is ungrateful and does not show herself. There seems no escape from her dilemmas.

At the centre of the experience, undergoing fears of a change of identity, she finds a drama of death and rebirth, of the restraint of murderous impulses, of reparation, of the necessity for gratitude. But gratitude does not come, and there is neither death, nor birth.

As often in Sylvia Plath we have an approach to a realisation of the capacity of love, and a way of escape from her death-circuit. Only a 'curtain of wax' (a wall of glass, a bell jar) seems to divide her from the 'bride flight', and the discovery of gratitude and touch with reality. Yet if she did find freedom it would mean murder—as it does to the bees who would mate in the air and then be killed by the queens. The old queen is merely being coerced into accepting her role for another year—yet she is unfound. So, even in such a poem, one of her best, Sylvia Plath fails to accomplish what Dostoevsky (another manifestly schizoid writer) managed to accomplish, a reaching out to find reality, going with an inward discovery of love and truth. Sylvia Plath can only record the perplexity of her exhaustion and the feeling of having merely survived, of merely having endured by an intellectual holding together, and of not running away:

I am exhausted, I am exhausted—
Pillar of white in a blackout of knives.
I am the magician's girl who does not flinch,
The villagers are untying their disguises, they are shaking
    hands.

> Whose is that long white box in the grove, what have they
> accomplished, why am I cold.

She has only maintained her purity, as a 'pillar of white', threatened by the surrounding black threatening forms of the devotees.
She has been the conjurer's victim, who survives the knives
thrown at her only by not flinching, not giving way to the horror
of implosion. (Had she panicked the bees might have killed her.)
The villagers change back their identities and shake hands, a
gesture of accomplishment which is alien to her. All she feels is
the presence of death (perhaps of the 'new virgins' who could have
replaced the old ungrateful self?). She finds no hope in the act of
care, only the schizoid sense of futility, and a feeling of coldness,
of exposure of soul. The old queen—the mother—on whom a
sense of be(e)ing could have been built, 'does not show herself',
and there is no source of new being, of honey, in the hive. We can
say of *The Bee Meeting* that it is a superb and sensitive portrayal of
how, to a schizoid individual, a normal social event can seem like a
nightmare of menace. The ritual also reminds her of being dealt
with as a depersonalised object in the operating theatre (or ECT
treatment room). So, it illuminates any experience in which we
become a victim, a 'piece of machinery in a repair shop', or
objectified in some other way. The 'long white box in the grove'
—is it hers, or Daddy's?

The pillar of white is the petrified woman: the long white box
is the purity of death. But 'ye are like unto whited sepulchres,
which indeed appear beautiful, outwardly, but are within full of
dead men's bones, and of all uncleanness' (*Matthew*, 23, 27). As
Sylvia Plath says,

> . . . A body of whiteness
> Rots and smells of rot under its headstone
> Though the body walk out in clean linen.
> (*Moonrise*, *The Colossus*, p. 66)

So, the coffin is hers, Daddy's and Christ's.

In the next poem, *The Arrival of the Bee Box* (*Ariel*, p. 63), the
bee box is a coffin:

> I ordered this, this clean wood box
> Square as a chair and almost too heavy to lift.

I would say it was the coffin of a midget
Or a square baby
Were there not such a din in it.

The box is locked, it is dangerous.
I have to live with it overnight
And I can't keep away from it.
There are no windows, so I can't see what is
     in there.
There is only a little grid, no exit.

Here, it is the underlying fear of implosion that makes for vividness in the imagery. The box of bees seems to contain a swarm of vital elements which threaten to invade her ('I wonder how hungry they are?'). She is fascinated by her own desire to be invaded by them ('I can't keep away from it'). As we have seen, to the schizoid individual who feels impelled to withdraw, 'the ultimate unconscious infantile weak ego is very clearly experienced consciously as *a fear of dying*' (Guntrip). There is an anxiety permanently present in such an individual, about 'feeling unable to cope', a struggle to 'master ... an ... internal breakdown threat', sometimes 'experienced as a *wish to die*'. Her own preoccupation with her potential internal breakdown draws her to this box of menace.

The box looks like the 'coffin of a midget/Or a square baby'. Does it contain her regressed libidinal ego? We may remember Guntrip's patients' dreams of babies in steel drawers, or puppies in boxes. She is fascinated by the buzzing vitality—and the promise of richness. By contrast, 'I am no source of honey'. A 'square baby' would be an inhuman one, which is why the phrase is comic and wry—but it is also horrible as an image of a dead *self-made* regressed ego, cubic, without live limbs and form. She does not know what shape her unborn self is (a puppy? a horse?). Her way of possibly escaping the enmity of the swarm is to be confused with seemingly feminine non-human objects, *fragments of herself*:

There is the laburnum, its blond colonnades,
And the petticoats of the cherry.

She is as depersonalised as she can be 'In my moon suit and funeral veil'. The bees in the box seem like black hands, from the

Congo. They are part-objects of 'male doing', clambering as if seeking to grasp her, and sting her: so, they are raping penises. They are 'Minute and shrunk for export',—just as 'the old man shrank to a doll'. In ancient Rome the mob demanded public rape and execution. She discusses her capacity to cope with the threat of being raped and annihilated. She cannot cope by swaying the mob: 'I am not a Caesar'. But she has power over the bees as their owner:

> I have simply ordered a box of maniacs.
> They can be sent back.
> They can die, I need feed them nothing, I am the owner.

She has the bees in her power, but she has in her power neither the implosive forces she feels to be in her environment, nor the wish to die in herself that makes her so fascinated by possible implosion. She strives towards overcoming her paranoia by merging with natural objects and becoming ignored, and by gratitude: 'To-morrow I will be sweet God, I will set them free.' By reparation she makes their imprisonment 'only temporary'. Because of this reparative urge we have one of the most 'normal' of Sylvia Plath's poems: she achieves here a significantly developed sense of distinction between herself and the bees—she discovers resources in herself by which to deal with reality, to *care* for the bees, as for children. The poem's images are of a rebirth, beginning with a dead baby, ending with free bees, and the escape from death. By her recognition of the bees not merely as aspects of her identity, but as creatures in themselves, she, as 'sweet God', can release them to be themselves (as in the end she released her children). In this we have something like the moment in *The Ancient Mariner* in which the Mariner blesses the watersnakes unawares in the tropical sea which previously seemed to be merely an aspect of the threatening sea of hate and are suddenly seen as manifestations of created life, and loved.

By clarity and care about meaning—not a word is wasted—Sylvia Plath here discovers something of her true self, records the perplexities of schizoid problems of identity, and explores the reparative urges that belong to the 'stage of concern'. Her irony here belongs to sanity, not to hebephrenic disdain nor to an abandonment to delicious hate.

In *Stings* (*Ariel*, p. 65), again about the quest for the self, the pull of her strange inner compulsions is less successfully countered:

> ...I
> Have a self to recover, a queen.
> Is she dead, is she sleeping?

In this poem she is not threatened by a box of vital creatures, or a swarm, but she is extracting the honey deposited during the time the bees have been in the hive. Symbolically, she is searching for her own sweetness: she has painted the hive lovingly, in a gesture she places as 'excessive'.

> ... the hive itself a teacup,
> White with pink flowers on it,
> With excessive love I enamelled it
>
> Thinking 'Sweetness, sweetness'.

The act of extraction 'to scour the creaming crests' is a sweet and pure activity: the man helping her is 'white', their gauntlets are 'neat and sweet'. Here we have the good Daddy: 'The throats of our wrists brave lilies.' There is a hope of flowering, of birth, of purity,—even if 'lilies' suggest death. Once again rebirth and the discovery of the self are linked with death. As well as seeking honey, they are exploring cells where there are grubs and queens. Something by way of 'inner contents' may emerge but it might be deathly:

> Brood cells grey as the fossils of shells
> Terrify me, they seem so old.

These grey cells resemble those in the grey paper self she is making in *Poem for a Birthday*. What she is looking for (she fears) may have died in the cell. Or perhaps it belongs to death and is fossilised?

> Is there any queen at all in it?

There seems too little hope:

> If there is, she is old,
> Her wings torn shawls, her long body
> Rubbed of its plush—

Poor and bare and unqueenly and even shameful.
I stand in a column

Of winged, unmiraculous women,
Honey-drudgers.
I am no drudge
Though for years I have eaten dust
And dried plates with my dense hair.

In seeking for her female element, she is full of distrust:

What am I buying, wormy mahogany?

If there is a 'queen' inside her, it will be an 'antique'—'Her wings
torn shawls' (in *Nick and the Candlestick* we remember she expresses a fear of being wrapped in 'raggy shawls, cold homicides').

Her femaleness is male ('I stand in a column'): she identifies
with women who have eaten dust and dried plates, seeking to be
feminine. In this, she has

. . . seen my strangeness evaporate,
Blue dew from dangerous skin.
Will they hate me,
These women who only scurry,
Whose news is the open cherry, the open clover?

The female bees are alive to the open flowers of cherry and
clover: they scurry at the work of fulfilling their role, of enjoying
and fertilising, as she has never been able to. Her own quest is not
satisfied by pursuing the generosity of blossom. She is different:
she hopes her 'blue dew from dangerous skin' (her animus
quality) will evaporate, and leave her purer. The be(e)ing seems a
threat to one who does not know how to be. The problem of
reparation is not her problem. The blossom satisfies the manic-
depressive: the schizoid has first to begin, by losing her 'strangeness' (without losing her identity). Will they hate her for this?

By disciplined effort she manages to overcome her fear,
identifying with the hive as a 'honey-machine' that works without thinking, so there is no conflict of will:

It is almost over.
I am in control.

Here is my honey-machine,
It will work without thinking,
Opening, in spring, like an industrious virgin

To scour the creaming crests
As the moon, for its ivory powders, scours the sea.
A third person is watching.
He has nothing to do with the bee-seller or with me.

The swarm will scour the crests of blossom as the moon scours the
sea. The image is characteristically arid: the moon-mother, who
draws the sea after her should be like the bees gathering honey
from flowers: but she is not, she only scours, for her 'ivory
powders' are a sterile, if beautiful, pure valuable dust—but not
honey. The poet's honey-machine is like her own striving to
make an identity ('I am no source of honey'), by an automatic
kind of male activity used to exert control.

Who is the 'third person'? The answer is suggested by Eliot's
line, 'Who is the third who always walks beside you?' It is Christ,
the 'great scapegoat'.

> . . . here the square of white linen
> He wore instead of a hat.

This square is that found by Simon Peter in the sepulchre: 'And
the napkin, that was about his head, not lying with the linen
clothes, but wrapped together in a place by itself' (*John*, 20, 6).
This napkin is perhaps also the Veronica, by tradition used to wipe
away Christ's sweat. But the word 'sweet' ('He was sweet'), by
many associations in her poetry, links Sylvia Plath's Christ with
Daddy: he is her source of honey and being. He must be resurrected: his sweetness is in his sweat, which springs from his
creative effort. The rain here is a reiteration of the golden rain
of *The Beekeeper's Daughter*, his semen, in which she is to find herself. The 'bees found him out' because they savoured the sweat
generated by his work. But they also found him out, as she
hopes to do, making what they could by way of honey out
of his sweat, as she hopes to. She works to reconstruct his
features, as Veronica captured the face of Christ on her napkin.
(At the same time, leaving his slippers behind, he is a little like
Cinderella):

Now he is gone

In eight great bounds, a great scapegoat
Here is his slipper, here is another,
And here the square of white linen
He wore instead of a hat.
He was sweet,

The sweat of his efforts a rain
Tugging the world to fruit,
The bees found him out,
Moulding onto his lips like lies,
Complicating his features.

As on an actual man, the bees die because they sting: so on the
father the work of taking in his sweetness is deathly (because it is
plunging into the grave). As hanging on Christ's lips is thinking
'death' is 'worth it', so the bees are glad to take the honey. It is as
if they want him to 'speak' them. They died.

At this moment, she is seeking life:

They thought death was worth it, but I
Have a self to recover, a queen.
Is she dead, is she sleeping?
Where has she been,
With her lion-red body, her wings of glass?

The Queen is a queen of hate: her body is red like a (male)
heraldic lion, her wings are transparent and brittle. Is she dead?
Is she sleeping? She is evasive and terrible—a red *scar* in the sky (a
wounded identity), a red *comet*—not an aspect of the normal
structure of the firmament, but rather a threatening portent—a
menacing sign instead of a confirming gesture as in *The Night
Dances* (though even there 'The comets . . . have such a space to
cross'—they are in dreadful isolation).

The final lines are a contradiction: the 'wax house', the cells,
'killed her', but she is flying. The place of storing honey, and of
generation, is also a 'mausoleum'. Death is a rebirth: being in
touch with being is a death, because 'Daddy' is dead. The search
for the true identity is also to be faced with its deadness: penetrating to the heart of reality, for the schizoid individual, is to

discover the empty feeling of being unreal. Is there any female element of being in me at all? If I find it, won't it kill me? No wonder she is baffled.

Is there any queen in it at all? The answer is equivocal, ambivalent: there is only a queen of hate 'more terrible than she ever was'.

In the next poem, *Wintering* (*Ariel*, p. 68), there is a re-enactment of the despair in which Esther Greenwood enters the cellar before her suicide attempt in *The Bell Jar*. The honey is in the dark cellar next to empty gin bottles, empty *glitters*. In the winter, in the cellar, at a time of minimum activity, she contemplates the stored honey—obtained by the midwife's extractor, as if it was a child from a womb, squeezed out by a machine:

> This is the easy time, there is nothing doing.
> I have whirled the midwife's extractor,
> I have my honey,
> Six jars of it,
> Six cat's eyes in the wine cellar,
>
> Wintering in a dark without window
> At the heart of the house
> Next to the last tenant's rancid jam
> And the bottles of empty glitters
> Sir So-and-So's gin

It is at the heart of the house, where inner goodness should be. The jars shine like 'cats' eyes' which can see in the dark: will the honey reflect her? The last tenant's jam is rancid: the new honey has by contrast the promise of sweetness. But will the honey reflect substantially in her? Or will it only be an empty glitter, like the bottles which once held Sir So-and-So's gin, a manic stimulant, but which are now not even any good for honey?

Because her hopefulness evaporates, the cellar becomes a place of darkness, of menace, and a horror possesses her.

Despite her intention to fill it with honey, and so with reflecting light (from the golden rain) there is only the partial light of her dim torch, that throws no meaning over the things there. They simply threaten to impose their stupidity on her.

This is the room I have never been in.
This is the room I could never breathe in.
The black bunched in there like a bat,
No light
But the torch and its faint

Chinese yellow on appalling objects—
Black asininity. Decay.
Possession.
It is they who own me.
Neither cruel nor indifferent.

Only ignorant.

The room is like one that can recur in dreams—the room of the
self that one fears is empty, decayed, deathly—the room which
symbolises the fear of internal breakdown. A patient of Guntrip's
'awoke one night in a state of terror, feeling that she was looking
into a black abyss yawning at her feet and could not escape falling
into it'. Sylvia Plath has never been in the room because to enter
it might mean never being able to escape again. To breathe in it
would be possibly to let one's breath (identified with one's soul)
escape into its maw, or to experience it rushing into one's empty
self by implosion. We have feelings expressed like these of being
stifled, or being in the 'black bag of the self': and of a meaningless
world thrusting itself on her. A black bunch of nothing gathers
there like a bat, threatening to rush at her, the regressed ego—the
'cry' that 'flaps out'.

There is paranoia in the word *asininity*, and it is as if she fears an
animal predator in the dark, which she projects from her inner
world—as Mahler does when he sees (and hears) the howling ape
of existential nothingness in *Das Lied von der Erde*. The black
malignant dark things in the cellar are appalling and 'asinine'
because they are ignorant: yet they own her and are 'neither
cruel nor indifferent'. They belong to a primitive stage before
reparation could (as in *The Ancient Mariner*) redeem the world:
belonging to the era before concern has developed, and before the
world is found as benign. They are pure, ruthless incorporative
savagery: *hate*.

Here, in this moment of collapse, we glimpse the 'unthinkable anxieties' that can threaten the schizoid individual—for which her desperate paranoia endeavours to compensate. The bees keep going throughout the winter in this cellar, like a hoarded activity of thought hidden within oneself: it is a question of surviving, till the true self can be found:

> This is the time of hanging on for the bees—the bees
> So slow I hardly know them,
> Filing like soldiers
> To the syrup tin
>
> To make up for the honey I've taken.
> Tate and Lyle keeps them going,
> The refined show.

She has taken their honey for herself, for her own vitality. They keep going, slowly, on the purified snowlike sugar she has given them which is inert and refined. It is pure like hate, while honey and the flowers are like love.

> It is Tate and Lyle they live on, instead of flowers.
> They take it. The cold sets in.

'Tate and Lyle' is not sugar, honey, or flowers, but a limited company—a corporate organisation. The bees too are a 'limited company'. Underlying the symbolism here is the advertising slogan on the golden syrup tin, 'Out of the strong came forth sweetness'. Daddy ('he was sweet') is the lion, and the inside of his corpse breeds the source of new life.

The bees are living in the cellar, where Sylvia Plath has stored her honey. The cellar is a womb which gives a 'second chance to be reborn', into which she wants to regress. The honey she stores there is the hopeful unborn true self, to be made from female element being.

But this has had to be made out of doing—and so out of the male element. Here there are many subtle ambiguities. The swarm consists of worker bees, and they 'taste the spring' by doing—storing their being in the breast-like hive. Again she is trying to achieve femaleness by desperate male doing methods, which are all she knows. But will it do? 'Will the hive survive?' 'It is Tate and Lyle they live on, instead of flowers'—that is, 'my swarm-identity is made up of such sweetness as I can gather from the swarm of doing that flies forth from my father's dead image'—it lives on this kind of honey, instead of on true self being.*

At the same time, the mass of wintering bees is like the pseudo-male compulsive thinking-as-doing of a schizoid individual, who hoards her dissociated conglomeration of fragments as a self-'system'. Outside, the snow-covered landscape resembles a porcelain pastoral, denatured and ceramic; the swarm identity is exerted against the pure seductive death and forgetfulness of the snow:

> Now they ball in a mass,
> Black
> Mind against all that white.
> The smile of the snow is white
> It spreads itself out, a mile-long body of Meissen,
>
> Into which, on warm days,
> They can only carry their dead.

The bees survive on the basis of their femininity, hibernating at the cradle side, like Patient Griselda:

> The bees are all women,
> Maids and the long royal lady
> They have got rid of the men,
>
> The blunt, clumsy stumblers, the boors.
> Winter is for women—
> The woman, still at her knitting,
> At the cradle of Spanish walnut,
> Her body a bulb in the cold and too dumb to think.

There will be a return to doing, in the spring. But can they survive? Will there be blossoms to warm them? Can they survive on the Christmas promise?

> Will the hive survive, will the gladiolas
> Succeed in banking their fires
> To enter another year?

* Did Sylvia Plath know that an ordinary worker bee larva can develop into a queen if reared under special conditions?

What will they taste of, the Christmas roses?
The bees are flying. They taste the spring.

The imagery of seasonal renewal, of Christ's rebirth (Christmas roses, sugar roses at Easter), of sweetness, honey, effort and love, give these Bee poems a creative impulse and an 'intentionality' widely lacking in Sylvia Plath's work. Andrew Brink says 'The renewal of life remains a possibility' in *Wintering*, though he does not find the other bee poems reassuring. But surely, taken as a whole, they belong to the positive direction in her life, towards the discovery of the rich potentialities of being human? Moreover, the bee poems lead to one of the most successful of all her poems, which extends the bee theme to problems of collective psychic infection, in *The Swarm* (*Winter Trees*, p. 37).*

For the schizoid individual the problem of inward ego-weakness is exacerbated by external events that are manifestations of hate. Since such manifestations are false solutions of moral inversion they make the identity problem more difficult to solve for each of us. Our problem, however, is to see that false (hate) solutions *are* false. Sylvia Plath here is able to see the dreadful ambiguity of this problem. Hearing shooting, she has fantasies of some menacing warlike hate:

Somebody is shooting at something in our town
A dull pom, pom in the Sunday street.

For some reason the next word is 'jealousy': why? Such violence seems to her like hate-envy, an urge to get inside another ('open the blood') or to extract 'inner contents' as flowers bursting forth (which would be flowers of bad stuff, of hate—'black roses'). It is the shrike.

Jealousy can open the blood,
It can make black roses.
Who are they shooting at?

It is as if someone were asleep, and is wakened by this hostile noise. They stumble to the window, dreaming of the Napoleonic wars, and see a man shooting at a swarm of bees, to get it down from a tree. Jealousy is the envy of the man shooting at the bees: it is the envy of the bees, which is like the envy of Napoleon, who

* Published in *Encounter*, October 1963, but not included in *Ariel*.

caused so many wounds to flow. At the same time the bees in
their swarm on the tree are like a black flower.

One source of hate is directed against another, as so often in her
work. As soon as she forms images of hate she forms the image of a
colossus, a man in some depersonalising rig-out. Here it is the man
dealing with the swarm. The other identity involved is dissipated
into a swarm that menaces. So we have 'the man with grey hands'
whose hands turn out to be asbestos gloves: it is he who is shooting.
He is the practical man, and he is dealing with a collective
infection—the black mind of the hive.

The swarm does not respond at first to the shooting, thinking
it is thunder. The bees think that the hate directed at them
confirms, by the voice of God, their own impulse to attack, to
implode, to tear out the insides of things, to invade, to kill. Both
the shooting and the swarm stand for that confrontation which
threatens annihilation, because such hunger (jealousy) will 'empty'.
The bees feel they are confirmed in their sadism by the hate-noise
of the gunshots: the attack on them hardens their paranoid
response, condoning the beak, the claw, the grin of the dog.

> Yellow-haunched, a pack-dog
> Grinning over its bone of ivory
> Like the pack, the pack, like everybody.

The grin of the dog is sadism. It grins over the bone from which
all the flesh has been gnawed leaving only bony ivory*—a white
pure sterile value, already referred to in another poem, as an image
of the characteristics of herself (the moon's 'ivory powders'). In
animal existence there is a sadistic hate-urge to prey, and in truth
like all living creatures we exist at the expense of others. This
becomes most frightening in a pack—or swarm. Everyone belongs
to this pack, because everyone has a hate-problem, of a hunger
that threatens others.

This pack, in its collective identity, echoing as threatening
object the petrified (asbestos-gloved) man who is shooting at it,
seems to her like the colossus. In *The Colossus* Daddy is 'pithy and

---

* In the background of her mind, I believe, is the phrase 'Boney was a warrior'
and also the objects (some of them chessmen) carved from bone by prisoners of
the Napoleonic wars, on show in Peterborough Museum and elsewhere, as at
Buckland Abbey.

historical', and elsewhere he is like a ruin from history, a tumulus. Here he is Napoleon:

> It is you the knives are out for
> At Waterloo, Waterloo, Napoleon
> The hump of Elba on your short back,
> And the snow, marshalling its brilliant cutlery
> Mass after mass, saying Shh!

She has been awoken out of a dream by the shooting and before her half-awake vision spreads an image of war, 'Shh!' is the noise of the snow and its crystals are knives that are capable of cutting up the Napoleonic armies.* She is horrified both by the way the Father of Hate plays with people as if they were (petrified) chessmen, and by the vision of the real human throats trampled by the collective psychopathology of the Napoleonic wars:

> Shh! These are chess people you play with,
> Still figures of ivory.
> The mud squirms with throats,
> Stepping stones for French bootsoles.

People in the mass have been used in history as stepping stones, for ambitions that arise from envy, the voraciousness of 'jealousy', in the schizoid fanatic. In such mass manifestations Sylvia Plath saw how the individual's hungry need would bring about the 'loss of all objects'. Napoleon is chasing the gold and pink breasts of the phantom mother:

> The gilt and pink domes of Russia melt and float off
>
> In the furnace of greed.

Hate threatens to melt the substantial world like ice or gold melting in a furnace. Napoleon sees the domes in the clouds, yet dissipating like clouds ('Clouds, clouds'): by such evanescent delusions of hate a world can be wrecked.

What is amazing about this poem is the confidence with which the distorted surrealistic images are set down, and the mastery by

---

* Cf. in the early version of *All the Dead Dears*, the 'footless woman' who 'flies against the wind when the snow hisses . . . to vamp in the guise of my sister'. This death-witch is the Mother-imago who, like the North Wind, in George Macdonald's fairy-story, brings oblivion.

which they are united. What unites them is not a historical perspective, so much as an anguish of identity to which every image is grist, in the quest for insight. So Sylvia Plath here created a profound vision of the consequences of schizoid hate in the world at large. She sees with vision into the worst possibilities in our world of 'collective infection'—a phrase from Jung who also associated this with the destructive animus (see *Man and his Symbols*, p. 185).

The dream of the collective mind of the bees is like the group psychopathology of Napoleonic France:

> So the swarm balls and deserts
> Seventy feet up, in a black pine tree.
> It must be shot down. Pom! Pom!
> So dumb it thinks bullets are thunder.

Its collective infection is also 'like everybody'. We all share the capacity to enter into such modes of hate behaviour, which Sylvia Plath sees with uncanny insight as manifestations of the urge to discover and exert a false (colossus) identity. She sees their ambitions with irony, as false solutions. Just as Napoleon and his forces felt Big (to no purpose) by invading Europe, so the bees feel Big at being *seventy feet up*! From this height the surrounding territory seems puny and easily conquered,

> The bees have gone so far, Seventy feet high!
> Russia, Poland and Germany!
> The mild hills, the same old magenta
> Fields shrunk to a penny
> Spun into a river, the river crossed.

The bees argue about their territorial gains, spiky with the manifestations of hate (which is also a self-defence, as with a hedgehog). The man with a gun in his self-defensive asbestos hands stands below, threatening their dreams of Empire. In their dreams they build a vision of hives like railway stations (?Waterloo) to and from which bees fly like trains on their faithful orientations, into a countryside to be exploited for honey, with no end.

> The bees argue, in their black hall,
> A flying hedgehog, all prickles.

The man with grey hands stands under the honeycomb
Of their dream, the hived station
Where trains, faithful to their steel arcs,

Leave and arrive, and there is no end to the country.

The man shoots them down:

Pom! Pom! They fall
Dismembered, to a tod of ivy.
So much for the chariots, the outsiders, the Grand Army!
A red tatter, Napoleon!

History is reduced to the collective insanity of schizoid dreams:
it is reduced to men shooting into the bodies of dreamers. Identities become tattered rags of flesh and once the delusion is shattered
they become mere conformist selves again:

The last badge of victory.
The swarm is knocked into a cocked straw hat.
Elba, Elba, bleb on the sea!
The white knots of marshals, admirals, generals
Worming themselves into niches.

The swarm is 'knocked into a cocked hat'—knocked into a straw
hive which looks like a hat. The cap of office is as much a thing of
straw. Victory, aspirations, and defeat become group identities
reduced to their components: after defeat the military leaders become mere petrified busts which move into place like white grubs
in the hive, petrified remnants of the live incidents of history.
They 'worm' themselves into their niches in order to seem to have
an identity which *réclame* celebrates: their living identity, which
was but a schizoid dream of territory and of the satisfaction of
greed ('no end to the country'), is confirmed by the dead white
bust.

How instructive this is!
The dumb, banded bodies
Walking the plank draped with Mother France's upholstery
Into a new mausoleum,
An ivory palace, a crotch pine.

The bees enter their new hive docilely. It is also a mausoleum, where the hibernating grubs are sealed as if in death (but actually for rebirth). The living identity of the Napoleonic swarm, based on hate, is trapped in a mausoleum, which is also a palace of petrifaction and it is made of pine. Compared with their seventy foot pine in the open air it is like the coffin that haunts us all through the bee poems.

The schizoid pseudo-revolution provokes a pragmatic reaction:

> The man with grey hands smiles——
> The smile of a man of business, intensely practical.
> They are not hands at all
> But asbestos receptacles.
> Pom! Pom! 'They would have killed *me*!'

He is those defence forces which are obliged to become petrified themselves in order to resist the Napoleonic invasion. Hate and moral inversion oblige a morally inverted hate-reaction on those who deal with it: the Blitz begets Dresden. Once hate has become immanent, it is 'intractable':

> Stings big as drawing pins!
> It seems bees have a notion of honour,
> A black intractable mind . . .

When bees sting, they die. Their hate is noble, black and fixed—a self-sacrifice. But having been defeated, they are pleased to be in Elba, pleased to be insignificant, in the 'bleb on the sea' ('Able was I ere I saw Elba': 'bleb' anagrams as 'bble' or 'elbb' and in the word-play at the back of Sylvia Plath's mind lapses into blabbering noises of inarticulate impracticability).

> Napoleon is pleased, he is pleased with everything.
> O Europe! O ton of honey!

The hive see their lot is satisfactory, though it is a sad come-down from the dreams in the pine-tree, 'knocked into a cocked hat'. The collective identity makes the 'crotch-pine'-hive Europe. What Napoleon dreamed of is equated with the bees' dream: a ton of honey. In the 'bleb' of Elba Napoleon was glad to be a mere bleb of flesh. The depersonalised bee-man is pleased with his work. Great ambitions come in the end to this—a deflated docility—

after all the madness of collective envy and its human consequences in pursuit of the gilt and pink domes of pleasure.

What is instructive is Sylvia Plath's insight into the self-deceptive processes of schizoid false solutions. From her own deep need to feel real, to be human, she can see the Napoleonic impulse to be Great through Hate with irony. Yet the deluded vision seems magnificent, too, except that it is also the puffed-up vision of self-deluded bees 'seventy feet high'. She sees the bees' easy satisfaction with the hive ironically too, no less a self-delusion however much less dangerous to the world. They become 'falsely socialised', by being shot down and ushered into a captive hive. In the bee poems Sylvia Plath turns her 'existence anxiety' into an exploration of the universal predicament—of our potentiality for solving our inward sense of vacancy and weakness, like Napoleon, at the expense of others. *The Swarm* is a profound and remarkable work of art.

There is no room to explore it here, but Sylvia Plath's bee symbolism echoes remarkably some bee symbolism in George Macdonald's *At the Back of the North Wind*. See the dream story Chapter XX.

We came to a small box against the wall of a tiny room. The little man told me to put my ear against it. I did so and heard a noise something like the purring of a cat, only not so loud, and much sweeter. 'What is it like?' I asked. 'Don't you know the sound?' returned the little man. 'No,' I answered. 'Don't you know the sound of bees?' he said. I had never heard bees, and could not know the sound of them. 'Those are my lady's bees,' he went on. I had heard that bees gather honey from the flowers. 'But where are the flowers for them?' I asked. 'My lady's bees gather their honey from the sun and the stars,' said the little man. 'Do let me see them,' I said. 'No, I daren't do that,' he answered. 'I have no business with them. I don't under-stand them. Besides, they are so bright that if one were to fly into your eye, it would blind you altogether.' 'Then you have seen them?' 'Oh, yes, once or twice, I think. But I don't quite know; they are so very bright—like buttons of lightning . . .

Sometimes in Sylvia Plath bees are associated with lightning and thunder.

> Lightning licked in a yellow lather
> But missed the mark with snaking fangs:
> The sting of bees took away my father.
> > (*Lament*, Poems submitted for the
> > Cambridge English Tripos, p. 52)

> A man used to clench
> Bees in his fist
> And outrant the thundercrack . . .
> > (*All the Dead Dears*, ibid., p. 57)

In Macdonald's story the bees are 'buttons of lightning' and when they are released they fill the room with light: to reach them, the protagonist must climb to the top of the moon:

> The little box had a door like a closet. I opened it—the tiniest crack—when out came the light with such a sting that I closed it again in terror—not, however, before three bees had shot out into the room, where they darted about like flashes of lightning.

They dash into the lady's hair, and she catches them in her hand, as Sylvia Plath's father caught bees in his hand. One wonders whether she had read Macdonald's strange fantasy about the ice-mother.

9
Psychotic Poetry

The 'bee' poems represent the sanest of Sylvia Plath's poems: indeed, in some of her insights, as in *The Swarm*, she transcends mere sanity. There are, however, certain poems in her *oeuvre*—some of them highly praised at large—which distort reality and follow such a sick logic that they must be declared pathological. My task must be to try to demonstrate that these are psychotic and why: and to try to demonstrate how and why the poet fell victim to these tendencies.

There are 'maenad' elements in some early poems. Sylvia Plath persuades us by the purity and clarity of her verse, to take the 'donnés' of her mythology. But it is a very private and personal world—many of whose aspects are esoteric, and can only be understood by a laborious decoding, such as I have attempted here.

A glimpse into this private world is given in the nightmarish poem *The Disquieting Muses* (*The Colossus*, p. 58). The mother failed to invite some 'disfigured and unsightly cousin' to her christening, so, like the princess in *The Sleeping Beauty*, the protagonist is cursed. This disfigured cousin appears as the three ladies in *The Disquieting Muses* who have always haunted her 'With heads like darning-eggs . . .' These 'nod and nod and nod' at the left (sinister) side of her crib. These 'muses' have not only brought disaster: their wooden, non-reflecting faces burst the windows in a hurricane. They are preventing her from becoming a woman. Furthermore, they have killed her creativity. While other children danced she 'could not lift a foot'—and her mother 'cried and cried'. 'And the shadow stretched, the lights went out . . .'. The mother sent her to piano lessons but the 'muses' made her tone deaf. One day she woke to a vision of faery—in her efforts to create a beautiful, ideal mother:

> I woke one day to see you, mother,
> Floating above me in bluest air
> On a green balloon bright with a million
> Flowers and bluebirds that never were
> Never, never found anywhere.
> But the little planet bobbed away
> Like a soap-bubble as you called: Come here!
> As I faced my travelling companions.—
>
> . . .
> They stand their vigil in gowns of stone,
> Faces blank as the day I was born,
>
> . . .
> And this is the kingdom you bore me to,
> Mother, mother . . .

It is not the image of the blank faces that stand around that make the poem paranoid—but the way in which the nightmare fantasy is presented as a truth of her world—and there is a sense in which she literally means it. The stone, club-like, petrified, malignant sister-witches do *haunt* her world, and deaden it. We take her to belong to life, but there is a sense in which like one of the sisters in *Two Sisters of Persephone* (*The Colossus*, p. 63), Sylvia Plath remains, psychically, 'Worm-husbanded,* yet no woman'—wedded to death. Many of the women in her poems are menacing death-women, and nightmare predators, as in the early *All the Dead Dears* (*The Colossus*, p. 27). A note to the poem says:

> In the Archeological Museum in Cambridge is a stone coffin of the fourth century A.D. containing the skeletons of a woman, a mouse and a shrew. The ankle-bone of the woman has been slightly gnawn.

This dead woman, like the moon, becomes a symbol of the mother, who has proved psychically sterile, and has thus condemned the poet to a living death, and 'funeral veil', a 'moon suit' as she calls her garments in *The Arrival of the Bee Box*.

---

* This phrase gives us the clue to the sexuality in *Daddy* 'The voices just can't worm through'.

Looking at the skeleton, Sylvia Plath sees how the generations drop away into the past and become skeletons. But she also looks back into her own psychic prehistory. She needed to eat the mother: all she managed to do was to nibble a dry fragment, like the mouse in the coffin. She is like the dead little animal (Little-soul) who gnawed at a dead woman. The great hunger in her, as symbolised by the black shadows of doors and tombs, yearns to pass again through the womb, as Esther yearned to pass through caves and tombs.

The continual death of generations is seen as 'the gross eating game'. Looking in the coffin she sees this 'game' unmasked. She confronts our existential 'nothingness', which we ignore in the passage of normal everyday life. We could not live confronted by our mortality every minute of the day. But however much we laugh at death, clownishly and from a blind eye, we cannot ever really escape the problem of our mortality. It's a game

> We'd wink at if we didn't hear
> Stars grinding, crumb by crumb,
> Our own grist down to its bony face.

But the gross eating game is not merely Time wearing us away. The schizoid horror of voracious envy, and the paranoid fear of being 'emptied' by the castrating mother of primitive fantasy, un-humanised, makes the skeleton more predatory: she menaces.

> . . . yet kin she is: she'll suck
> Blood and whistle my marrow clean
> To prove it.

The poet tries to clothe the skull with flesh and a face, so she can be seen. As she tries to reflect creatively the kin-woman, so the glass over the exhibit seems to be a mirror, or the surface of a pool into which mother and stepmother seek to draw her.* In the version of this poem which appears in the collection handed in for the English Tripos at Cambridge (*Two Lovers and a Beachcomber*, p. 58), she recalls a childish fantasy of her father's death:

> And an image looms under the fishpond surface
> Where the daft father went down
> With orange duck-feet winnowing his hair . . .

---

* The analogy with the paintings of Francis Bacon is striking here.

What follows is so personal that it is as if she is talking to herself, in a psychotic way:

> That one: not known enough: death's trench
> Digs him into my quick:
> At each move I confront his ready ghost . . .

To make her psyche alive ('quick') she has had to dig him into her,
and death's trench enabled her to do it. But she doesn't know him
enough: she can't hold him together. But she cries out like Lady
Macbeth at Banquo's ghost, that she sees him among his hives,
blackberrying

> Glaring sun-flower-eyed
> From the glade of hives,
> Antlered by a bramble-hat,
> Berry-juice purpling his thumbs: O I'd
> Run time aground before I met
> His match . . .

The blackberries appear here again, as an image of a male doing
which she loved and in which she feels there is a clue to love.
Daddy's 'thumbs' picking and eating the blackberry 'eyes' is a
symbol of Daddy 'masturbating a glitter': i.e. it is imagery of
parental sex in which she feels there may be a clue to the 'seeing'
love that could bring her alive.

But the stanza (omitted from the published form of the poem
in *The Colossus*) is personal and esoteric and belongs to the element
of madness in her utterance, that grows as time goes on. The
desperateness of her situation, she realises, brings many dangers,
for one's identity is thus built on ghosts that bring death with them
whenever they are evoked:

> Luck's hard which falls to love

> Such long gone darlings: they
> Get back, though, soon,
> Soon: be it by wakes, weddings,
> Childbirths or a family barbecue:
> Any touch, taste, tangs
> Fit for those outlaws to ride home on,

And to sanctuary:

. . .

      . . . Still they'll swarm in

. . .

      . . . until we go
Riddled with ghosts, to lie
Deadlocked with them, taking root as cradles rock.

To her, the newborn child is the soil in which the ghosts of the dead take root: one's identity is composed of death, 'deadlocked'. This is a characteristic schizoid feeling—like that expressed by Sartre's image of the self in the family being a baby 'sewn up in a dead man's skin'.

To her it is 'hard luck' to love a 'long-gone darling' like the father so much: the intense emotions that seem to lie beneath this poem, judging by its rhythm, suggest powerful unconscious feelings to do with the 'other world' where the dead are, and the need to be always searching for him ('O, I'd run time *aground* before I met/His match'). At the same time 'death's trench/Digs him into my quick'—the father is 'inside' her as a split-off male element which she cannot include in her personality.

Her self being so divided and disintegrated, Sylvia Plath found it difficult to hold her world together: it would become invaded by split-off projections, or perception would fail altogether. Out of her confusion, she could at times write poems like *The Eye-Mote*, *Sheep in Fog*, *Child*, and *Balloons*, which resulted from her capacity to go beyond the limits of normal perception. In these poems there is also a penetrating conscious awareness that our perception of reality is deeply subjective in origin. But in other passages the dissolution of perception becomes menacing, and she lapses into a wild rapture of dissolution. One remembers how Esther Greenwood faced the ordeal of having her photograph taken: 'I fixed my eyes on the largest cloud, as if, when it passed out of sight, I might have the good luck to pass with it' (*The Bell Jar*, pp. 106–7).

What seems to be penetrating insight may suddenly get out of hand and invest the world with a paranoia projected from her inner world. Thus in the poem *The Thin People* (*The Colossus*, p. 30), there is an exploration of the fact that, in our world, so deeply have we been shocked by the images of the victims of concentration-camp brutality, such as we have seen on film, that grey figures are present all the time in our perception of the world. We cannot see the world without it being sadder to look at because of our having seen the wasted bodies of Belsen. I have, however, just stated what the poem says in a sane way and I have spoken of it as if it were a sane poem. But the thin people in Sylvia Plath's poem do not remain in the memory, nor do they merely exist in terms of subjective anxieties colouring perception. They enter real experience—they are really 'there': they get out of hand, and become psychotic delusions.

Of course, most of us would take this as hyperbole and we all refer to ghosts or figures in the landscape which are not really 'there'. But Sylvia Plath's figures are more pressing than that: they are not content to be *felt* or conjured by mere hyperbole to sit in the moonlight, threatening the meaning of life. They actually escape and run about the world, and, as we read the poetry, grapple how we may with its logic, we find ourselves wondering whether they haven't taken on a life of their own and won't disappear when we say 'It was only a poem', or shut our eyes. As with the paranoid patient, who really sees what isn't there (and it won't go away), so we are brought to believe magical things about the nature of reality, as we did when we believed fairy tales:

> So weedy a race could not remain in dreams,
> Could not remain outlandish victims
>
> In the contracted country of the head
> Any more than the old woman in her mud hut could
>
> Keep from cutting fat meat
> Out of the side of the generous moon when it
>
> Set foot nightly in her yard
> Until her knife had pared
>
> The moon to a rind of little light.
> Now the thin people do not obliterate
>
> Themselves as the dawn
> Greyness blues . . .

The thin people, like ghosts unafraid of the dawn light, do not disappear when we have finished dreaming. They will not stay in our heads—they are out in the world. They can't stop going out and engaging with reality like the old woman in the fairy story who went out to cut pieces off the moon as it set foot nightly in her yard, so that it became a thin crescent. Is this a dream? It is like a dream. But by placing it alongside the reality Sylvia Plath traps us, by making us feel that when we turn back to reality, the thin people will still be 'there'. So, reality is a dream: we live in a nightmare. The world of fantasy threatens to take over the world of reality, as with the psychotic who really sees apes where there are none and (as Sylvia Plath says in many of her poems) we cannot close our eyes to a horror that presses on us.

Exactly what is the parallel between the thin people and the old woman? If we examine this question I believe we find ourselves strangely imprisoned. The dawn light is real—but the thin people persist. The old woman and the moon are imaginary, yet the words 'fat meat', and 'generous' suggest strongly that her illusory belief yielded substantial flesh. Actually the old woman does not fit easily into the logic of the poem, even admitting the logic to be poetic and irrational. There is no inevitable connection between the wasted forms of the thin people and the gradual etiolation of the moon as the old woman cuts pieces off it. The image, however, confuses us as to what is real and what is not, and what seems to be a clear-headed poetic logic leads us into a strange feeling that the world contains both old women who cut fat pieces off the moon, and thin people who have got out of our heads. From an acceptable (and seemingly rational) insight we are led into irrationality, and into a somewhat paranoid vision—close to a psychotic state, out of which we have to struggle to regain our sanity.

There *is* a connection between the old woman and the thin people, at a deeper level, which we can find by making a phenomenological interpretation of the slightly mad poem. Both are images arising from the hunger which is hate—the greedy old woman who cuts pieces off the moon may be related to us who look at the thin people, for whose emaciation we feel responsible and guilty. In the images of the old woman and the grey people, what is 'inside' us—greed, hate—is projected outside us. What the old woman and the thin people share is the fact that they are both paranoid projections of this dark inward force of which the poet was afraid and of which we are all afraid—afraid of perhaps more than any other thing in life.

'There is no capacity for reparation in us big enough ever to overcome the emptiness which the thin people, and our guilt for what happened to them, cause in our experience of the world.' This is what the poem says and by the comparison with the old woman it makes it seem the most natural thing in the world that we cannot rid our world of predatory creatures which are not mere hallucinations *but are really there*, like the moon in the old woman's yard. There is no wilderness in which we can 'lose' them, and even the 'tree boles flatten and lose their good browns': the thin people make the world thin as a wasps' nest—and destroy the very fabric of our 'life world'. We can only despair of ever over-coming the 'thinness'.

This may be true—insofar as we take it to mean that *our guilt which we feel for the victims of human hate will always cloud our perception of our world:* this is a poignant and sane observation. But it is not true that *our world is full of actual malignant shadowy creatures which haunt and discolour it, and which we can never appease or eradicate.* If we accept this as a fact we enter into madness. Or perhaps we should rather say, there are some people who can never feel normal security about what is real and what is unreal, and these are people we call mad. The problem is to determine when an abnormal view can illuminate aspects of experience, and when it is disastrous, as it certainly is in *Edge*. In *The Thin People* it is illuminating, generating an outward-going compassion prompted by shock—it enables us to see that it was a madness to create the camp victims, while this collective madness is something of which we could be capable at any time.

Sylvia Plath tells us that the world is full of hate, this may be valuable. But where she suggests that this hate can get out of hand and cannot be dealt with by our own efforts within ourselves, she is promoting irrationality and paranoia. She tells us that there are chasms between us: this may deepen our awareness of our predicament. Insofar as she suggests these chasms cannot be crossed she is denying the evident, and fundamental, truths of human love. Where she suggests that painful efforts have to be made, to reject the conformist self urged on us by 'society', and to find our true self —which may still be waiting to be born—she is being profound.

But where she urges us, with rapture, to take to the false solutions of hate, rage and self-destruction, she is pressing her sick logic on us and contributing to the same nihilism that made the thin people.

This raises wider questions, of course, about the nature of art. For the moment, perhaps, we can accept that creativity is concerned with redemption, with the pursuit of the questions 'What is it to be human?' and 'What is the point of life?' When art becomes psychotic it is cut off from 'true redemption', and ceases to interact, in a creative way, with the self and the world. Andrew Brink (1968) writes of Sylvia Plath,

> If art is to heal it must communicate distress to the significant others whose acts are implied in its genesis. It must change interpersonal relations and improve community. For all the privacy of his reactions the artist remains a social being, whose acute perception of relationships is basic to ordering of words, no matter how obliquely they speak about the actual distress. Time and again in *Ariel* we are returned to the basic fact of broken love, complicated by hatred and feelings of abandonment. There is an ambivalence because the resulting isolation is delicious, the condition of art and despair, whose accompanying self-pity is an inescapable part of the suicide syndrome. (p. 65)

The failings of her relationships, he believes, propel thinking into lethally repetitious patterns.

She felt abandoned, and gave way to abandonment. This abandoned element provokes the wild defiance in her more psychotic poems, in which the bombastic tone is a denial of all real needs, and of existential realities and responsibilities, as in *Lady Lazarus* (*Ariel*, p. 18):

> It's the theatrical
>
> Comeback in broad day
> To the same place, the same face, the same brute
> Amused shout:
>
> 'A miracle!'
> That knocks me out.
> There is a charge
>
> For the eyeing of my scars . . .

9

We may remember Dr Robert Daly's remark quoted above
(p. 126) about the impulse of the schizoid woman to seduce. Here
she enacts a strip-tease ('eyeing') by which she seduces us ('brutes')
into believing she *can* commit suicide every ten years, and come
back. For coming into any closer contact there is a penalty—which
she wants us to pay:

> And there is a charge, a very large charge
> For a word or a touch
> Or a bit of blood . . .

This sardonic reference to the relic cults of martyrdom reveals the
element of vengeance in her suicide. But this sarcastic hostility is
itself a defence against intolerable fear. If we listen to her reading
this poem on the British Council recording we can hear in her
voice a tremble of fear that gradually mounts to a quiver of rage.

Thrusting her hate into us, is, of course, a defence: it helps her
to overcome her fear that if we loved or comprehended her we
would engulf her. In fever (*Fever 103°*, *Ariel*, p. 59) she escapes
from corporeal existence into a dimension of existence beyond our
reach:

> I am too pure for you or anyone.
> . . . I am a lantern . . .
> Of Japanese paper, my gold beaten skin
> Infinitely delicate and infinitely expensive.

In the attempt to keep us away by alienation she seeks to preserve
her own chaos. Yet she makes her own encapsulated world so
consistent that by the cunning of her art we become involved in
dissociation before we realise it.

Commentators on Sylvia Plath often speak of her quest for an
absolute reality, and for a purity of vision that was intolerant of
shams. It is true that she displays great integrity. But in *Lady
Lazarus* the quest for a golden purity has a desperate and often
negative quality, as if she were seeking the purity of being no
longer human—ambivalent, full of conflict, fragments, blood and
mess. At the end of *Getting There* (*Ariel*, p. 44) she steps 'from the
black car of Lethe,/Pure as a baby'. Elsewhere she uses the image
'Pure and clear as the cry of a baby . . .' In *Lady Lazarus* she is
Herr Doktor's

opus
I am your valuable,
The pure gold baby . . .

So, the pure gold baby she hopes to be is newly born, but also one which is totally pure and so inhuman. In *Fever 103°* the state of purity is so unearthly that it is untouchable: 'I am too pure for you or anyone.'

Sylvia Plath's preoccupation with purity can, I believe, be illuminated by Fairbairn's discussion of the perplexities of the schizoid individual. In circumstances of deprivation he says 'emptiness comes to assume quite special significance for the child'. Not only does he feel empty, but he fears that his inward hunger may empty the mother—and 'involve the disappearance and destruction of his libidinal object'. The ambivalence of being human therefore to the schizoid individual means that he has within him such a strong hunger that it may spoil all goodness. Out of this arises a struggle to keep the goodness 'pure'. Sylvia Plath's use of gold as a symbol moves between these poles. In Freudian terms gold is a symbol of 'inner contents'. As an export from one's inner substance it can be something which it is good to give. But it can also be something which is to be got rid of, and which may be pure hate.

The search for an unearthly purity may be studied in *Fever 103°* (*Ariel*, p. 58). Brink (1968) notes how

> She explained that, 'This poem is about two kinds of fire—the fires of hell, which merely antagonise, and the fires of heaven, which purify. During the poem, the first sort of fire suffers itself into the second.' This shows promise of release; such suffering should prompt an affirmation of spiritual energies and greater than human hope.
>
> (p. 60. The phrases from Sylvia Plath are quoted by A. Alvarez in his *Tri-Quarterly* article.)

She is trying to say that it is possible to turn the fires of hell into the fires of heaven, by schizoid inversion. The one can merge into the other, so that death becomes birth: hate can be purging love, as by 'Radiation' and 'Hiroshima ash . . . eating in'. In the heat of the sickness she turns to reject her false self: ('My selves dissolving, old whore petticoats'). The dangers of being alive and human are too great: it is 'the aguey tendon', the sin of impure flesh. But as

> ... the low smokes roll
> From me like Isadora's scarves, I'm in a fright
>
> One scarf will catch and anchor in the wheel.*

She fears that the scarves of smoke from her purgation will actually bring her death. In this poem she sees that the tongues of hell 'will not rise'

> But trundle round the globe
> Choking the aged and the meek,
> The weak
>
> Hothouse baby in its crib,
> The ghastly orchid
> Hanging its hanging garden in the air,
>
> Devilish leopard!

This 'ghastly orchid' is surely the female element itself—the sexual organ of the negative anima, the 'devilish leopard' in herself of which she is terribly afraid, is associated with the 'weak hothouse baby', the regressed libidinal ego. Its 'hanging garden' is surely the genital. Like the newts in *Nick and the Candlestick* it is turned white by death:

> Radiation turned it white
> And killed it in an hour.
>
> Greasing the bodies of adulterers
> Like Hiroshima ash and eating in.
> The sin. The sin.

The patterns in the mind released by the delirium of fever, so accurately recorded here, are not only those of sexual guilt, but also feelings of sin, of a deep inner badness.† Her fears of dependence and ambivalence are exacerbated: 'Your body', she cries, 'Hurts me as the world hurts God'. The purity she yearns for is the purity of not being human any longer: 'I am too pure for you or anyone.'

---

* Isadora Duncan was strangled when her scarf caught in the wheel of a car.
† The reference is evidently to the film *Hiroshima Mon Amour* which merges the act of love with that of the ultimate hate.

> ... my gold beaten skin
> Infinitely delicate and infinitely expensive.

> I

> Am a pure acetylene
> Virgin ...

The poem is ironic: a comment on the deranged feelings one-experiences in fever. But yet the poet cannot distinguish between her life-feelings and those which impel her to become something non-human—a moon of paper, a lantern. In fever she is a 'huge camellia/Glowing and coming and going, flush on flush', and tormented by the beads of hot metal, pure flaming gas. The fires of hell may have been meant to become the fires of heaven, in the poem, but they are welcomed as transforming her out of the human state—a transformation into refined purity which involves the burning: she is only bewildered by the things with which she is attended

> By kisses, by cherubim,
> By whatever these pink things mean.
> Not you, nor him

> Not him, nor him
> (My selves dissolving ...)

Again, the selves sound like males.

To return to *Lady Lazarus* (*Ariel*, p. 16), we can see that the posture in it belongs to a desperate quest for such new purity, as of Lazarus raised from the dead. But the delusion is plain enough, though she tries to delude us by her Barnum and Bailey barking:

> I have done it again
> One year in every ten
> I manage it—

The absurd boast is made in a tone of hysterical pride, utterly remote from that of the quiet and acutely observed self-knowledge of (say) the bee poems, which move in the direction of being rather than not-being. This 'black flip' mode destroys capacities for meaning; and carries us into moral inversion of a dehumanised kind:

> A sort of walking miracle, my skin
> Bright as a Nazi lampshade . . .

There is a gloating satisfaction both in the inversion of appropriate
feeling and in prompting disgust in the reader. The exhibitionism
becomes offensive, like much of the schizoid destructiveness in
contemporary art:

> Peel off the napkin
> O my enemy.
> Do I terrify?

But such postures belong to weakness not strength. To use a
phrase from Guntrip there is a 'fear of being found', so that anyone
who seeks genuinely to bring her back to life and contact is an
enemy. There is thus a resistance to the reader who shares her
penetrating schizoid vision elsewhere: there is a new note here of
abandonment to 'dark rationalisations':

> Soon, soon the flesh
> The grave cave ate will be
> At home on me . . .

'grave cave ate' is the kind of 'chaos-play' on words we meet in
Laing's patient Julie, for example her 'leally lovely lifely life' or
'I'm a no un'.*

> And I a smiling woman.
> I am only thirty
> And like the cat I have nine times to die.
>
> This is Number Three . . .

As Fairbairn tells us of such schizoid modes, showing is substituted
for doing, exhibitionism for relationship. She puts herself beyond
relationship with the reader, who is contemptuously rejected as
one of the

> —peanut-crunching crowd . . .

She 'plays another scene which may seduce yet another audience'
(to use Daly's phrase)—but despite the apparent confidence (the

---

* I.e. no-one, a noun (a word not a person) and a (pure) nun. See *The Divided
Self*, p. 223.

writing is skilfully controlled) she is not now placing her own destructiveness so much as revelling in it: she is ringmaster and promotion agent to her own suicide:

> Dying
> Is an art, like everything else.
> I do it exceptionally well.
>
> I do it so it feels like hell.
> I do it so it feels real.
> I guess you could say I've a call.

As Laing points out, attempts by the schizoid individual to experience real alive feelings may be made by subjecting oneself to intense pain or terror. However, a horror of real ordinary living can develop, which will then seem ridiculous to the true self, and so repugnant. This explains the appeal in Sylvia Plath's psychotic poems: like a great deal of art in our time, she encourages us to feel that ordinary life and its satisfactions are piffling affairs—'neutrality'. The big inversions, hostilities and forms of destructiveness are the only way to live. What Laing (1960) says illuminates both Sylvia Plath's more psychotic poems and our own increasingly psychotic culture:

> The individual's . . . adaptation to ordinary living [comes] to be conceived by his 'true' self as a more and more shameful and/or ridiculous pretence. *Pari passu* his 'self', in its own fantasied relationship, has become more and more volatilized, free from the contingencies and necessities that encumber it as an object among others in the world, where he knows he would be committed to be of this time and this place, subject to life and death, and embedded in this flesh and these bones. If the 'self' thus volatilized in fantasy now conceives the desire to escape from its shut-upness, to end the pretence, to be honest, to reveal and declare and let itself be known without equivocation one may be witness to the onset of an acute psychosis.
> *Such a person though sane outside has been becoming progressively insane inside . . .* (p. 160, my italics)

Lady Lazarus is, in this sense, a psychotic poem. 'Volatilized' is a key word: she 'melts to a shriek'. She has here ceased even to play

at being sane. Laing also says: 'It is not uncommon for depersonalized patients . . . to speak of having murdered their selves . . .
Such statements are usually called delusions, they are delusions
which contain existential truth' (ibid., p. 162). The patient who
says he has 'committed suicide' may be perfectly clear about the
fact that he has not cut his throat. We find the same kind of dissociation in Sylvia Plath when she (to us, cold-bloodedly) cannot
see the evident dangers to her body and being of suicide. It is
difficult for us to discuss this kind of ambiguity, because we are
accustomed to accept statements in terms of logical, sane, argu-
ment. With such statements, however, we have to enter into the
ambiguous logic of insanity. Laing speaks of the 'denial of being
as a means to preserve being', and of 'fending off the threat of
castration' by pretending to be castrated already. Obviously, here
we regress to early infantile procedures, to avoid intolerable
threats, rather like a child calling out 'I'm not here!' in a game of
hide-and-seek. *Lady Lazarus* is a psychotic fantasy, that a person
who has committed suicide can talk about it.

Another motive for the self-castration in this poem is clear in
the aggression directed at the Father, in vengeance, and, behind
him, the castrating mother. All these are ways of dealing with
menacing figures, who are threatening her with talion revenge for
her hatred directed against them. Daddy has merged with the
psychiatrist who tried to cure her by ECT:

> So, so Herr Doktor.
> So, Herr Enemy.
>
> I am your opus,
> I am your valuable . . .

The bitterness comes from the fact (which we can see in *Poem for
a Birthday*) that the psychotherapist tried to make a pure gold
baby, 'good as gold', rather than bring the real baby self, Fido
Littlesoul, to birth. But there is no longer any hope for that
regressed libidinal ego: he could not be found in this farrago of
hate. We are in the ultimate hate-dynamics of the concentration
camp. The Nazis were heartless enough to throw babies into
furnaces: her internalised Daddy is like that, too, since he has condemned his baby to a living death.

So, what is the final product? In the hands of the doers she has become nothing, she

> . . . melts to a shriek.
> I turn and burn.
> Do not think I underestimate your great concern.

Here she completely reverses the concept of *concern*, for Herr Doktor's 'concern' is not a giving in reparation which seeks to prevent or remedy the damage or annihilation (caused by envy). It is a 'concern' that she should be entirely annihilated, the reverse of ruth. He is only concerned to eradicate her from the world in a 'final solution'. In the end Daddy merges with God and the Devil who have 'done' to her, and given her flesh, bone, but nothing essential there—only a pseudo-morality (soap), conventional relationship (a wedding ring) and 'a gold filling'—something to stop a hole, a stop-gap, pure, plug: the purgation she seeks in the fire of death reduces her to nothing. In revenge she threatens to re-emerge as pure hate.

> Ash, ash—
> You poke and stir.
> Flesh, bone, there is nothing there—
>
> A cake of soap,
> A wedding ring,
> A gold filling.

But there is something which, as Winnicott says, 'cannot be destroyed'—the true core of the self. This self is mingled with the voracious mouth-ego: we meet her in the bee poems. She is the 'red, terrible girl' whose cries are hooks. She is the essential female self, who does not often show herself—and her immediate impulse is to rise like a flame from the ashes of a false life to consume the false male imagos.

> Herr God, Herr Lucifer
> Beware
> Beware.
>
> Out of the ash
> I rise with my red hair
> And I eat men like air.

She is a salamander or Phoenix: she also has the characteristics of the chameleon which was supposed to eat air. She has also appeared 'more terrible than she ever was' in *Stings*.

In *Lady Lazarus*, Daddy-Doktor 'pokes and stirs', as if having intercourse with the mother who is ash and a vortex: but there is 'nothing there'. The triumphant note in *Lady Lazarus* is false: there is no real triumph, but a shriek of desperation, bewilderment and despair—a despair so schizoid, so deep, that it is utterly without hope, and this hopelessness can only find relief in recklessness. It is the immoral motive of the schizoid individual diagnosed by Fairbairn—'since the joy of loving seems hopelessly barred to him, he may as well deliver himself over to the joy of hating and obtain what satisfaction he can out of that'. While this is a poignant tragedy for the individual, it is also an anti-human development, and inauthentic.

If we listen acutely to Sylvia Plath we can see that she was aware that what faced her was appalling and dreadful because, even in the heart of loss of confidence, she preserved clarity of insight and expression. But because she leaves out the unrecognised factor of actual annihilation, her poetry can turn towards the psychotic, yet still remain clear and convincing in its logic—though that logic is utterly false. One sees this happening, I believe, in *Elm* (*Ariel*, p. 25). In this poem there is a powerful expression of a deep dread of the regressed libidinal ego, which, in its hunger, seems to threaten loss of all objects, and of the world itself:

> I am inhabited by a cry.
> Nightly it flaps out
> Looking, with its hooks, for something to love.
>
> I am terrified by this dark thing
> That sleeps in me;
> All day I feel its soft, feathery turnings, its malignity.

The hunger is so ferocious that there can be no confidence in love.

> Love is a shadow
> How you lie and cry after it
> Listen: these are its hooves: it has gone off, like a horse.

Though the self desperately yearns for the confirmation of love, it always seems to gallop away, like a runaway horse, and all she hears is the echoes of its hoof-beats. Again, we touch on the origin of this failure of confirmation in the mother, for whom the moon is a symbol:

> The moon, also, is merciless: she would drag me
> Cruelly, being barren.
> Her radiance scathes me. Or perhaps I have caught her.
>
> I let her go. I let her go
> Diminished and flat, as after radical surgery.

The face that should reflect is felt to be one that threatens annihilation by impingement. So, perhaps, I have 'caught her' she says— that is, 'perhaps I have become a person with her manner'. 'I let her go' means, 'I forfeit for ever any hope that I can find love there. By a kind of amputation I give up this possibility and see the moon as diminished and flat, and become diminished and flat myself' ('a cut paper shadow').

Where can the reflection be found? As in *Little Fugue* there seems only a 'featureless cloud' offering no human response. So, the identity in *Elm* seems as evanescent:

> Clouds pass and disperse.
> Are those the faces of love, those pale irretrievables?

—one gets nothing of oneself back.

> Is it for such I agitate my heart?

Surely the rhythm of this evokes a literary reference, from Tourneur,

> Does the silkworm expend her yellow labours
> For thee? For thee does she undo her self?

and also from Eliot, echoing Tourneur, 'Blood shaking my heart . . .' In Tourneur the character is looking at a skull, and the question is an existential one. In Sylvia Plath's line we have a characteristic image of reflection. 'Is my need for love, which shakes me so, and terrifies me so, a yearning for nothing more than pale passing dissipating featurelessnesses in clouds?'

In her puzzlement, she realises that she has all the insights, but
can do nothing for herself:

> I am incapable of more knowledge.

She has experienced the worst that can be experienced, and still all
she knows is hate. Without any confidence in love, how can she
ever feel 'ontological security'?

> I know the bottom, she says. I know it with my great tap root:
> It is what you fear.
> I do not fear it: I have been there.
>
> Is it the sea you hear in me,
> Its dissatisfactions?
> Or the voice of nothing, that was your madness?

She herself is only too familiar with the 'bottom': being a schizoid
individual she knows it with strange insight. But her dissatisfaction is as immense as the sea and her voice is a voice of non-being.
From her utter incapacity to find love or believe in it, she is only
amazed that the person she is addressing still cries out for it.

She doesn't know what to say to someone who yearns for love.
In telling her that love is only the echoes of disappearing hoof-
beats, she recognises that she herself is only offering hate and
despair, which may have the effect of petrifying the 'she' she is
addressing:

> All night I shall gallop thus, impetuously,
> Till your head is a stone, your pillow a little turf,
> Echoing, echoing.

She has only hate to offer:

> Or shall I bring you the sound of poisons?
> This is rain now, this big hush.
> And this is the fruit of it: tin-white, like arsenic.

Some of the images are familiar—'acetic acid in a sealed tin', the
white mushrooms growing, perhaps. But for the moment the
verse has gone garbled, and we have something more frightening
than confusion—for the words have become psychotic. The daily
experience of sunrise and sunset—as in the 'dew that flies/Suicidal

... Into the red/Eye, the cauldron of morning' (*Ariel*) becomes an atrocious series of sunsets:

> Scorched to the root
> My red filaments burn and stand, a hand of wires.

We can make gestures at meaning. There is a memory of being 'lit up like an electric bulb' by shock therapy. There is the feeling of being burnt like a witch, when 'the devil was eating the devil out'. There is a feeling of days being an agony, so that when the sun goes down red one experiences this kind of torment. But the images are wild and incoherent. The self now only exists as a series of fragmentary pieces of aggression:

> Now I break up in pieces that fly about like clubs.
> A wind of such violence
> Will tolerate no bystanding: I must shriek.

As the identity breaks up, so it is impossible to find any focus of confidence. Perception itself breaks down and everything disperses: the intentional will is paralysed. The face she sees in the branches—is it her own? Is it the moon? Certainly, it is the face of the unreflecting mother which is all one gets if one seeks love:

> What is this, this face
> So murderous in its strangle of branches?—
>
> Its snaky acids hiss.*
> It petrifies the will.

Instead of reflection there is a Medusa to petrify, a murderous image of hate. This deep fault in the psychic tissue overcomes her (for, as she says elsewhere 'fixed stars govern a life').

> ... These are the isolate slow faults
> That kill, that kill, that kill.

Berck-plage (*Ariel*, p. 30) shows the same inability to hold experience together, written under the impact of a death, about a nightmare encounter with crippled people the previous year. The topography of the summer resort around her is coloured by a sense of doom. The poem ends:

---

* The word 'kiss' in *Ariel*, in earlier editions, is a misprint.

For a minute the sky pours into the hole like plasma.
There is no hope, it is given up.

The images merge here, of a coffin going down into a grave, of
hostile faces in implosion of the identity, and of a cosmic orgasm
of annihilation. The images are psychotic in intensity. Mackerel
fishers are seen as if they are carrying parts out of a body, taken out
of the Thalassal source:

> . . . the mackerel gatherers

> Who wall up their backs against him.
> They are handling the black and green lozenges like the
>   parts of a body.

—'handling', 'parts'—the dead fish are castrated penises. They are
her inner stolen libidinal penis amputated. The landscape of this
seaside place, seen as through the eyes of a priest who has denied
love in himself (and others), is full of shrieking and surreal images
of physical intercourse:

> . . . Behind the concrete bunkers
> Two lovers unstick themselves.

The priest (like her imago of her father) has black boots:

> This black boot has no mercy for anybody.
> Why should it, it is the hearse of a dead foot,

> The high, dead, toeless foot of this priest
> Who plumbs the well of his book,

> The bent print bulging before him like scenery.

Sylvia Plath tries consciously to write a poem as if about a priest
who is distressed and obsessed by the libidinal delight he has
denied in himself. 'He' becomes, however, the dead father and so
the bad internalised father in herself. Thus the horror felt at the
normal gay seaside scene is her horror, that physical love is sick,
threatening and repulsive—because it brings the dangers feared in
parental intercourse. The toeless foot is castrated. Merged with the
titillating images

> Obscene bikinis hid in the dunes,

> Breasts and hips a confectioner's sugar
> Of little crystals, titillating the light . . .

is that of a fearsome pool that is 'sick with what it has swallowed'
—'Limbs, images, shrieks'. It is as if the noises and images of the
primal scene are evoked in fantasy, bringing an arousal of the
infantile belief that some loss of limbs is involved, when the
parents eat one another (as if they were sugar). The lovers 'unstick'
in a sterile place (concrete bunkers): their bodies are 'sea-crockery'
—vessels for a kind of depersonalised ingustation (cf. the slang
term 'dish').

The priest-protagonist is almost consumed, by the incorporative threat itself, and by his own envy:

> . . . trembling,
> Drawn like a long material
>
> Through a still virulence,
> And a weed, hairy as privates.

Beneath the imagery of recoil is that of castration (A 'long
material' 'drawn' . . .) and of being eaten by a huge female sexual
organ. The castrating father and mother are both present and they
are attacking the poet's own identity because she feels involved in
the (threatening) love activity around her on the beach, which
evokes the menace of the combined parents, castrating the
mackerel 'parts'.

Berck-plage (a resort in northern France) is a place which has
many orthopaedic convalescent homes and the crippled patients
are wheeled about the shore. They have silvery crutches and
wheel-chairs. The glitter of these takes on a menacing quality, like
her ubiquitous 'hooks instead of hands'. The castrating damage all
round her has been caused by love needs ('where are the eye-
stones'). She sees a funeral and a grave ('a naked mouth, red and
awkward'), that is the mouth of Mother Earth, the ultimate
castrator. So, this poem is full of unreconciled and unplaced
images of horror: castrated and wrecked organs: 'Old blood of
limb stumps, burnt hearts.' There is no hope of rebirth: we can
only become involved in the final paranoia and sense of futility of
the psychotic.

In one of his strange epigrams Blake said:

When a man marries a wife he finds out whether
Her knees and elbows are only glewed together.

In *The Applicant* (*Ariel*, p. 14), Sylvia Plath sets out (consciously)
as if to write an ironic poem, caricaturing the expectations of a
conventional man, who regards woman as a thing, in a society
which puts a premium on human functions rather than personal
value. But while readers try to take it in this vein of satire they are,
I believe, clinging to this notion of its 'social content' to prevent
themselves seeing how psychotic the poem is. The poem is written
with the same hostile irony as *The Tour*—in which a (normal)
genteel aunt is menaced with the brutal savagery that underlies the
world of the schizoid individual who depends on hate. We
remember that in the end the aunt is introduced to the pink rubber
bald nurse, with no eyes (see above p. 145). This nurse is all at once
Lady Lazarus, the 'blank' mother, and one of the pink torsos from
Poem for a Birthday. She is a bitterly ironic comment on the unreflecting mother who functions by pseudo-male doing. She is one
of the terrifying mannekins, darning dollies and other horrible
dehumanised figures that haunt Sylvia Plath's world—and menace
her creative life. There is a hint even of masturbating the dead to
life.

It is as spare parts of this automaton that the bits of woman are
presented to the Applicant, by a creature who bears more than a
faint resemblance to Ted Hughes's Crow: a kind of huckster who
is also a trickster. First, the protagonist asks, are you one of us?
Are you a disabled, depersonalised person?

> Do you wear
> A glass eye, false teeth or a crutch,
> A brace or a hook,
> Rubber breasts or a rubber crotch,
>
> Stitches to show something's missing?

Are you one of us crippled by society? Impaired by our less-than-
human state? *Are you like me*, a pink torso automaton, fitted with
spare parts? No, no? 'Then/How can we give you a thing?' This
means, how can we be generous to you (if you are not Fallen Man
like us)? But also, as we have seen, how can we fit you with a
(male) sexual organ? Defining someone's being, then, is seen here

as stitching something on, or applying a mechanism (as sex super-
markets supply women with a penis-shaped vibrator, or men with
a life-size doll with which it is possible to have sexual intercourse).
The protagonist could be a sexologist—or any kind of expert
offering 'treatment' of a dehumanized kind in the politics of
experience: offering 'being for the others'.

The applicant feels deprived when, having no faults he/she cannot be given a thing. He/she can produce no physical evidence of
his/her needs. So, he/she weeps—and is told

> Stop crying.
> Open your hand.
> Empty? Empty . . .

The hand has grasped no answers to the problem of life, and the
applicant comes empty-handed to the problem of meaningful
relationship.

> . . . Here is a hand

> To fill it and willing
> To bring teacups and roll away headaches
> And do whatever you tell it.

Significantly, instead of a person we have a part-object—a hand.
And what is offered is a 'thing', an 'it'.

> Will you marry it?
> It is guaranteed

> To thumb shut your eyes at the end
> And dissolve of sorrow.

It is as though the woman writing the poem is saying: 'That's all
you want of me. I am part of the stock of woman, available to
applicants.'

The lines mock the lovely phrase 'Till death do us part', in the
marriage service. This 'thing' that is being provided is as sub-
servient to the applicant's needs as a wife in ancient India who was
obliged to perform suttee at her husband's funeral. When the
applicant dies, she will dissolve in tears. She was always replaceable,
anyway.

We make a new stock from the salt. The applicant is naked,
like Adam

> I notice you are stark naked
> How about this suit——
>
> Black and stiff, but not a bad fit
> Will you marry it?

Sylvia Plath, in another poem, is married to her plaster cast. Here the applicant is being offered a black casing, like a frogman's wet suit. What is it? It is the black tegument of a schizoid identity:

> It is waterproof, shatterproof, proof
> Against fire and bombs through the roof.
> Believe me, they'll bury you in it.

It is, in fact, the black shiny shoe, in which 'I have lived'—Daddy's shoe-identity. The dispenser now turns to the inner realm:

> Now your head, excuse me, is empty.
> I have the ticket for that.
> Come here, sweetie, out of the closet.

Here we have something akin to an advertisement for *Playboy* or *Penthouse*, a magazine of paper wives.

> Well, what do you think of *that*?
> Naked as paper to start
>
> But in twenty-five years she'll be silver
> In fifty, gold.

The woman supplied is equated with the marriage certificate or paper image of woman. Her value appreciates to that of the silver and gold wedding, which is (of course) nothing.

> A living doll, everywhere you look.
> It can sew, it can cook.
> It can talk, talk, talk.
>
> It works, there is nothing wrong with it.

This physical partner is totally dehumanised, so that love and kindness became horrifying mechanical activities (as they do, of course, in a sex show or blue film).

> You have a hole, it's a poultice.
> You have an eye, it's an image.
> My boy, it's your last resort.
> Will you marry it, marry it, marry it.

The rhythmic repetition in the last line expresses a repugnance, at coition, as a mechanical jigging act which is the basis of marriage. The recommendation of relationship is seen as a sell, or cheat, while our needs are mere functions—have a hole poulticed, or a voyeuristic urge satisfied. Sylvia Plath's attitude to sexuality often belongs very clearly to the age of a pornography explosion, itself a schizoid and even pychotic manifestation.

Implicitly in this poem the normal processes of finding a sense of identity and meaning in relationship are rejected. The esoteric image of Daddy's black shoe shows how private the poem is and this brings us to a crux in our critical estimation of the poetry of a writer like Sylvia Plath. She is utterly sincere to her lights: but at times these are 'not light but rather darkness visible'. Some of her poems, too, are in 'a code of night', like Dylan Thomas's, and some exist inside the dimension of a totally inverted morality. Her experience is recorded with utter faithfulness—but falls at times within the context of a psychotic encapsulation, so that her experience is not true to 'agreed reality', however consistent it may be within itself. We need to read her poetry, then, with the awareness that sometimes every value is inverted: and that in such a poem as The Applicant we have poetry which has gone over into 'sick logic'.

Her ultimate delusions may often be found closely stated in her poems. It is sometimes argued that she exerted artistic control over them. This is not so. Certainly organisation and effort went into the poems: but the logic is pathological. Yet the delusions may be so attractively and clearly stated (and so uninhibited by reason) that they seem like sane sense—even because of the encapsulated completeness of the deranged conviction. In Last Words (Crossing the Water, p. 63), for instance, she writes that she wants a sarcophagus for her coffin.

> With tigery stripes, and a face on it
> Round as the moon, to stare up.

The 'tigery stripes' are her pseudo-male (waspish) identity—
which she aggressively adopts here as her monument when she
dies. But she asserts that when she is dead she will be able to see.

> I want to be looking at them when they come
> Picking among the dumb minerals, the roots.
> I see them already—the pale, star-distance faces.
> Now they are nothing, they are not even babies.
> I imagine them without fathers or mothers, like the first gods.
> They will wonder if I was important.

At first, the coffin is buried, and she sees the roots coming through
the soil. But 'them' refers next to the people who are to look at her
sarcophagus in several thousand years' time, when she is discovered. What she looks forward to is *being found*, and so she finds
herself looking into a mirror in which she sees babies, without
mothers or fathers—god-like. But now her hopelessness takes
over: creative reflection fades.

> My mirror is clouding over—
> A few more breaths, and it will reflect nothing at all.
> The flowers and the faces whiten to a sheet.

The mirror becomes a white sheet, which is the shroud over the
face of a corpse. It is her own breath that does this to it—the
reminder of her own mortality.

As Winnicott has indicated, the child is fascinated by breath, in
which he finds the idea of 'spirit, soul, anima'. Having contem-
plated death-as-rebirth, Sylvia Plath here becomes full of distrust:

> I do not trust the spirit. It escapes like steam
> In dreams, through mouth-hole or eye-hole. I can't stop it.

We still put our hands over our mouths when we yawn, to
prevent the soul escaping. Sylvia Plath feels, like every young
infant, that the price of being mortal is to be vulnerable enough
to be able to lose one's soul (a theme explored in many nursery
rhymes): 'One day it won't come back . . .'. 'Things aren't like
that', she continues. So, to become 'petrified' in R. D. Laing's
sense, is to be safely non-human and durable:

> They stay, their little particular lustres
> Warmed by much handling. They almost purr.

Here we have a touch of her fetishism over glittering objects.

> When the soles of my feet grow cold,
> The blue eye of my turquoise will comfort me.

She will become a mummy, and her heart (her feeling of 'being') will be stored away until she needs it.

> They will roll me up in bandages, they will store my heart
> Under my feet in a neat parcel.
> I shall hardly know myself.

When people say, 'I shall hardly know myself', they usually mean that when they try on their new clothes or jewels they will be so splendid that it will be as if they were a new person. So, with Sylvia Plath, here, she feels as if the new-born self after death will be so splendid that she will hardly recognise it—like (of course) the resplendent images of a Tutankahmun after death.

The psychotic delusion is that what is necessary is the destruction of an old self, and the rebirth of a new. In truth she won't be there to know herself. There are two other poems on parallel themes. One is *Face Lift* (*Crossing the Water*, p. 17), in which the protagonist becomes newborn, 'Pink and smooth as a baby'—by undergoing an operation. The old self is sloughed:

> Now she's done for, the dewlapped lady
> I watched settle, line by line, in my mirror—
> Old sock-face, sagged as a darning egg.
> They've trapped her in some laboratory jar.
> Let her die there, or wither incessantly for the next fifty years . . .

She has brought herself to rebirth:

> Mother to myself, I wake swaddled in gauze . . .

By contrast, another poem about the same schizoid division in herself takes a sane direction. This is *In Plaster* (*Crossing the Water*, p. 30): 'there are two of me now/This new absolutely white person and the old yellow one'. The new one is superior, 'one of the real saints'—because she is non-human. Here again is the feeling of being a case with a face painted on:

> And secretly she began to hope I'd die.
> Then she could cover my mouth and eyes, cover me entirely

And wear my painted face the way a mummy-case
Wears the face of a pharaoh . . .
. . . Living with her was like living with my own coffin . . .

It was a kind of marriage. But the choice here is to be human.

She may be a saint, and I may be ugly and hairy,
But she'll soon find out that that doesn't matter a bit.
I'm collecting my strength; one day I shall manage without
    her . . .

—so this poem follows a path back to the world, rather than that
which leads through the delusions of rebirth into the tomb.

In this confusion, what was Sylvia Plath's attitude to her own
poems? Though the words are but 'echoes', her creative activity
at best was an heroic attempt to break out of schizoid dissociation.
At the same time it seems as if she felt that her words themselves
were like worms coming alive from a corpse—by-products of
death, like manifestations of the identity squirming with their own
life, out of a body, manifestations of both life and death ('The
voices just can't worm through . . .'). In *Lady Lazarus* the narrator
notes how in hospital after an attempt at suicide:

They had to call and call
And pick the worms off me like sticky pearls.

The words again are both worms and pearls: and yet an identity
to live in too.

Her self-mothering took the form of mothering poems—as she
tells us in *Stillborn* (*Crossing the Water*, p. 35):

They are proper in shape and number and every part.
They sit so nicely in the pickling fluid!
They smile and smile and smile and smile at me.
And still the lungs won't fill and the heart won't start.

Again, we have an image of a foetus in a bottle, which is also the
regressed libidinal ego in the bell jar. Again we have the image of a
staring that is not reflection: 'And they stupidly stare, and do not
speak of her.' The poems are not, this time, being spoken out of
her mouth.

Words on the page take on at times, for her, a strange life of their own: and this evidently has something to do with the way in which her perceived world could dissolve, or turn malevolent. The priest reading at Berck-plage is trying to read his book despite the voyeuristic scenes around him. In *The Wishing Box*, as the protagonist loses her sense of a meaningfully perceived world, despite her efforts to find meaning through reading, she suddenly finds that 'to her terror' 'her eyes had scanned five pages without taking in the meaning of a single word'. 'She tried again, but the letters separated, writhing in malevolent little black snakes across the page in a kind of hissing, untranslatable jargon...' This perhaps was her worst fear of all: that the breakdown of apperception, whereby the universe had become 'dark and fatherless', should affect the one realm in which she found hope of restoring meaning. The suicide whose mind is destroyed by a vision of death (*Suicide Off Egg Rock, The Colossus.* p. 33) seems to be driven to his final act by the breakdown of reading:

> Flies filing in through a dead skate's eyehole
> Buzzed and assailed the vaulted brain-chamber.
> The words in his book wormed off the pages.
> Everything glittered like blank paper.

The sky can become blank, when there is a total loss of any sense of possible meaning in the universe: the bald eye is forced to stare at white, meaningless light. If the horror of death as nothingness overwhelms one, the quest for meaning can become so pointless that the world, as it were, packs up and leaves, crawling off like maggots from a corpse—leaving a blank white page which glitters not in reflection, but with a final mocking sterility.

At this point, having tried to define what we mean by her psychotic poerty, we may perhaps return by contrast to a sane poem—one which couldn't, however, have been written without the torment of experiencing a life without feeling alive. The mushrooms (*Mushrooms, The Colossus*, p. 34) which grow

> Overnight, very
> Whitely, discreetly
> Very quietly—

seem to her to have an uncanny power of manifesting substance:

> Our kind multiplies:
>
> We shall by morning
> Inherit the earth.
> Our foot's in the door.

The mushrooms are

> Perfectly voiceless,
>
> . . .
>
>   . . . asking
> Little or nothing.

They are also inhuman, depersonalised, mercifully not involved in relationship:

> Nobody sees us
> Stops us, betrays us . . .

She could never feel secure, in a secure world: all she could do was to allow her poems to grow, like the mushrooms, with their power of strange vitality.

> Soft fists insist on
> Heaving the needles,
> The leafy bedding . . .

Here the symbols belong to the organising power of creativity: the mushrooms symbolise 'intentionality'. But elsewhere, as Andrew Brink says she comes to 'falter on the edge of traditional archetypal problems of regeneration and then fall away into an area of psychotic transformation almost beyond the reach of art . And then we have to defend ourselves.

10

The Artist, Responsibility and Freedom

Not long ago I was talking about Sylvia Plath to the mother of some young children. I could not get her to see that in giving assent to the poem *Edge* (*Ariel*, p. 85), which she admired, she was giving assent to a poetic logic which argued conclusively that there was 'perfection' in committing suicide, and in 'folding' into one's dead body those children who had emerged from it. She could not see that one could not enjoy the poem without being troubled by doubt, as to where it might be taking the reader in admiring it.

The word 'emerged' when applied to children seems just 'not right' enough in the sentence above to provide us with a thread of a clue—to lead us out of the labyrinth, for it is a labyrinth into which Sylvia Plath lures us. The poem *Edge* is beautiful but psychotic: or, to restrict the discussion within the compass of literary criticism, delusory. Its appeal lies in the delusive purity of the logical inversion of all human values, that is logical only according to a morality based on hate.

The delusion is there in the phrase 'folded back'. Psychically speaking, it is possible to explore the experience of a mother who wants to fold back her children into herself. But insofar as this takes any physical reference, as with the word 'body', it is delusory, because children, once they have been born cannot be put back into the womb. They can, of course, be pushed back emotionally, in a manner of speaking. But, embodied, they have a 'life of their own' and their own claim to freedom.

The children in *Edge* have emerged from the protagonist's womb. The poem regards them as if they had not—as if they were still essentially part of the mother. If they were still part of the mother, there could be no moral objection to their destruction— that is, if one accepts that an individual has the right to kill himself. But if one believes that a child, once conceived, or certainly once born, has a right to live, then *Edge* is a poem which idolizes infanticide. In denying the right of a child to exist, it is denying human freedom in a very deep way. The schizoid diagnosis enables us to understand such confusions without either condoning or condemning them.

As Fairbairn tells us, schizoid women often have difficulties in giving birth. Either they will not let their children go out of their insides: or when they do release them, they lose all interest in them: or they treat them as still parts of themselves. Such 'black and white' oversimplifications of the relationship between oneself and others belong to the theme of purity, of pure hate, which in *Edge* takes on a terrifying perfectionism: the perfectionism of turning things into beautiful stone, in death.

Sylvia Plath says of the mother in *Edge*, and her dead children, that

She has folded

Them back into her body as petals
Of a rose close when the garden

Stiffens and odours bleed
From the sweet, deep throats of the night flower.

Giving sweetness, as from a flower, is to bleed: here the rose closes on itself, as the garden (body) 'stiffens', and the children she gave birth to are folded back into her body. To use a phrase from Guntrip, she is 'unable to accord them the status of separate persons'. Yet, in life, Sylvia Plath was able to accord her children sufficient separate status to avoid treating them as part of herself at her suicide. In *Edge* the children are folded back at each breast— each pitcher of milk. In life she took her children mugs of milk before taking her life. This act of provision was a recognition of their separate existence—their not-me-ness, which the poem denies. For her to care also seems an earnest of her belief that she would be there with them tomorrow—reborn. It was, of course, of psychotic disproportion to care about the children's immediate need for milk, but not to care that they were to be deprived of their mother forever after: though, unconsciously, in my view, she expected them to have a newborn mother. But there is also an underlying energy of vengeance in the poem—vengeance which, again, has a phenomenological meaning. She hopes to turn the mother into a 'sorry mother'. I take the phrase from the poem *Sleep in the Mojave Desert* (*Crossing the Water*, p. 47), in which 'the day moon lights up like a sorry mother'—and she is happy for a moment.

It will be evident from the many quotations I have given that the moon is a mother-symbol in Sylvia Plath's poetry, but that this moon-mother is not the redeeming light she is, say, in Coleridge's *Ancient Mariner*. She is rather a creature who is attending a terminal case:

> The moon lays a hand on my forehead,
> Blank-faced and mum as a nurse.
> (*Small Hours, Crossing the Water*, p. 46)

This mother is a menace:

> The moon, also, is merciless: she would drag me
> Cruelly, being barren.
> Her radiance scathes me . . .
> (*Elm, Ariel*, p. 25)

> . . . her cancerous pallors . . .
> (*Purdah, Winter Trees*, p. 17)

> What is this, this face
> So murderous in its strangle of branches?
> (*Elm, Ariel*, p. 26)

In *The Moon and the Yew Tree* (*Ariel*, p. 47) the moon-mother offers no creative opening to potentialities through love:

> The moon is no door . . .
> . . . it is quiet
> With the O-gape of complete despair . . .

> The moon is my mother. She is not sweet like Mary.
> Her blue garments unloose small bats and owls.
> How I would like to believe in tenderness . . .

In *Edge*, she is not even sorry: 'She is used to this sort of thing'. And perhaps if a sorry expression can be brought into that blank face, by a desperate measure like suicide, it will be some kind of expression at least, and so there will be some hope of being seen (but how?) by a softened face? And behind this there may be an even stranger motive. Perhaps this time, by contrast with the time of her father's death, when the mother didn't seem to care enough, she *will* now care. What anguished bewilderment! Who could applaud it?

Yet today, such confusion is *taught*. There is obviously a relationship between art and life: what happens when we are dealing with art that is so seductively delusory? If, as I believe, culture is a primary human need, what happens if we supply that need with persuasive artefacts which seek to involve us in rejecting the basic drive to go on existing? Or push into us what Brink calls 'demonic symbolism tending towards disintegration', perhaps 'overburdening consciousness with material it cannot handle' by 'dangerous art'? (Consider the series of suicides in poetry and the other arts in recent years. Hasn't the chosen position of asserting the impossibility of finding meaning something to do with that? See Masud Khan, 1975, in *The Black Rainbow*.)

With such a poem as *Edge*, there is a serious problem for criticism, when the work threatens to persuade us, by its very effectiveness as art, into a dynamic of negation. The critic can surely only endorse such art if he is prepared to endorse the essential denial of humanness and freedom?

A. Alvarez, in his book *The Savage God*, says that *Edge* is 'one of her most beautiful poems' and is 'specifically about the act that she was about to perform'. He goes on:

> It is a poem of great peace and resignation, utterly without self-pity. Even with a subject so appallingly close she remains an artist, absorbed in the practical task of letting each image develop a full, still life of its own. *That she is writing about her own death is almost irrelevant.* (p. 30, my italics)

Alvarez sees no conflict between his evaluation of the poem *Edge* and the tragic events of which he gives us a poignant account:

Around 6 a.m. she went up to the children's room and left a

plate of bread and butter and two mugs of milk, in case they should wake hungry before the *au pair* girl arrived. Then she went back down to the kitchen, sealed the door and window as best she could with towels, opened the oven, laid her head in it and turned on the gas. (p. 30)

He also says, 'she must have accepted the logic of the life she was leading and come to terms with its terrible necessities'. Yet, as he relates, she 'left a note saying, "Please call Dr ——" and giving his telephone number' (p. 31)—as if she did not want to die. She is anxious to give the children the 'breast'—but not as in *Edge*, in such a way as to make them into asps. She seems to have expected herself to be there next day.

There is surely no logic in anyone's life, or in the way they lead it, which obliges them to come to an inescapable conclusion that they *must* commit suicide? Whatever Alvarez says, there can be no 'terrible necessity' to end one's life. How can one call a mistaken suicide attempt, which succeeds against a person's intentions, a 'coming to terms'? Doesn't pity itself require us to try to unravel the false solution that suicide nearly always must be?

As Andrew Brink (1968) points out, Sylvia Plath finds infant innocence in *The Night Dances*, 'with Coleridgean overtones', as a manifestation of new beginnings. The children were certainly a challenge to her nihilistic solipsism. But yet, tragically, she was still overcome by her illogic, of believing 'perfection' required death:

> The old self, so unsatisfactory in its functioning, could not be put aside by the new-mother-self, only just fledged. A rationalization therefore had to be devised to the effect that any hope in self-perpetuation was a missing of the true meaning of perfection. At some point nullification of all took over from qualified acceptance of new life offered by the children. (p. 59)

Perhaps what gave her hope was her capacity as a woman to create being, in her children. Schizoid purity, 'perfection', she sees in *The Munich Mannequins* as 'terrible, it cannot have children'. In *Magi* she is deeply critical of abstracts of perfection. In *Edge* 'the woman is perfected' in death and her children are folded within her. But, as Brink also says, 'the children already existed in their own right', and so discovering this enabled her to *leave them alive.*

> Even in extremity to deny them was impossible, and indeed there had been a time when the children seemed to remove the general curse. In a BBC broadcast talk she had said of her poem *Nick and the Candlestick* that 'a mother nurses her baby son by candlelight and finds in him a beauty which, while it may not ward off the world's ills, does redeem her share of it'. This idea is startlingly developed in *Edge*, written in the last week of her life when everything had gathered on impending self-extinction. It is a poem of active resolve to break out of the vicarious circle of torment, and it openly speaks of death as the only remaining perfection. All sense of continuity is put aside as the children, *reduced to extensions of self*, are caught up in the same drive to finality. (Ibid., my italics)

Here Brink points to the fundamental ethical objection to the delusions: children are not mere 'extensions of self' and a woman who chooses 'finality' has no right to inflict it on them. Yet, as Brink indicates, the art seems so perfect that we can easily become involved in its 'sick logic': it is true that dust returns to dust by the nature of things, but it is not true that suicide and infanticide are 'natural' in the same way:

> Return to the earth is in the nature *of things, but not as it is put in 'Edge', whose art is so accomplished that its darkest-rationalization fully passes scrutiny. Sick logic establishes itself through suffering and the power of metaphor.* (Ibid., pp. 59–60, my italics)

The problem is how to make the 'schizoid diagnosis' and to unravel the sick logic, while giving recognition to the creative effort. In an article in *The Cambridge Review* (7 February 1969, p. 246) A. Alvarez wrote a denunciation of the kind of analysis I have made here:

> Not, alas, that this will discourage the amateur analysts: no doubt they will ransack these poems, as they have others, for their own devious, undiscriminating and wholly uncritical ends. So it might be as well to point out that here [in the collection of poems handed in for the Tripos at Cambridge] as in her later

work, when Sylvia takes as her subject a couple of mildly persecuted dreams, she was able to use the material positively, creatively and with very great objectivity in order to make autonomous poems. Which is an activity a good deal less sick and uncontrolled than the interpretations which will, almost certainly be wished on it.

In this, it would seem, interpretation is itself seen as 'sick'. That suicide is sick is hotly denied in Alvarez's book. But phenomenological interpretation, as a way of 'listening' to meanings, might have provided clues to ways of saving Sylvia Plath herself, by indicating that, if not 'sick', her logic was deluded and false. As Brink says, 'Had Sylvia Plath's hopefulessness and helplessness found relief, had the existential situation altered just slightly, natural forces might have intervened'. Who would not feel concern, over someone who wanted to take their own life, 'sick' or not? And who would not want the forces of survival cherished by 'relief'—in her, in poetry, and in us?

Even Alvarez appreciates that Sylvia Plath did not really want to die. But he never detects that strange manifestation which is *schizoid* suicide. It is important to emphasise the truth (which should be clear enough when looking at the corpse, as Alvarez did) that suicide is not birth. It does not set you free: it kills you. One must not be seduced into the (false) belief that it represents a beginning, however much one may understand how there seemed no other authentic path to take.

In his book Alvarez personifies suicide as a 'savage god'. This seems to be almost a kind of paranoid projection of the destructive dynamic which is essentially within ourselves. The 'meaning' which suicide is supposed to give a life is really a false meaning— bound up with turning against the true self and the fundamental ego-weakness.

I have tried to expose the flaws in Sylvia Plath's logic. She was anxious that her children should have their drinks next morning. A parallel anxiety did not stop her from orphaning them. In this we see the radical dissociation in her. She was exposing others to the possibilities of brain damage, serious injury, or death by explosion. She risked killing a neighbour, as is made clear from the biographical details in Alvarez's book.

Only a plea of being deluded by a totally mistaken logic into supposing she was making a new world for herself can absolve her and lead us to her pain. It is not possible to absolve her simply on the grounds that she was an artist. To applaud her more nihilistic poems (and her suicide) is to fail to encounter her suffering, as Alvarez really does when he says: 'her suicide becomes the whole point of the story, the act which validates her poems, gives them their interest, and proves her seriousness' (*The Savage God*, p. 33). Is this not (in George Orwell's words) 'shrinking from the implications of the fact that an artist is also a citizen and a human being'?

The consequent critical dilemma haunts the symposium *The Art of Sylvia Plath* without being exorcised. A. R. Jones writes of the *Ariel* poems: 'We are persuaded almost to cooperate with the destructive principle, indeed to love the principle as life itself . . .' (p. 236). Some of the contributors to this book show themselves to be aware of a problem: but they tend to shrink from it with an aggressive defiance of any attempt to comprehend the nature of Sylvia Plath's distortions of experience. So agitated are they to protect her against being called 'ill' that they manage effectively to prevent themselves and others from understanding her existential anguish. They are afraid that if she is called 'ill' her art will be dismissed as sick, but they do not see that in simply accepting her work without discrimination they are failing themselves to suffer and choose, in recognition of the deeper and more painful aspects of her predicament, while betraying art.

Charles Newman, the editor, asks, 'Given the premises of *her* poetry, what good is art?' But, he says, that question 'cannot be answered in criticism'. 'Criticism', apparently, must be limited to that which does not concern itself with meaning. If we did concern ourselves with meaning we might 'find [her] impulse anti-humanistic or indicative of mental illness'. Though Newman quotes (at least three times) Freud's observation that 'the state of being in love threatens to obliterate the boundaries between ego and object', he does not try to distinguish between pathological and normal manifestations of the schizoid fear of merging with the object, or the impulse to annihilate the 'other' associated with it—and the consequent impulse to turn against life altogether.

Newman's only way of avoiding these problems is by becoming a cold-blooded aesthete: 'It is the form of the expression, and not the neurosis from which it may or may not issue, which concerns us, and which we can evaluate, celebrate' (p. 24). Newman sees that there is in her a kind of detachment which is 'schizophrenic'. 'This aesthetic detachment . . . isolated her in the outside world': but he wants us to isolate ourselves in the same way, in our responses. Her dissociation conferred on her 'a peculiar sense of strength'. So, we are to find even her most nihilistic work 'one of the most astonishing creative outbursts of our generation—a breakthrough in modern poetry', or even a 'triumphal surge of affirmation'. This is nonsense: her psychotic poems are a defence against weakness and her blackest poetry is the opposite of affirmation.

There is one voice which stands out in *The Art of Sylvia Plath*; the decent and obviously pained voice of her husband, Ted Hughes. In his notes in the *Poetry Society Bulletin* (February 1965), Hughes pays tribute to the astonishing power of her will, which sought to wring creativity and love out of impossibility:

> Her whole tremendous will was bent on excelling. Finally, she emerged like the survivor of an evolutionary ordeal: at no point could she let herself be negligent or inadequate. What she was most afraid of was that she might come to live outside her genius for love, which she also equated with courage, or 'guts', to use her word. This genius for love she certainly had, and not in the abstract. She didn't quite know how to manage it: it possessed her. It fastened her to cups, plants, creatures, vistas, people in a steady ecstasy. As much of all that she could, she hoarded into her poems, into those incredibly beautiful lines and hallucinatory evocations.

Yet they are hallucinatory, and her muse, as he sees, was often virtually death himself:

> Behind these poems there is a fierce and uncompromising nature. There is also a child desperately infatuated with the world. And there is a strange muse, bald, white and wild, in her 'hood of bone', floating over a landscape like that of the Primitive Painters, a burningly luminous vision of Paradise. A Paradise which is at the same time eerily frightening, an unalterably spot-lit vision of death.

10

In the face of this enigma, while trying to understand madness, we need to discriminate, for the sake of art as well as for the sake of the tormented person, for this vision is surely a vision of an Anti-Paradise? With her we must establish, to quote Masud Khan:

> a *sanity* to humanistic values that need so urgently to be re-instated if literature and art are not to become the ruthless and ultimate vehicles for the dissolution of human individualism, respect for life and pain, belief in the necessity of the *other* for one to be real and to be a person, and faith in zest and joy which alone make mind and its symbolic logic creative.
>
> (Private communication)

The posture of *la grande désorientation* may seem heroic, but it may be a false and desperate stance of flight from our essential nature. The mentally ill individual who leaps from the skyscraper or cuts out his mistress's heart, or pours petrol over himself and becomes a 'human torch', for no rational cause or justified passion, may seem to be making a heroic gesture. Yet, by a phenomeno-logical analysis, when such 'solutions' are based on false self strategies, though they may seem heroic, they may really be a *denial* of what the individual knows deep down to be his 'own business' (which is why we try to 'talk down' a suicide). As Guntrip says, a 'defensive system' which motivates such actions, may be defensive 'against the dangers of the inner world', so that what is being acted out symbolises an inner drama, but the falsity is in the delusion that this can be achieved by outer demonstra-tions. Of course, as Guntrip (1968) also says, a self-system that has 'gone wrong'

> perhaps deserves a better label than Winnicott's term 'false self'. It is the result of an often heroic struggle to stay alive and discover a modus vivendi. But it is not really the patient's true and proper self for it finds no room for his uniqueness and individuality . . . (p. 190)

While the 'inauthentic' may seem heroic, it can also be cruel and inhibiting. The negative dynamics of the self may become sadistic, attacking the hidden weak regressed libidinal ego, disrupting the whole 'psychic tissue', as a person divides against herself.

An inability to tolerate weakness in oneself can be turned on others. This kind of futile destructiveness (so prevalent in the arts today) is not essentially creative and differs totally from the positive destructiveness described by Marion Milner (1969) who speaks of 'creative fury that will not let individuals rest content with a merely compliant adaptation', that may need 'temporary chaos' when there is hope of a 'better' self and a 'growth towards one's own shape', beyond the chaos (p. 389).

The dynamics of destructive hate may be seen as 'strategies of survival'. But the danger is that the cycles of hate can become encapsulated. An individual may feel as Guntrip says, 'I can't change, I feel hopeless'. There can develop a 'hopelessness about putting any of the existential questions to rest', with a consequent disintegration of all effort to 'be something'. In such a situation, *in clinical therapy*, the psychotherapist has to be an 'interventionist' —to break into the system of 'internal reality in which the patient's symptoms are entrenched'.

With Sylvia Plath, I believe, the literary world failed to offer any such 'intervention' which could break into her encapsulation, to provide 'relief'. Alvarez seems now to believe that Sylvia Plath felt that 'help might be acceptable if you were willing to make the offer', and that he let her down by failing to understand her meaning in *Death & Co.* (see *The Savage God*). This seems remote from his earlier point of view: 'Whether her involvement with suicide . . . was real or imaginary is beside the point so far as her art is concerned' (*Times Literary Supplement*, 23 March 1967, p. 231).

But it may be the case, as Andrew Brink (1968) believes, that the poetry defined a course: 'The truth is that poetry became so completely the vehicle for feeling and willing that it simultaneously opened up and pursued a course of action' (p. 54). This raises, of course, wide social, cultural, and political issues. Few critics have raised the question of the moral effects of Sylvia Plath's work.

Irving Feldman (in *Book Week*, 19 June 1966) said that her words were 'the motions of the disembodied will'—and 'this disembodiment takes the form of a sort of pure style, of words released from their weight of meaning, or moral concern'. He is attacked for this in *The Art of Sylvia Plath*: his linking of the aesthetic problems and her madness is dismissed as 'super-psychologised nonsense' (p. 298). P. N. Furbank pointed to the resemblance between Sylvia Plath's poetry and 'black' cinema (*The Listener*, 11 March 1965). But the fashionable view, represented by Newman's book, is that such objections cannot be sustained, and in her life it seems clear that what may be called the fashionable *avant garde encouraged* her negative dynamics, as they did Dylan Thomas's. At the same time they failed to see where her real courage lay.

Our only hope of recovering discrimination is in demonstrating that the view of man underlying the present 'black' fashion is false and not at all 'realistic'. The assumption behind such contemporary criticism of the fashionable kind is that man's fundamental reality is aggressive and sensual—brutish. Thus in his essay in *Encounter* in June 1965 ('American After-thoughts') Alvarez says that most of Sylvia Plath's later poems are 'about the unleashing of power, about tapping the roots of her own inner violence . . .' As we have seen, Sylvia Plath's 'violence' is by no means an 'unleashing of power', or 'tapping of roots'. It is a manifestation of failure. It belongs rather to the rejection of the 'importunate cricket'—her hungry Littlesoul—and a flight from the existential problem, into chaos. Misled by his model of man, which is that of the scientific reductionism of the 'Naked Ape' school, Alvarez virtually makes the tapping of the *roots* of violence a requirement for all the best modern art. 'There is, of course, nothing extraordinary about this, I think that this, in general, is the direction all the best contemporary poetry is taking.' He adds: 'this kind of writing involves an element of risk . . . the very source of her self-destructiveness. But it was precisely a source of *living* energy, of her imaginative creative power . . .' (*Triquarterly* (1966), p. 73).

The assumption is that violence in the 'animal' self is a source of vitality—a theory Alvarez shows he accepts elsewhere in writing of Ted Hughes:

> There was a sense of his being in touch with some primitive area, some dark side of the self . . . This, after all, was what his poems were about: an immediate, physical apprehension of the violence both of animal life and of the self—of the animality of the self. (*The Savage God*, p. 24)

This belief in the animal violence in us as the spring of creativity is not borne out by psychoanalysis, *Dasein* analysis, the new existentialism or philosophical biology. Alvarez points more clearly to the origins of poetic energy when he says her expression is a 'by-product of a compulsive need to understand'. The motto to Alvarez's book on suicide is a sentence from Bakhunin: 'The passion for destruction is also a creative passion': but surely this is only acceptable if 'destructiveness' leads to something new? Our counter-quotation, from Guntrip, must be, 'only the strong can love: it is the weak who hate'. From philosophical anthropology it is becoming clear that consciousness and civilised values are primary aspects of human nature, and products of evolution in its higher stages. It is natural to man to be good and to strive towards transcendence. In this light of this and the 'schizoid diagnosis', the emphasis in contemporary fashionable culture on man's brutishness, and the accompanying cynicism about values are obscurantist falsifications.*

One critic in *The Art of Sylvia Plath* declares that 'in a deranged world a deranged response is the only possible reaction of the sensitive mind'. But there have been those—Anne Frank, Viktor Frankl, Pastor Bonhoffer—who did not respond in such a hopeless way to appalling circumstances. Why should it not be possible for the sensitive mind to 'hold fast to what it means to be a man'—as Kierkegaard urged? From the point of view of philosophical anthropology, our primary reality is not aggression but the need for meaning, and this should be the last thing to give up. If we accept the view that derangement is justified by a deranged society, then may we not, by nourishing destructiveness, allow ourselves to be cut off from our deepest resources? These questions are well discussed by such critics as Theodore Roszak and Philip Rieff. Entrapped in a pessimistic functional view of man, many people today, like Ted Hughes, seem to think it is only realistic to lose hope in civilisation, since there is no hope of redeeming man: Hughes has spoken of 'a pervasive and deep feeling that civilisation has disappeared completely' (*London Magazine*, January, 1971). He also refers to the need to have one's spirit 'invested in something

* See *Naked Ape—or Homo Sapiens?* Towers and Lewis, Garnstone, 1969; John Vyvyan, op. cit.; *Towards a Psychology of Being*, Abraham Maslow, Van Nostrand, 1968; and the present author's *Human Hope and the Death Instinct*, Pergamon, 1971.

that will not vanish . . . a new divinity . . .'. Yet in *Crow*, his latest work, there is little that may be called divinity, but rather surely a cultivation of the desperation of an encapsulated nihilism ('Nothing escaped him. Nothing could escape.')

While it is true that there is a curative impulse in *Orghast*, isn't the effect of *Crow*, like that of Sylvia Plath's final lapse into nihilism, to promote hopelessness and a 'longing for non-being'? In *Orghast in Persepolis* we read that, 'Agoluz . . . works out in physical and mortal terms what Sogis works out in spiritual terms. Agoluz's role is to convert the Krogonishness inherent in himself (his real father being Krogon) to a sane, rational, albeit limited and partial order, which is workable' (p. 96). But even in this, there is a suggestion that ordinary, positive existence implies a compromise, and the expression of a Heideggerian contempt for natural existence. It is true that, according to Smith, 'The cure, for Man, will be to understand this bird (Krogon) and come to some final reconciliation . . . not to heroify the sickness . . .'. But doesn't *Crow* heroify the psychotic and glamourise false solutions? And doesn't the elated bravado of the poetry endorse this posture: *Song for a Phallus* bearing a significant relationship to the aggressive assertiveness of *Daddy* and *Lady Lazarus*? Aren't they both a 'giving way to the joys of hating and getting what satisfaction one can out of that'? And aren't suicide and its cult aspects of this idolisation of false solutions and terribly dangerous in our world which could well commit suicide entirely, and now has the technology to do so?

Alvarez, for his part, rejects at the end of *The Savage God* any suggestion that suicide is 'diseased'. It is, he believes, cleaner and less nasty than natural death. Obviously for him suicide has the appeal of showing that one is existentially big and strong. As a patient of Guntrip's said, 'If I were man enough I'd do it'. To Alvarez, suicide is 'a terrible but utterly natural reaction to the strained, narrow, unnatural necessities we sometimes create for ourselves' (p. 237). But suicide is not larger than life, nor is it the only reaction to 'narrow necessities'. Nor is ordinary life 'unnatural', even in the hygienic mundanity of suburbia, whatever Heidegger may feel about *Das Mann*. It is no solution to the deadness and conformity of the dehumanised life of Western Society, to go over to the braggadoccio postures of false solution.

This is not courage. The courage we require is the courage to be human.

Is our use of the word 'false' in 'false self' merely a semantic trick? Discussing the whole concept of 'false self' Peter Lomas says: 'it would perhaps be least confusing to restrict the term "false" to behaviour designed, for whatever reason, to conceal the existence of the true self and therefore to deny meaning' (in Rycroft (1966), p. 137). Here it is important to emphasise, as Lomas does in *True and False Experience*, that to be false is to deny one's truth—and so to forfeit one's freedom and authenticity: to shirk human responsibilities: to lose potentialities. Some critics represent Sylvia Plath as a martyr because she seems the victim of a society which oppressed her 'freedom'. Thus Alvarez writes in *The Art of Sylvia Plath* about *Daddy*:

> She goes right down to the deep spring of her sickness and describes it purely. What comes through most powerfully, I think, is the terrible *unforgivingness* of her verse, the continual sense not so much of violence—although there is a good deal of that—as of violent resentment that this should have been done to *her*. What she does in the poem is, with a weird detachment, to turn the violence against herself, so as to show that she can equal her oppressors with her self-inflicted oppression. And this is the strategy of the concentration camps. When suffering is there whatever you do, by inflicting it upon yourself you achieve your identity, you set yourself free. (p. 66)

But Sylvia Plath did not set herself free, nor was she 'oppressed', however much her deluded decision was a quest for freedom. Alvarez sees that her tone is one of 'manic defence': but he goes on, 'But what, in a neurotic, is a means of avoiding reality, can become, for an artist, a source of creative strength . . . presenting the situation in all its fullness' (p. 66). But, as we have also seen, she is *not* able to present the 'situation in all its fullness': she gives herself up to a partial view in which certain terms in the logic are disastrously missing. Alvarez continues: 'There is a kind of cooing tenderness in this which complicates the other, more savage note of resentment. It brings in an element of pity, less for herself and her own suffering than for the person who made her suffer. Despite everything, '*Daddy*' is a love poem' (p. 66).

But, as I have shown, I trust, *Daddy* is a desperate rejection of the essential negative energy that kept her alive, when hope came to be lost. Alvarez later seems to have looked at his own conclusions more closely and adds a postscript to his remark, 'Poetry of this order is a murderous art' (p. 67):

> These final remarks seem to have caused some confusion. I was *not* in any sense meaning to imply that breakdown or suicide is a validation of what I now call Extremist poetry . . .
>
> But I did mean that this kind of writing involves an element of risk. The Extremist artist sets out deliberately to explore the roots of his emotions, the remotest springs of his personality, maybe even the sickness he feels himself to be a prey to, 'giving himself over to it,' as I have written elsewhere, 'for the sake of the range and intensity of his art.' It is precisely here that the risk lies. (p. 67)

Everything depends, of course, on what is meant by 'giving himself over to'—a phrase which disturbingly echoes Fairbairn's words about the fanatical immoralism of the schizoid individual who gives himself up to the joys of hating in ruthless despair of ever finding love. Alvarez goes on,

> I do not personally believe in the classical Freudian argument that art is therapeutic, that the artist is relieved of his fantasies by expressing them. The very source of her creative energy was, it turned out, her self-destructiveness. But it was, precisely, a source of *living* energy of her imaginative, creative power. So, though death itself may have been a side-issue, it was also an unavoidable risk in writing her kind of poem. My own impression of the circumstances surrounding her eventual death is that she gambled, not much caring whether she won or lost; and she lost. (pp. 67–8)

How, in life or art, can death ever be a 'side-issue'? It is surely at the centre of all human effort, in the sense that it challenges us with the problem of the meaning of our existence, because it is the focus of our greatest dread. But again, as I hope I have shown, Sylvia Plath by no means gambled with death, but, rather, held death at the centre of her living and her art: but, certainly, no-one can call her final energy of nullification a 'living energy'.

Alvarez, like the contributors to *The Art of Sylvia Plath*, is anxious to preserve her created work from being dismissed because it is 'sick'. But this is to confuse the psychopathology of the person with the implicit world-view in the works. As Viktor Frankl (1969) says, '. . . it is self-evident that no . . . psychopathology can ever pass judgement on the validity or invalidity of a world-view' (p. 15). That we make a diagnostic statement about the psychopathology of a person does not exonerate us from the need to come to grips philosophically with his world view and examine it for its rightness or wrongness. Elsewhere Frankl makes the point that a person may be mentally ill, and in desperate need at times, because he cannot cope with existence. But whether he is ill, or whether he is for the time being healthy, psychically speaking, he may have an anguished preoccupation with the problem of existence, or even a dread, which is not sick, but a natural manifestation of his human self-awareness and consciousness of the nature of life. To be tormented by the dreadful nature of existence is not to be ill, but human. Death obliges us to find meaning, in order to assert the *Dasein*. But false-solutions and destructiveness cannot achieve the *Dasein*. They solve nothing.

Alas, enormous creative effort did not save Sylvia Plath. Few psychotherapists today would subscribe to the 'Freudian' theory which Alvarez dismisses. The deep scars in the psychic tissue which cause mental illness may not be healed by a lifetime of creative effort, while no-one expects any man's spiritual anguish ever to be healed of its tragic truth. There can be no doubt that to be as deluded as she was about the nature of death and re-birth was psychopathological as was (whatever Alvarez may say) her suicide. But this does not mean that in all her poetry the attitude to human existence is psychopathological, nor can it be rejected on the grounds of psychotherapeutic theory. At times, as I hope I have shown, in *The Swarm* and *The Night Dances*, for example, she offers us acute perspectives which enhance our sanity. But there are other poems in which she 'gives herself over'—to her psychosis, and in these the element she most dangerously abandons is the organisational, creative quality—that which Andrew Brink calls the 'redemptive'. In these the same self-defeat which killed the woman also defeats the art, by diverting the pursuit of meaning towards a hopeless sensationalism. And it is this problem in contemporary art to which Alvarez's kind of encouragement of derangement is no service. Everywhere the very context in which art can exist at all is being destroyed by the abandonment of those redemptive and meaning-seeking qualities which alone make art worth having at all: indeed, many avant-gardists attack the greatest works of art out of sheer envy of their creative power, and in feeble malice.*

The failure of the redemptive elements in the poetry of Sylvia Plath is explored by Andrew Brink (1968) in the essay from which I have quoted. He cites William Law:

> every life . . . must bear and torment itself with its own inward-burning Strife, and yet be unable to reach, touch, or obtain any Spark of Light and Love to make its Fire-life sweet and amiable . . .
>
> (*The Grounds and Reasons of Christian Regeneration*, 1759)

Brink says of Sylvia Plath that 'these poems [*Ariel*] came out of a state fully answering Law's description of "inward burning strife" but they attempt its overcoming by means of conventional re-demptive symbols which are imagistically potent *without being effective*'. The private language 'looks like something redemptive but is not'. 'The result is a curiously synthetic language doing little or nothing to pull together the community of relationships and meaning so desperately needed if life was to continue' (p. 49). Brink accepts the problem of Sylvia Plath's ineffectiveness in creativity as Alvarez does not. Brink continues:

> The life at risk is real and not a sham, hence the unmatched directness and poignancy with which complicated states of mind are revealed. Naked feeling is conveyed with hallucinatory force—we are brought alarmingly close to a burning, self-consuming centre. But why do the poems stop at this when seeming to promise release? (p. 49)

Because, in the end, the destructive energies triumph,

> her poems release self-destructive thoughts of increasing magnitude. As they penetrate with ever truer aim to the core of mental distress, they reveal the one thing needful, a pathological

---

* The account at the end of *Orghast in Persepolis* is relevant here.

wish not to be resisted. In the end intention and act are inseparable as the poems fabricate a deed and justify it. (p. 54)

Brink virtually sees that in this drive there is an underlying symbolism of schizoid suicide: 'the artist embarks on a self-destructive journey *which might have brought rebirth*' (my italics). He observes that the poetry became encapsulated—cut off from love and forgiveness. 'With this essential ingredient missing . . .', the myth of eternal return, 'the engendering and making new, is all but invalidated.' Intentionality is corrupted, in terms of being —and only the intention to negate triumphs: in Brink's phrase 'At some point nullification of all took over'. How can those concerned with culture *approve* of *nullification*? Alvarez says, 'It was only by her determination to face her most inward and terrifying experiences, and to use her intelligence in doing so—so as not to be overwhelmed by them—that she managed to write these extraordinary poems' (review in *The Observer*, 14 March 1965). But whatever he says, and despite her courage, she *was* 'overwhelmed' by her experiences, and her delusory assault on Daddy is a way of *not* facing the needs of the regressed libidinal ego. She gave herself over instead into the hands of the malignant animus, and lost hope of solving the problem of existence altogether.

That Sylvia Plath was encouraged in this path by literary fashion is clear. In a British Council recorded interview she admitted that

> I've been very excited by what I feel is the new breakthrough that came with say Robert Lowell's *Life-Studies*. This intense breakthrough into very serious, very personal emotional experience, which I feel has been partly taboo. Robert Lowell's poems about his experiences in a mental hospital, for example, interest me very much. These peculiarly private and taboo subjects I feel have been explored in recent American poetry—I think particularly of the poetess Anne Sexton, who writes also about her experiences as a mother: as a mother who's had a nervous breakdown . . . (*The Poet Speaks*)

Alvarez believes that Sylvia Plath took further than Lowell and Anne Sexton her 'analysis of the intolerable' and the 'taboo'. But what in our culture was 'taboo'? He refers to the film *Hiroshima Mon Amour,* in which 'adultery, radiation and expiation were also inextricably mixed together'. In Sylvia Plath's *Fever 103°* says Alvarez: 'The idea of the individual and the world purged of sin is established, and the poem is free to move on to the realms of purification' (*Art of Sylvia Plath*, p. 63).

We have looked at the logic of pure hate in such poems as *Lady Lazarus* and the flip 'cool' of references in it to 'my skin/Bright as a Nazi lampshade'. In this there is a disturbing lack of a sense of human proportion. The zany light-heartedness, as with some passages in *The Bell Jar* about death, display a cold intellectual callousness. But it isn't that Sylvia Plath meant to be callous: the failure of tone is a manifestation of a certain emotional failure to know how to respond, of what the psychotherapists call a 'diminution of affect', or 'absence of appropriate feeling tone'.

Sylvia Plath seems to have felt that existence should be controllable by the mind:

> I believe that one should be able to control and manipulate experiences, even the most terrifying—like madness, being tortured, this kind of experience—and one should be able to manipulate these experiences with an informed and intelligent mind. I think that personal experience shouldn't be a kind of shut box and mirror-looking narcissistic experience. I believe it should be generally relevant, to such things as Hiroshima and and Dachau, and so on. (British Council interview)

Hiroshima and Dachau were themselves terrible acts of dissociated mental hate. There is a dreadful relevance in what she says: but intellectual control is no answer, because it belongs to hate.

Alvarez finds remarkable the objectivity with which she handles such personal material. But the objectivity she displays in some poems is like the cold-bloodedness of a schizoid individual who simply does not know how to respond to human suffering. In psychoanalytical terms, she had in some areas not completed the 'stage of concern', and so could not experience the capacity to make reparation, to feel for others: hence her hopeless failures of tone, at times. Elsewhere, it must also be said, however, she does experience concern—and reparation, as in *Nick and the Candlestick*.

We have the same kind of failure of appropriate feeling response in Sylvia Plath's connoisseurship of methods of suicide.

The subject of *Lady Lazarus* for Alvarez is 'the total purification of achieved death' whatever that may mean (*Art*, p. 64). In this poem, he says, Sylvia Plath becomes an 'imaginary Jew'. More closely examined, this seems an indulgence in a schizoid-paranoid delusion of oppression.

> Dying
> Is an art, like everything else.
> I do it exceptionally well.
>
> I do it so it feels like hell.
> I do it so it feels real.

We are almost invited to a seductive conclusion that those who suffered death in concentration camps were lucky, because they experienced a resurrection:

> Out of the ash
> I rise . . .

But, of course, the whole falsity of the poems is in the failure to recognise that one cannot *repeat* suicide, as she believed one could. To do it well is the end.

The fascination with death-camps finally gives her (and Alvarez) away. Alvarez declares that

> anyone whose subject is suffering has a ready-made modern example of hell on earth in the concentration camps. And what matters in them is not so much the physical torture—since sadism is general and perennial—but the way modern, as it were industrial, techniques can be used to destroy utterly the human identity. Individual suffering can be heroic provided it leaves the person who suffers a sense of his own individuality—provided, that is, there is an illusion of choice remaining to him. But when suffering is mass-produced, men and women become as equal and identity-less as objects on an assembly line, and nothing remains—certainly no values, no humanity. This anonymity of pain, which makes all dignity impossible, was Sylvia Plath's subject. (*Art*, p. 65)

But does Sylvia Plath invoke the death-camp phenomena in poems like *Lady Lazarus* to find insight into nihilistic impulses (as she does in *The Swarm*)? Or to justify her libidinal attachment to her death-circuit? To celebrate freedom as Solzhenitsyn and Viktor Frankl do? Or to posture at being 'oppressed' and 'identify with the aggressor' in masochistic self-indulgence as so much of today's art does?

To Alvarez her paranoid delusions themselves are heroic:

> Second, she seemed convinced, in these last poems, that the root of her suffering was the death of her father, whom she loved, who abandoned her, and who dragged her after him into death. And in her fantasies* her father was pure German, pure Aryan, pure anti-semite. (*Art*, p. 65)

Of course, Sylvia Plath tries herself to make out that her poem *Daddy* is 'spoken by a girl with an Electra complex. Her father died while she thought he was God'.

> Her case is complicated by the fact that her father was also a Nazi and her mother was very possibly part Jewish. In the daughter the two strains marry and paralyse each other—she has to act out the awful little allegory before she is free of it.
> (British Council interview)

But this 'story' is surely merely a thin disguise over her own obsessive and hostile attachment to the 'internalised bad object'. Since Otto Plath went to America at the age of fifteen and had his book *Bumblebees and their Ways* published there in 1934, there seems no occasion to suppose he was a Nazi, or to commend fantasies that he was 'pure Aryan, pure anti-semite'.

Alvarez is correct in seeing that the poem is motivated by 'vengeance'. But who deserves it? Alvarez seems to imply that if one suffers oppression and torture then the way to choose one's freedom is to cultivate an 'internal fascism'. But Viktor Frankl's (1957) account of his experience of Auschwitz concentration camp makes it quite clear that it was the Nazis in whom the 'internal fascism' was to be found. Yet even then, once you knew them, these individuals were only mixed and imperfect human beings. Frankl's way of preserving meaning, not least by 'taking his

---

* The phrase 'in her fantasies' is not in the essay in the *Tri-quarterly* and must have been added when it was edited for *The Art of Sylvia Plath*.

suffering upon himself', was by cherishing human qualities in himself and others through the processes of love.

I have dealt elsewhere with Alvarez's commendations of the nihilism in contemporary art.* Here I would simply like to concentrate on the problem of meaning. In his death camp Viktor Frankl came to ponder the 'living' nihilism of our 'homun-culism'—the implicit model of man held by those who can see no meaning in their personal existence.

> and therefore think it valueless . . . And let us not forget, homunculism can make history—has already done so . . . I believe it to be a straight path from that homunculist image of man to the gas chambers of Auschwitz, Treblinka, and Maidenek. (p. 109)

But Sylvia Plath contributes to homunculism when she aban-dons herself to nihilism. It is not difficult to see her problem in relation to the fact that:

> the average man of today seems to be haunted by a feeling of the meaninglessness of life . . . what we can observe in the majority of people is not so much the feeling of being less valuable than others, but the feeling that life no longer has any meaning . . . (p. 109)

Both Frankl and Alvarez refer to the problem of boredom: the latter refers to the 'bored moral nihilism' of the contemporary artist. And in this aspect of the modern world we can I believe find a clue to the solution of the problem with which Sylvia Plath presents us. As Rollo May (1971) says, 'There is a dialectical relationship between apathy and violence' (p. 30), and this is related to the need for meaning.† To cultivate the self 'beyond a certain point', admits Alvarez, is 'also boring'. (*Encounter*, June 1965). To solve his problems of existence the artist needs to escape from solipsism, because only in pursuing his life-tasks can anyone realise his potentialities and find a sense of meaning in having existed which is imperishable. Surely then, if we urge the artist to 'give himself over to his sickness for the sake of the range

---

* 'Out of the Ash', *The Human World*, Vol. 5, November 1971.
† Discussed further in his *Power and Innocence*, 1974.

and intensity of his art', which is what Alvarez says most contemporary artists do, may we not be urging him into a fatal encapsulation? 'He cultivates', says Alvarez, 'not only his own garden but his psychosis, or at the very least his psychopathic tendencies' (1965). The world, being urban-industrial, is itself schizoid and causes apathy and dehumanisation. The artist is driven in on himself, and he becomes more extreme and solipsistic. In this state, declares Alvarez, artists have 'performed an endless series of underground tests on themselves'. In the poetry of Robert Lowell and Sylvia Plath this 'extraordinary self-awareness is delicately counter-balanced by an utter indifference'. But in general, they belong to the movement in the modern arts to 'press deeper and deeper into the subterranean world of psychic isolation, to live out in the arts the personal extremism of breakdown, paranoia and depression'.

Alvarez writes as if these tendencies were commendable for the sake of the art. But this can only be endorsed, surely, in the mode of the monstrous aesthete, like Gilbert Osmond in James's *Portrait of a Lady*, whose delectable sensations have nothing to do with responsibility to life. As we have seen, the extremism of breakdown, paranoia and other forms of negative emotion, including the cold-bloodedness Alvarez refers to as 'indifference', are desperate falsifications of experience, and forfeitures of intentionality, often impelled into hate. The great value of Frankl's work (especially his *From Death Camp to Existentialism*) is that it makes clear, from actual experiences of concentration camp life, that, even in such circumstances, 'encounter', responsiveness to and responsibility for those we love are the experiences by which we find our greatest sense of meaning, of *Dasein*. By contrast, the fascination of Alvarez and Sylvia Plath with death camps seems to belong to the kind of obsession with nihilism, indifference, psychosis, hate, and death that has become a diversion for the *avant garde*, in forgetfulness at times of all responsibility for humanity. The trouble is—as should be clear from her meanings—hate cannot help us solve any of our existence problems, because it cannot find meanings, only 'endless violence' as a substitute.

What we seek by creativity is a sense of meaning, of 'being there' to set against nothingness, and in the light of the new existentialism this is possible. Rollo May invokes Pascal's words:

'When I consider the brief span of my life, swallowed up in the eternity before and behind it, the small space that I fill, or even see, engulfed in the infinite immensity of spaces which I know not, and which know not me, I am afraid, and wonder to see myself here rather than there, now rather than then' (*Pensées*). 'The comets have such a space to cross'; it is this kind of dread that is to be found in some of Sylvia Plath's poems, such as *The Night Dances*, not as the expression of a schizoid condition but rather as the perception, albeit by a schizoid individual, of the dreadful truth of our existence in the universe.

To recognise our predicament is a first step towards asserting and claiming our autonomy and freedom as human beings, however, and it is here that the schizoid individual finds such difficulty, because of his lack of confidence in his own existence and potentialities. As Rollo May says (1958),

> Composed of *sein* (being) plus *da* (there), *Dasein* indicates that man is the being who is *there* and implies also that he has a 'there' in the sense that he can know he is there and can take a stand with reference to that fact. The 'there' is moreover not just any place, but the particular 'there' that is mine, the particular point *in time* as well as space of my existence at this given moment. Man is the being who can be conscious of, and therefore responsible for, his existence. (p. 41)

May goes on, 'the full meaning of the term "human being" will be clearer if the reader will keep in mind that "being" is a participle, a verb form implying that someone is in the process of *being something*' (p. 41). It is over this that Sylvia Plath was bewildered, as we have seen. Her most decisive act, existentially speaking, was to reject the *Dasein* altogether, and to choose non-being, although she was deluded by her sick logic that this was to choose to begin. But this was to forfeit creative hope for the future, and so to be overwhelmed as she feared to be. Her best poems represent an existential choice, in that they were an attempt *to be*, and to *be something*. Her psychotic poems, and her suicide, by contrast, move towards *being nothing*. Being, as May says, should mean *potentia*—the potentiality of what we truly might be. 'The significant tense for human beings is the future— for this belongs to intentionality.' Sylvia Plath's existential confusion is that what she took to point forward in this way actually pointed to the termination of being and potentiality.

But Sylvia Plath offers us 'intentionality', at times, as when in *Nick and the Candlestick*, among all the symbols of nothingness, he is, in his here-ness and now-ness, the 'one/Solid the spaces lean on' —her love for her baby is an assertion of 'me in the here and now', the *Dasein*. Even the love-blessings in *The Night Dances* confront the void. Her portrayal of the mechanical and meaningless nature of our rituals (as in *The Bell Jar*) is by implication an accusation that our world is loveless and thus cannot find meaning. In her poems, and from her continual images of yearning for tender care, she virtually tells us that true rebirth can only be achieved in terms of being, the individual finding and seeing himself, and accepting dependence on others and the need for love and meaning.

Moreover, in her meticulous creativity, she gave herself to the processes of love, for such creative effort in symbolism is a form of human interaction and an insistence on the here and now: here is her 'living energy'—not in the pursuit of death. She is at her best when she creates for others, not in the encapsulations of hate.

For all her harrowing and courageous record of suffering, Sylvia Plath died in the end because she could not sustain confidence in her true potentialities which could free her. The ripe plums all rotted and fell: there were no more telegraph poles. She found enough responsibility to leave her children alive as independent beings, and to create her poetry—'saving and storing from transitoriness' her suffering which she 'could not change or avoid'. In this sense her life work was a 'salvaging'—but it ceased to be a 'salvaging of *possibilities*'. What decayed in her was *potentia*. After a point, perhaps *Elm*, she lost hope, and 'possibilities' is no longer the word. Moreover, the terms 'creative deeds', 'loving' and 'effective action' seem foreign: her characteristic stance is at best that of standing like the magician's girl who does not flinch: a contender or survivor.* At best, she is trying to find her children and to love. At worst she gives herself up to a black and furious contempt for her existential needs.

But Sylvia Plath also often records that strange feeling of being

---

* Cf. the significant poem *The Contender* in the second edition of Ted Hughes's *Crow*.

aware of her heart saying 'I am', as if her body and being were unconvinced about what her intellect believed. And in this we have a glimpse of the 'formative principle'* in her, that created the poetry. To write poetry was 'what it means to be alive'. Almost in spite of herself she recognises the impulse to find meaning in her life emerging as a pulse from the cosmos, and as belonging to an urge to establish meaning rising from one's deepest bodily being.

There is no more valuable contribution to human survival than the courageous creative quest for the 'formative principle' within oneself, working from the pulse of meaning in the true self towards *potentia*, rejecting all mere conformities or falsifications, in the search to make something significant of one's moment. This is the creative fury, belonging to the engagement with nothingness, in exerting the *Dasein*. We have this spiritual integrity in Sylvia Plath's best work. She knew what the mind was for—even though she displayed such lack of confidence in being. On the other hand, there is no greater tragedy than rejecting the voice of the essence of one's being, and giving way to the moral inversions of 'Evil be thou my good!' In tribute to her anguish and fortitude it is essential that we should distinguish in her work between the one and the other.

* This phrase is taken from Marion Milner, who found this dynamic in her patients, and takes the phrase itself in her turn from L. L. Whyte. See Milner (1969), p. 384.

Bibliography

SYLVIA PLATH

(A very complete bibliography is given in *The Art of Sylvia Plath*, London, Faber and Faber, 1970, including a list of the titles of all her poems and where they may be found.)

Books

Two Lovers and a Beachcomber, Sylvia Plath Hughes, a typescript collection of poems handed in for the English Tripos, Part II, Cambridge University, 1956. Some of the poems in this differ from the published versions. Not all are listed in *The Art of Sylvia Plath*.

The Colossus, London, Faber and Faber, 1967. (Originally published as *The Colossus and Other Poems*, London, Heinemann, 1960.)

Ariel, London, Faber and Faber, 1965

The Bell Jar, London, Faber and Faber, 1966. (Originally published under the pseudonym Victoria Lucas, London, Heinemann, 1963.)

Crossing the Water, London, Faber and Faber, 1971

Winter Trees, London, Faber and Faber, 1971

Crystal Gazer and Other Poems, London, Rainbow Press, 1971

Short Pieces

'The Wishing Box', *Granta*, Vol. 61, No. 1166, 20 October 1956, also in *Atlantic*, Vol. 214, No. 4, October 1964

'Context', *London Magazine*, No. 1, February 1962

'Ocean 1212-W', *The Listener*, No. 70, 29 August 1963

Ten poems in *Encounter*, October 1963

British Council Interview, 'The Poet Speaks'

Books and Articles about her

Alvarez, A., 1963. 'A Poet's Epitaph', *The Observer*, 17 February

—, 1965. 'Poetry in Extremis', *The Observer*, 14 March

—, 1966. 'Sylvia Plath', *Triquarterly*, Evanston, USA, No. 7, Fall

—, 1969. 'Sylvia Plath', *The Cambridge Review*, 7 February

—, 1971. *The Savage God*, London, Weidenfeld and Nicolson

Brink, Andrew, 1968. 'Sylvia Plath and the Art of Redemption', *Alphabet*, No. 15, December, London, Ontario, c/o English Department, University of Western Ontario, Canada

Holbrook, David, 1971. 'Out of the Ash', *The Human World*, No. 5, November, Swansea

—, 1973. 'Sylvia Plath, Pathological Morality, and the Avant Garde', *Penguin Guide to English Literature, The Modern Age*, Vol. 7, London, Penguin Books

Homberger, E., 1970. *A Chronological Checklist of the Periodical Publications of Sylvia Plath*, Exeter

Hughes, Ted, 1965. 'Sylvia Plath', *Poetry Book Society Bulletin*, February

—, 1966. 'The Chronological Order of Sylvia Plath's Poems', *Triquarterly*, No. 7, Fall

Melander, I., 1972. *The Poetry of Sylvia Plath, a study of themes*, Acta Univ. Gothoburgensis, Gothenburg Studies in English,25, Stockholm

Newman, Charles (ed.), 1970. *The Art of Sylvia Plath*, a symposium, London, Faber and Faber

Richmond, Connie, 1973. 'The Worlds of Sylvia Plath', essay for the Certificate of Education, University of Kent, England

Steiner, George, 1965. 'Dying is an Art', *The Reporter*, Vol. 33, No. 8, 7 October (reprinted in *Language and Silence*, London, Faber and Faber, 1967)

Steiner, Nancy Hunter, 1973. *A Closer Look at Ariel: a memory of Sylvia Plath*, London, Faber and Faber

TED HUGHES
Books by and about Ted Hughes

Wodwo, London, Faber and Faber, 1967

Crow: From the Life and Songs of the Crow, London, Faber and Faber, 1970

Holbrook, David, 1975. 'Ted Hughes's *Crow* and the Longing for Nonbeing' in *The Black Rainbow*, ed. Peter Abbs, London, Heinemann

Smith, A. C. H., 1972. *Orghast in Persepolis*, London, Eyre Methuen

GENERAL
Books relevant to the theme of this study

Balint, Michael, 1952. *Primary Love and Psychoanalytical Technique*, London, Tavistock

Bowlby, John, 1965. *Child Care and the Growth of Love*, London, Penguin Books

Caws, Mary Ann, 1966. *Surrealism and the Literary Imagination*, Paris, Mouton

Coate, Morag, 1964. *Beyond all Reason*, London, Constable

Esterson, Aaron, 1970. *The Leaves of Spring*, London, Tavistock

Fairbairn, W. R. D., 1952. *Psychoanalytical Studies of the Personality*, London, Tavistock

Farber, Leslie H., 1966. *The Ways of the Will*, London, Constable

Frankl, Viktor, 1957. *From Death Camp to Existentialism*, Boston, Beacon Press

—, 1967. *Psychotherapy and Existentialism*, London, Souvenir Press

—, 1969. *The Doctor and the Soul*, London, Souvenir Press
(See also his contribution 'Nothing but . . .' in *The Alpbach Seminar on reductionism*, eds. Koestler, A. and Smithies, R., London, Hutchinson, 1969.)

Grene, Marjorie, 1966. *Dreadful Freedom*, later called *Introduction to Existentialism*, Chicago, University of Chicago Press

—, 1968. *Approaches to a Philosophical Biology*, especially her translations of excerpts from F. J. J. Buytendijk, New York, Basic Books

Guntrip, Harry, 1961. *Personality Structure and Human Interaction*, London, Hogarth Press

—, 1968. *Schizoid Phenomena, Object-relations, and the Self*, London, Hogarth Press

Henry, Jules, 1966. *Culture against Man*, London, Tavistock

Holbrook, David, 1971. *Human Hope and the Death Instinct*, Oxford, Pergamon Press

—, 1972. *The Masks of Hate*, Oxford, Pergamon Press

—, 1972. *Dylan Thomas, The Code of Night*, London, Athlone Press

—, 1972. *Sex and Dehumanization*, London, Pitman

— (ed.), 1972. *The Case Against Pornography*, London, Stacey

—, 1972. *The Pseudo-revolution*, London, Stacey

—, 1975. *Gustav Mahler and the Courage to Be*, London Vision Press

Jung, C. G. and von Franz, M. L., 1964. *Man and his Symbols*, London, Aldus Books

Klein, Melanie, 1950. *Contributions to Psychoanalysis*, London, Hogarth Press

—, 1955. *New Directions in Psychoanalysis*, London, Tavistock

—, 1959. *The Psychoanalysis of Children*, London, Hogarth Press

—, 1962. *Our Adult World and Other Essays*, London, Heinemann

— (with Joan Riviere), 1935. *Love, Hate and Reparation*, London, Hogarth Press

Laing, R. D., 1960. *The Divided Self*, London, Tavistock (available in Penguin Books)

Laing, R. D., 1967. *The Politics of Experience*, London, Penguin
—, 1969. *The Self and Others*. London, Tavistock
Laing, R. D. and Esterson, Aaron, 1964. *Sanity, Madness and the Family*, London, Tavistock
Ledermann, E. K., 1972. *Existential Neurosis*, London, Butterworth
Lomas, Peter, 1966. 'Psychoanalysis—Freudian or Existentialist' in Rycroft (1966)
— (ed.), 1967. *The Predicament of the Family*, London, Hogarth Press
—, 1973. *True and False Experience*, London, Allen Lane
May, Rollo, 1971. *Love and Will*, London, Souvenir Press
—, 1974. *Power and Innocence*, London, Souvenir Press
May, Rollo and others (eds.), 1958. *Existence—a New Dimension in Psychiatry*, New York, Basic Books
Menninger, Karl, n.d., *Man Against Himself*, London, Hart-Davis, Harvest Books (originally published 1938)
Millet, Kate, 1969. *Sexual Politics*, London, Hart-Davis
Milner, Marion, 1969. *In the Hands of the Living God: An Account of a Psychoanalytical Treatment*, London, Hogarth Press
Poole, Roger, 1972. *Towards Deep Subjectivity*, London, Allen Lane
Rieff, Philip, 1975. *Fellow Teachers*, London, Faber and Faber
Robinson, Ian, 1973. *The Survival of English*, Cambridge, Cambridge University Press
Roszak, Theodore, 1973. *Where the Wasteland Ends*, London, Faber and Faber
Rycroft, Charles (ed.), 1966. *Psychoanalysis Observed*, London, Constable
—, 1969. *A Critical Dictionary of Psychoanalysis*, London, Nelson
Straus, Erwin, 1966. *Phenomenological Psychology*, London, Tavistock
Vyvyan, J., 1972. *Sketch for a World-picture, a Study of Evolution*, London, Michael Joseph
Winnicott, D. W., 1957a. *The Child and the Family*, London, Tavistock
—, 1957b. *The Child and the Outside World*, London, Tavistock
—, 1965. *The Maturational Processes and the Facilitating Environment*, London, Hogarth Press
—, 1968a. *Collected Papers: Through Pediatrics to Psycho-analysis*, London, Tavistock
—, 1968b. *The Family and Individual Development*, London, Tavistock
—, 1969. *The Child, the Family and the Outside World*, London, Penguin Books
—, 1971a. *Playing and Reality*, London, Tavistock
—, 1971b. *Therapeutic Consultations in Child Psychiatry*, London, Hogarth Press
(The most relevant essay by Winnicott is 'The Mirror Role of the

Mother' in *Playing and Reality*: see also 'Creativity and its Origins' in the same.)

Papers

Alvarez, A., 1965. 'American Afterthoughts', *Encounter*, June

Daly, Robert, 1968. 'Schizoid Rule-following', *The Psychoanalytical Review*, Vol. 55, 3, Fall

Fairbairn, W. R. D., 1958. 'On the Nature and Aims of Psychoanalytical Treatment', *International Journal of Psychoanalysis*, Vol. 29, 5

Khan, Masud, 1971. 'L'Oeil Entend', *Nouvelle Revue de Psychanalyse*, Paris, Printemps (translated as 'To Hear with Eyes' in *The Privacy of the Self*, Hogarth Press 1974)

Solomon, J. C., 1963. 'Alice and the Red King: a psychoanalytical View of Existence', *International Journal of Psychoanalysis*, Vol. 44.

Index